MYTHS OF DEMILITARIZATION IN POSTREVOLUTIONARY MEXICO, 1920–1960

MYTHS OF DEMILITARIZATION IN POSTREVOLUTIONARY MEXICO, 1920–1960

THOMAS RATH

Parts of this book have been reprinted with permission in revised form from "'Que el cielo un soldado en cada hijo te dio . . . ' : Conscription, Recalcitrance and Resistance in Mexico in the 1940s," *Journal of Latin American Studies* 37, no. 3 (2005): 507–32, and "Revolutionary Citizenship versus Institutional Inertia: Cardenismo and the Mexican Army, 1934–1940," in *Forced Marches: Soldiers and Military Caciques in Modern Mexico*, edited by Ben Fallaw and Terry Rugeley (Tucson: University of Arizona Press, 2012).

Designed and set in Calluna and Block T by Rebecca Evans.

The paper in this book meets the guidelines for permanence and durability of the Committee on Production Guidelines for Book Longevity of the Council on Library Resources. The University of North Carolina Press has been a member of the Green Press Initiative since 2003.

Library of Congress Cataloging-in-Publication Data
Rath, Thomas
Myths of demilitarization in postrevolutionary Mexico, 1920–1960/Thomas Rath.
p. cm.
Includes bibliographical references and index.
ISBN 978-0-8078-3928-7 (cloth : alk. paper)—ISBN 978-0-8078-3929-4 (pbk. : alk. paper)
1. Civil-military relations—Mexico—History—20th century. 2. Civil supremacy over the military—Mexico—History—20th century. 3. Mexico—Armed Forces—Political activity—History—20th century. 4. Mexico. Ejército—History—20th century.
5. Mexico—Politics and government—1910–1946. 6. Mexico—Politics and government—1946–1970. I. Title.
JL1220.C58R37   2013
322'.5097209041—dc23   2012034768

The publisher has made every effort to contact the rightsholder for the cover image. The rightsholder is invited to write to the publisher so that a full acknowledgment may be given in subsequent printings.

CONTENTS

TABLES

ACKNOWLEDGMENTS

Like Napoleon's generals, historians require a great deal of luck to make any headway. I am fortunate to have crossed paths with numerous talented and inspiring historians and have enjoyed the support of many colleagues and friends. I am particularly grateful for the friendship, guidance, and high standards of Pablo Piccato. My thanks also to Alan Knight, who has supported this project, tolerated my prose, and provided me with many insights into Mexican history. Nara Milanich, Caterina Pizzigoni, and Paul Gootenberg provided welcome guidance and encouragement at an important stage. Paul Gillingham has also provided unrelenting encouragement and numerous insights from his own superb scholarship. At University College London, Nicola Miller and Christopher Abel first introduced me to Latin American history and culture. Before that, Pelham Lindfield Roberts's classes at Atlantic College introduced me to questions about global historical development that I still think about. Many other colleagues have offered support, advice, and encouragement, including, in no particular order, Dennis Gilbert, Ben Fallaw, Ben Smith, Pilar Zazueta, Carlos Gálvez-Peña, Julia del Palacio Langer, Cisco Bradley, Jim Krippner, Elena Jackson-Albarrán, Susanne Eineigel, Louise Walker, Bill Beezley, Ingrid Bleynat, Andrew Paxman, Ernie Capello, Matthew Brown, Paulo Drinot, Sinclair Thompson, Jonathan Ablard, Ray Craib, Karin Rosemblatt, Luciano Ciravegna, Kunle Owolabi, Mary Kay Vaughan, Nancy Appelbaum, David Sartorious, Wil Pansters, Kristina Boylan, Taco Terpstra, and Rebecca Bodenheimer.

At different points my research has been supported by the Economic and Social Sciences Research Council, the Latin American Centre (Oxford), the Columbia University Graduate School of Arts and Sciences, the Tinker Foundation, the Whiting Foundation, a visiting fellowship at the University of Maryland (College Park), and a Mellon Foundation Postdoctoral Fellowship in the Arts and Humanities at Hamilton College. I would also like to thank the archival and library staff at the Secretaría de la Defensa Nacional, Fideicomiso Archivos Plutarco Elías Calles y Fernando Torreblanca, Archivo

General de la Nación, Secretaría de Educación Pública, Biblioteca Miguel Lerdo de Tejada, New York Public Library, National Archives and Records Administration, and National Archives (UK). I am also grateful to Elaine Maisner and the staff of the University of North Carolina Press for their professionalism and interest in this project. Over the years the hospitality of the Quiroz Flores family and the distinctive ethos of the Casa de los Amigos have made trips to Mexico doubly inviting and enjoyable.

Friends have provided welcome breaks from academic life: Wil Grace laid on an enjoyable wedding and occasionally sent music; Alex Quiroz provided football, tacos, movies, and assorted other adventures. My parents and sisters have put up with long absences, transatlantic flights, and the no doubt baffling experience of listening to the details of peculiar historical research in a distant land over the phone. They did so with unstinting patience, love, and support, which I can only hope to repay someday. My son, Dev, arrived the same day as my book contract; he has disrupted and rearranged my life in the best possible sense since then. Hema Shenoi's contributions to this project are innumerable but are only a small fragment of the ways that she has enriched my life. I am grateful for that every day.

ABBREVIATIONS

CNC	Confederación Nacional Campesina
CROM	Confederación Regional Obrera Mexicana
CTM	Confederación de Trabajadores de México
DFS	Dirección Federal de Seguridad
DGIPS	Dirección General de Investigaciones Políticas y Sociales
FROC	Federación Regional de Obreros y Campesinos
PARM	Partido Auténtico de la Revolución Mexicana
PNR	Partido Nacional Revolucionario
PRI	Partido Revolucionario Institucional
SDN	Secretaría de la Defensa Nacional
SEP	Secretaría de Educación Pública
UGOCM	Unión General de Obreros y Campesinos de México
UNVR	Unión Nacional de Veteranos de la Revolución

MYTHS OF DEMILITARIZATION IN POSTREVOLUTIONARY MEXICO, 1920–1960

INTRODUCTION

On March 10, 1957, twenty soldiers drove into Cuauxocota, a small village in the foothills of the Sierra Norte de Puebla. After threatening to burn the village to the ground, the soldiers rounded up seventeen men, beating a few up in the process, and drove them to the jail in Teziutlán, the main town of the region. The lands around Cuauxocota were part of the numerous properties seized by state boss General Maximino Ávila Camacho and his allies in the late 1930s and early 1940s.[1] The raid was triggered by the villagers' plans to contact the federal agrarian department to request that the government accord their settlement its own *ejido*, a community land grant.

Four days later the remaining villagers wrote a petition to the president of Mexico. They denounced the raid as an arbitrary abuse that was unjustified since they had committed no crime, and they reported that they had started to fear for the men's lives. The petitioners did not primarily blame the army for the raid—they saw it as the result of the connivance of local landowners and municipal authorities—but neither did they entirely exempt the soldiers from responsibility. In the petitioners' version of events the soldiers' relationship with these other actors was far from clear, and the villagers argued that the army shared responsibility for the raid even if the soldiers had been following orders, since the orders were "inhumane." Finally, the petitioners noted that "we also know that the army is the defender of the nation and the law, because it has been repeated to us so many times during civic parades."[2]

This raid in the backwoods of the state of Puebla—small in scale, ignored by the Mexican press, but ultimately effective in quelling demands for land reform—raises a number of questions about the army's role in Mexico's political system. How important was the army as an instrument of political and social control? The incident reveals something of the variety of roles the army was expected to fulfill, as a coercive force and a potent nationalist symbol paraded before the public. What was the relationship between the army and other sources of authority? The petitioners believed that the army was collaborating with local elites and perhaps with federal authorities, but the exact relationship between these parties remained opaque. With their wry aside contrasting their own experiences with the state's efforts to associate the army with the "nation and the law," the petitioners also raised the crucial question of the army's legitimacy. This was a controversial but unavoidable topic in a political system whose leaders insisted they had banished militarism from the country, but whose soldiers remained all too visible as participants and enforcers of the new order. Finally, the act of writing the complaint itself illustrates how some people sought to protest and shape military policy and practice. To be sure, the families of Cuauxocota were unsuccessful; the men remained in jail for several days and were fined, and the locality avoided any substantial land reform into the mid-1960s.[3] However, they assumed that some sort of political space existed for the redress of perceived military abuses, otherwise they presumably would not have bothered to write at all.

This book tries to answer these questions: what the Mexican army did, why, and what people thought about it. In doing so, it seeks to challenge the dominant story of successful, top-down demilitarization that was promoted by the postrevolutionary regime and adopted by many subsequent historians. I argue that the process of demilitarization that Mexico experienced occurred after 1940, the traditional endpoint of histories of state formation. Demilitarization was shaped not simply by official policy but by a range of forces within state and society, including factional and ideological conflict within the government, tensions between the central state and the regions, and popular protest and public opinion. Most important, demilitarization was markedly incomplete.

This book defines demilitarization as a process by which the military's role in a political system declines in importance. It focuses on formal military institutions rather than on all organized, violent groups, although I argue that the army formed a major subset of that larger sociological category.[4] This book also approaches demilitarization as a multifaceted political, social, and cultural process, "both material and discursive."[5] The Mexican army, as we shall see, was in the business of organizing violence, but it also sought to control the cultural meaning attached to it. Scholarship on the Mexican army has tended to focus on officers and elite national politics.[6] This book explores how the army shaped Mexico's political system at different levels and in different places, combining an analysis of national and provincial politics, military factionalism, recruitment, policing, and veteran policies.

As Mexico emerged from the experience of mass mobilization and the civil war of 1910–20, a new governing elite agreed, at least in public, that the revolution had been fought to rid Mexico of militarism. However, Mexico's revolutionaries disagreed about the sources of militarism and how to insert the army into the new regime's institutions and ideology.[7] Drawing on different national experiences and foreign models of military organization, some sought to create a politically neutral army suitable for a liberal state. Some experimented with socialist ideas about creating a class-conscious and politically engaged army, while others imagined the army as a disciplinary school of revolutionary citizenship or sought to reinvigorate older liberal traditions of local militia. At the same time, the postrevolutionary regime confronted peasant communities, students, townspeople, journalists, revolutionary veterans, and dissident parties who seized on the revolution's multifaceted ideology to protest military policies and perceived abuses.

By the mid-1950s, the main features of the army and postrevolutionary state had crystallized. A new elite consensus emerged in which civilians increasingly dominated national politics and the government disseminated an official image of military neutrality that eclipsed earlier experiments in military policy. However, the government relied on military force to contain social unrest and political dissent. This allowed officers to retain power within the system, as they traded national obedience for impunity, provincial and operational autonomy, and the perks of systemic corruption. Despite these continuities, popular protest encouraged the regime to curb more ambitious policies such as conscription and to open up symbolic recognition to a broader swath of revolutionary veterans. It also encouraged the government to reduce the visibility of military bloodshed and to exert more control over public discussion of the army, which partly helped to mask the limits of demilitarization.

By retelling the story of Mexico's demilitarization in this way, I seek to answer broader questions about postrevolutionary state formation and politics: principally, how and why Mexicans came to exchange popular revolution for a durable, authoritarian regime that oversaw a profoundly inequitable model of development. A focus on the formative decades of the 1930s to the 1950s also helps us place more famous episodes of state violence in the 1960s and 1970s, and the militarization of domestic security since the 1980s, in historical perspective. To be sure, much would change in the army's relationship to Mexican society after the 1950s; but much would stay the same.

The Mexican Revolution left a paradoxical legacy. It brought massive popular mobilization, sweeping social reform, cultural experimentation, and a political effervescence that lasted into the 1930s. By the 1960s, however, Mexico's regime enjoyed a reputation as the most stable, most centralized, and strongest government in mainland Latin America. Many observers believed that the political violence that had characterized earlier attempts at state building had been replaced by a combination of economic development, subtle bureaucratic incorporation, stable civilian rule, and a pervasive revolutionary legitimacy. The peculiar name adopted by the official party in 1946, the Institutional Revolutionary Party (Partido Revolucionario Institucional, PRI), seemed entirely appropriate. Many historians have argued that reformist President Lázaro Cárdenas (1934–40) laid the foundations of the regime's stability. According to this view, Cárdenas pacified the countryside with sweeping land reform; in 1938, he created a corporate revolutionary party capable of co-opting popular demands and inculcating a widespread legitimacy.[8] Not least, according to Edwin Lieuwen's pathbreaking and influential study, Cárdenas brought about the "bridling of the political generals."[9]

Since the 1990s, "postrevisionist" historians have painted a far more nuanced, dynamic picture of the political conflicts of the 1920s and 1930s and the complex dialogue between diverse regional societies and the national state. Gilbert Joseph and Daniel Nugent's landmark 1994 collection, *Everyday Forms of State Formation*, encouraged scholars to explore how state institutions and policies were selectively contested, appropriated, or rejected by different groups in society.[10] Using Gramscian theories of hegemony, scholars have also explored the cultural and discursive aspects of state building, focusing on public education, civic ritual, and the mass media. Indeed, many have argued that postrevolutionary cultural programs, particularly in the 1930s, helped to forge a shared hegemonic political culture and "language of contention" that would bind state and society and ultimately underpin PRI rule.[11] Scholars have generally not considered the national army within this more multilayered analytical framework, although the army was a core national institution central to the revolutionary state's power and legitimacy. Moreover, until recently, historians have by and large not extended their analyses beyond the boundary of 1940, revealing an assumption that the key features of the postrevolutionary state had been settled by that point.[12]

For historians writing about the 1920s and 1930s, the political role of the revolutionary army has long been a central concern for obvious reasons: the army provided the bulk of Mexico's political leadership, and spawned major rebellions against the central government in 1923–24, 1927, and 1929. However, scholars have focused on elite national politics and have emphasized, above all, the government's gradual institutionalization of the army and the officers' subordination to the president and civilian party by the 1940s.[13] Revolutionary officers' corruption and entrepreneurialism—well known at the time—have attracted some scholarly attention, although studies have focused on the 1920s.[14] In 1961, Edwin Lieuwen wrote that "Mexico has unquestionably solved its problems of militarism. . . . Militarism has been dead for over a generation."[15]

To be sure, at the national level, demilitarization was not entirely mythical. Mexico was ruled by a single civilian party from 1929 until 2000, had a civilian president after 1946, and suffered no coups or serious army rebellions after 1929. The army's gradually declining share of the federal budget—from 65 percent in 1920 to 15 percent in 1946—also seemed to support a story of smooth, relatively costless demilitarization.[16] This interpretation was not uncongenial to the PRI regime. Particularly after the civilian Miguel Alemán ascended to the presidency in 1946, official rhetoric portrayed the civilian dominance of national politics, military professionalism, and consensual rule as part of a virtuous circle of political modernization overseen by the postrevolutionary regime. In their memoirs, Mexican officers tended to praise the president-driven reform and subordination of the army.[17]

However, the demilitarization of Mexican politics was far more protracted, conflictive, and uneven than suggested by this familiar story of purposive military reform. Scholars such as Frank Brandenburg, Lyle McAlister, David Ronfeldt, and Franklin Margiotta raised some doubts about Lieuwen's thesis and discussed how officers retained important political roles after the 1940s, but detailed historical research has long been difficult and is sparse.[18] Roderic Camp offered an empirically rich analysis of long-term trends in the sociology of the officer corps and discussed the persistence of political officers in the PRI system. However, Camp's analysis tends toward the synchronic rather than the diachronic, and the primary research focuses on more recent trends. In this work I build on Elisa Servín and Aaron Navarro's recent studies of officers' participation in presidential elections in the 1940s and 1950s. However, by exploring how these *cupular* struggles affected provincial politics, military organization, repression, and the army's role in official myth making, I aim to provide a fuller account of the limits of demilitarization.[19]

This book is also an attempt to better understand the role of political violence in postrevolutionary state formation. With its focus on officer politics, scholarship on the army has implied that the army contributed to rule more by what it did not do (mutiny, stage coups) than by what it did (police, repress). Revisionist scholars of the 1970s, reacting to more visible state violence in and after 1968, acknowledged the importance of military repression to a much greater extent than earlier scholars. Jean Meyer, for example, published his study of the Cristiada, a massive rebellion of Catholics in the center-west of the country between 1926 and 1929 that triggered the largest and bloodiest counterinsurgency campaign of the postrevolutionary army.[20] However, public discussion of army repression was risky, and primary sources were scarce. Many revisionists also still tended to place the structures of party corporatism at the core of their analysis of the state after the 1930s.[21] Since the 1990s, while postrevisionist historians' interest in cultural hegemony has enhanced our understanding of key topics, it has tended to discourage analysis of violent actors and institutions.

In the last decade, however, the opening of new archives for the years after 1940, official attempts to investigate police and military violence during the 1960s and 1970s, and the growing militarization of the Mexican state have encouraged scholars to begin reassessing the significance of political violence in general, and the military in particular, to PRIísmo.[22] The army's role in suppressing left-wing guerilla movements in Chihuahua (1965) and Guerrero (1967–74) and in the repression of Mexico City's student movement in 1968 and 1971 is now well documented.[23] However, studies have not explored in depth how the increasingly visible, more urban repression of the 1960s built on a longer history of state violence, particularly in the countryside, in which the army was crucial.[24] Exploring the long, provincial antecedents of Mexico's "dirty war" will also help to place Mexico's experience in a larger Latin American context of political violence and authoritarianism from which it is often isolated.[25]

There are methodological advantages to writing about how different groups struggled to institutionalize and legitimize violence in the army. This approach moves us away from reifying violence as an "entity, an autonomous agent" that can be analyzed in itself and directs us to the more manageable questions of who or what is using force, how and for what purposes over time; in short, it takes us away from abstract nouns and into the territory of subjects, objects, and a range of forceful verbs.[26] The history of the Mexican army is significant precisely because, by helping suppress and contain political dissent and multiple forms of social conflict, it contributed to the two large transformations that defined postrevolutionary Mexico: the slow, fitful extension of state control over the country, and that state's management, after 1940, of an inequitable process of capitalist development.[27]

At the same time, a focus specifically on military institutions makes sense because they enjoyed some autonomy from macro-level processes of state building and capitalist development. Conflicts over the army reveal something of the messy "contingent political dynamics" that mediated social conflict, state building, and transnational influences and shaped Latin America's history of political violence.[28] This focus on state institutions and politics is unlikely to satisfy scholars who view power in modern societies as endlessly diffused and totalizing, or who prefer to study the state largely as a discursive effect or "fetish" that conceals local social relations of domination.[29] The state should certainly be understood, in part, as a discursive claim; official antimilitarism and *civilismo* were crucial components of this. However, it was also a set of institutions that, however uneven, contested, and cacique-ridden, organized society in relatively patterned and predictable ways.[30] A focus on the stuff of national and regional politics—factions, ideologies, alliances, institutions, popular protest—helps capture what Mexico's process of demilitarization was actually like. It also helps explain why people felt they had a stake in these conflicts and might bother to contest what the army did and how it was organized.

The army was not the only violent actor and institution in postrevolutionary Mexico, but it was central for the regime's authority and legitimacy. The sources are replete with references to an array of formal and informal violent actors: pistoleros, armed *agraristas*, intelligence services, territorially bound caciques, geographically mobile coyotes, student *porras*, and, particularly in cities, police. Postrevolutionary Mexico also produced its own lexicon of violent political practices such as *zafarranchos* (shoot-outs) and *carreterazos* (the practice of dumping the bodies of the victims of political murder on roadsides).[31] It is often very difficult to learn much about these actors, let alone trace their interactions over time. The state did not enjoy a monopoly, let alone a legitimate one, over violence.[32] However, focusing on the army provides a useful way to cut into this thicket of political violence and begin to detect patterns. The army occupied a crucial and underappreciated place in this panoply of agents of violence. It was not uncommon for pistoleros and, particularly, the police to enjoy some backing and institutional links to the army. The army enjoyed organizational and institutional powers that others did not; it could arm and train militia and rapidly dispatch well-armed reinforcements. Of course, relying on the army brought certain political costs. It could damage the regime's image and lend officers political leverage. However, in many places, particularly in the countryside, the army was the most reliable violent actor the central state had at its disposal. Some aspects of military policy, such as recruitment and veteran benefits, were susceptible to popular protest and public opinion. In its core role as a violent agency of social and political control, the government's responses to protest are harder to detect and were more a question of style than substance.

Writing about the army also entails methodological and conceptual problems. For decades the government systematically discouraged research on the topic and sought to project a monolithic image of coherence and unity based on formal institutional structures.[33] Fortunately, we now have access to a broader range of sources that can correct this official image. The presidential election of 2000 brought a certain opening of archives, although the files released by the army to aid investigations into police and military repression remain incomplete and contain few documents prior to 1960. However, access to the archives of Mexico's intelligence agencies for the 1930s to the 1950s is now, cataloging problems aside, reasonably straightforward. Access to military officers' service files in the Department of National Defense (Secretaría de la Defensa Nacional, SDN) is also now far easier than previously. These sources, read alongside correspondence in the presidential archives and the personal archive of Joaquín Amaro, diplomatic reports, assorted memoirs, press reports, and copious military texts and publications, shed new light on debates within the government over military policy, military politics, and factionalism.

This book uses many petitions and complaints to probe what the army did and what some people thought about it. Interpreting these sources is not straightforward. Far from representing a random sample, such correspondence was created by people who chose to write to the central government, or whose correspondence was forwarded to it by other state agencies, people whose probable motives and reliability are not easy to apprehend. However, as Hans-Werner Tobler noted in a survey of the army's role in agrarian reform in the 1920s, given that the political disincentives to condemning (or even discussing) the army were always considerable, it seems most likely that such correspondence if anything underestimates the everyday political involvement and interference by the army.[34] Moreover, sources of dubious reliability can provide extensive insights into the development of political culture.[35] Read alongside intelligence reports and military files, the press, published testimonies, and local studies, these petitions and complaints powerfully illuminate the importance of the army to the postrevolutionary regime and what different groups considered to be acceptable, plausible, and productive discourse with the government about the army.

In addition, this book combines an analysis of national trends with a case study of the state of Puebla. Several factors influenced my choice of Puebla as a case study. First, the state of Puebla was a single military zone, like most others. As a large, socially and geographically heterogeneous state, Puebla also seemed to comprise a range of variables such that whatever conclusions were drawn from the state would not be completely atypical. Puebla also provided a relatively large number of secondary studies to contextualize the sources with which I had to work. This case study illustrates how military institutions worked in different ways in national and regional contexts, variations the government was loath to discuss and about which its formal rules were silent. It also allowed me to analyze and contextualize military policing in a systematic way. The army published no manuals on how to intimidate and raid peasant communities, decapitate social movements, and break strikes, and its activities largely have to be reconstructed on the basis of complaints and intelligence reports, something that was feasible at the state level. The regional case study made it possible to understand the significance of military policing in the context of processes of political and social (particularly agrarian) conflict unfolding at the regional level. The case study does not claim to provide the rich, ethnographic detail of local studies; however, it allows for a glimpse of how army practices actually worked and were understood at the grass roots during the formative years of PRIísmo.

Chapter 1 explores the long history of conflicts about the army's role in Mexican society and how these conflicts culminated in the Mexican Revolution of 1910–20. It then describes the project of military reform undertaken by the first postrevolutionary Sonoran regime (1920–34) and the basic outlines of the army bequeathed by the revolution. The revolution brought unprecedented military mobilization of different kinds, and a ubiquitous but vague commitment to combating militarism among revolutionary leaders. After 1920, military reform would be crucial to the new regime's power and to its self-image as a progressive, modern regime that had broken with the past.

Subsequent chapters are thematic but arranged in broadly chronological order, moving between national and regional levels of analysis. Chapter 2 focuses on the military project of reformist president Lázaro Cárdenas (1934–40) and the government's attempt to impose on the army a new version of what it meant to be revolutionary—one based on class consciousness and revolutionary engagement. The chapter first surveys Cárdenas's innovations in military rhetoric, and party and militia organization, before focusing on the government's attempt to immerse soldiers and their families in socialist education. The chapter argues that Cardenismo did not mark the culmination of the regime's efforts to subdue the military and that the military resisted much of Cárdenas's project for the army. Chapter 3 analyzes the introduction of national conscription in 1942, a policy that exemplifies the Ávila Camacho administration's turn away from Cardenista radicalism and its efforts to instill national unity and discipline. By drawing on hundreds of petitions sent to the central government, alongside government and diplomatic reports, the chapter illustrates how Mexican society discussed, contested, and resisted military policy in different ways. It reveals how most Mexicans criticized conscription using the state's own official discourse of revolutionary citizenship and nationalism and shows that, by the late 1940s, popular resistance stymied conscription in many places and helped convince the government to scale back its use of conscription as a tool of social engineering.

Chapter 4 explores the regime's changing relationship with its officer corps in the 1940s and 1950s. The chapter contrasts the new apolitical image of the army crafted by the government during the Second World War with the persistence of military factionalism and officer politics using diplomatic and intelligence reports, and offers an analysis of the promotion and circulation of commanding officers. Between 1948 and 1952, the regime defeated two groups of dissident officers, and shifted national politics closer to rhetoric. However, the political marginalization of the army at the national level did not simply percolate down to the regions. Officers fought hard against the demilitarization of national politics and preserved political and entrepreneurial autonomy within the system. The chapter concludes with a discussion of how military officers helped to build and maintain the Avilacamachista political machine in the state of Puebla.

Chapter 5 analyzes the army's role in political and social control in the 1940s and 1950s, and people's responses to it. After a national overview, the chapter focuses on the state of Puebla and argues that the army's roles displayed profound continuities. Drawing on around 250 complaints and petitions, alongside intelligence reports and military service files, this chapter traces how the army broke strikes, controlled and dispersed crowds, managed agrarian conflict, took over municipal and university authorities, and intimidated and occasionally killed dissidents. As in conscription protests, people sought to contrast official rhetoric with the reality of military repression and corruption. The chapter concludes that complaints about military policing did occasionally counter gratuitous uses of military force and encourage the government to adopt somewhat subtler ways of ruling and repressing.

Finally, Chapter 6 shifts the focus away from violent provincial politics and examines how the army helped shape the official history. It shows how the army's publications, ceremonies, and veteran policies represented the new regime and its army as the legitimate heirs to the Mexican Revolution. However, the version of historical memory that underpinned veteran policy was subject to shifting political and social forces. In the 1920s, the army defined the category of veteran narrowly to include only male soldiers of the victorious Constitutionalist faction. However, the proliferation of other groups claiming benefits as revolutionary veterans, the growing self-identification of right-wing dissidents as veterans, and changes in the revolutionary party's own rhetoric all led, by the 1940s, to the army expanding the official category of revolutionary veteran to include men and women from other factions.

CHAPTER ONE

Antimilitarism and Revolution in Mexico

During the Mexican Revolution, it was risky to tell jokes about military offi-cers. Nevertheless, at night in Mexico City's cabarets and vaudeville theatres some did. Along with jibes about military leaders' uncouthness and vanity, a particularly reliable theme was officers' hypocritical embrace of antimil-itarism—their tendency to repeat an elevated liberal democratic rhetoric that disavowed military influence, all the while ruthlessly pursuing political offices and wealth.[1] In the months prior to the presidential election of 1920, the Spanish writer Vicente Blasco Ibáñez attended one of the "principal the-aters of Mexico City" and witnessed a portrayal of General Pablo González, then conducting an electoral campaign that boasted of his civilian-minded, peace-loving credentials: "Don Pablo came on in the last act, and in the most comic fashion. He wore a battle uniform. He had a scowl on his face. Black eye-glasses and an enormous mustache added to the ferocity of his appear-ance. Dragging an enormous cannon behind him, he advanced toward the footlights, and there, in a voice which was more like the roar of a hungry lion ready to eat the audience, he shouted: 'I am a pacifist!'"[2]

To understand the prevalence and appeal of antimilitarist rhetoric, why many saw it as empty and laughable, and why postrevolutionary leaders persisted in using it anyway, it is necessary to understand Mexico's earlier history. After 1920, political and ideological conflicts about the army were often fierce and wide ranging. However, few people understood the issues to be entirely new. Postrevolutionary debates were shaped by earlier conflicts over the central or local organization of violence, who should serve in the army, the political and legal rights that military service should entail, and the circumstances under which the army could coerce the nation's own citizens. This chapter provides an overview of these conflicts in Mexico after inde-pendence, and how they culminated in the revolution of 1910–20. It then ex-plores how the Sonorans who controlled the postrevolutionary regime from 1920 to 1934 were influenced by this earlier history in their efforts to reform the army. The chapter ends with a sketch of Mexico's army of the early 1930s that illustrates the limits of Sonoran reform and provides a baseline from which to plot subsequent changes.

The Origins of the Military in Mexico

The effort to create a permanent military apparatus at the service of the central state can be traced back to the Bourbon reforms of the late eighteenth century. For most of the colonial period New Spain was lightly garrisoned, except in isolated frontier regions in the north. Elsewhere, the crown relied on local militia units to put down unrest and defend its territories against the occasional forays of competing imperial powers. From the crown's perspective, the advantage of the militia was that it was cheap. However, militias were often hastily organized, poorly disciplined, and sometimes "entirely fictional."[3] The crown was also ambivalent about the colonial militia because subordinate groups, including free blacks and (particularly on the northern frontier) indigenous groups, sought to use their service to press for local and group rights and exemptions from taxation with some success.[4] As inter-imperial rivalries intensified after the 1760s, the Bourbons tried to increase their control of the American colonies and extract more revenue from them and created a permanent military force. Spain's military expenditures in the Americas increased through the eighteenth century, although they remained modest compared with those of Britain and France.[5] Between 1758 and 1800, the viceroyalty's regular army had grown from 3,000 to 6,150 men. This new force oversaw an expanded provincial militia of around 11,000 men. Its officers were a mix of *peninsulares* sent from Spain and creole elites attracted by the legal privileges ceded by the crown to officers in new military codes.[6]

For the first fifty years after independence, Mexico's army both reflected and exacerbated the political instability of the period. In 1821, Mexico became independent after a faction of the colonial army switched loyalties and allied with the remnants of the popular insurgency they had spent most of the previous decade fighting. Mexico's army was one of the largest national institutions, and its officers were ubiquitous figures in government offices and in frequent coups, rebellions, and *pronunciamientos*.[7] Many historians have viewed military politics as being devoid of ideological meaning, led by individual caudillos who lacked the classical virtue to sustain republican institutions, or simply an expression of soldiers' tendency to follow whoever promised to pay their wages.[8] Others have taken the ideological debates of the time more seriously but have emphasized officers' varied and complex alliances with civilian groups rather than the politics of the army as an institution, which they have seen as weak and fragmented.[9] While there is much truth to each of these interpretations, the Mexican army (or at least its leadership) also displayed a "certain corporateness" and political identity.[10] Shaped by the shared experience of fighting the insurgency of 1810, this outlook included a hierarchical conception of society, antagonism to widespread political participation, a marked reformism in military matters coupled with a defense of the ample legal privileges and autonomy inherited from the Bourbon reforms, and a pronounced hostility to local militias.[11]

Recent research suggests that conservative officers were correct to be concerned about Mexico's tradition of local militias and has confirmed that tradition's strength and importance in the nineteenth century. The first attempts to group local militias into a National Guard began in the 1820s, but the National Guard only emerged as a key political institution between the 1840s and 1860s, as Mexico suffered invasion and territorial dismemberment during war with the United States (1847–48), civil war between liberals and conservatives (1857–61), and a further conservative-backed French invasion and occupation (1862–67).[12] Mexican liberals, like their political brethren elsewhere, generally defined militarism as the praetorianism of a privileged caste of officers and tried to create institutional separations between military and civilian spheres. Liberal proposals were accompanied by a moral discourse, perhaps unusually strong in Latin America, that emphasized the dissolute, vicious habits of military men—promiscuity, alcoholism, gambling, and cockfighting in particular—and the need to eliminate these behaviors through improved training, moralization, and limits on the scope of military justice. Many liberals also understood local and state militias as useful counterweights to the political power and authoritarian tendencies of the federal army, although moderates were often hesitant about opening up militia service to too many of the lower classes.[13] Throughout the wars against conservatives and the French, liberals increasingly relied on the National Guard to recruit leaders and communities to the cause, allowing them to build political alliances among Mexico's diverse provincial leaders and eventually emerge triumphant in 1867.

In some indigenous regions, service in the National Guard helped to spread notions of national identity and a popular, patriotic brand of liberalism that emphasized local autonomy.[14] Whether soldiers hailed from Mexico City or a distant peasant community in the sierra, service in the National Guard was certainly more agreeable than serving as a draftee in the federal army; militia units could often elect their own officers and enjoyed some control over where and when they could be deployed.[15] Likewise, some peasant communities in the north of Mexico, initially established as military colonies in territories dominated by nomadic indigenous groups, also came to associate local military mobilization with their rights to land, citizenship, and masculine honor.[16]

The rule of General Porfirio Díaz, president for all but four years between 1876 and 1910, transformed Mexican society and the army's role in it in many ways. Since the 1820s, the federal army's leadership had often tried to reform military training and education, recruitment, provisioning, and medical services. These plans were usually stymied by the instability and insolvency of the government.[17] This was to change after the 1870s, as Mexico was transformed by twin processes of capitalist development and state building. Export-led economic growth boosted state revenues, which in turn enabled the state to enhance its capacities, both "cognitive" and coercive.[18] The Porfirian state mapped territories, subsidized infrastructure, took censuses, recruited ex-bandits to a glamorous new provincial police force, and tried to update, centralize, and professionalize the armed forces.[19] Of course, this meant curtailing the very National Guard in which Díaz had made his name as a patriot fighting the French, that had propelled him to national power in 1876, and that had formed the nucleus of federal army officers up to the 1880s. In the 1880s, federal officers increasingly hailed from new military academies, and Díaz decommissioned the National Guard. Like other governments at the time in Latin America dedicated to reaping the benefits of export-led growth, the Porfirian regime undertook a certain, selective demilitarization: the army's share of the budget was reduced, its forces shrank by 25 percent between 1884 and 1910, and the number of officers in political posts declined across the Porfiriato.[20] However, the army remained deeply involved in enforcing the Porfirian order, its smaller size compensated in part by organizational improvements and increased mobility thanks to the new railways.[21]

International politics reinforced this domestic role. To the south, Guatemala was always too weak in geopolitical terms and poor in resources to play the role of a compelling military adversary. To the north, the United States presented far too formidable an enemy to be confronted with primarily military means. Although the United States did not enjoy the prestige of France and Germany as an organizer and outfitter of armies until the 1940s, its dominance over Mexico in military terms was evident to most observers since at least the 1840s. Throughout the wars of the nineteenth century and the Mexican Revolution, the United States was evidently an important source of arms and aid for rebels. Any government that intended to rule Mexico would have to use a part of its armed forces to secure key border points and ports. However, it was obvious that a purely military approach to deflecting U.S. influence made little sense. The army would continue to be influenced by foreign models of military reform and organization into the postrevolutionary period, but a basic domestic orientation would remain. The importance of domestic policing in turn ensured the dominance of Mexico's army over its small navy and later its air force.[22]

Despite this absence of international war, the Porfirian regime sought to use its newly reformed army to spread a particular (conservative, Europhile, racist) version of national identity and illustrate the "Order and Progress" that the government had brought to Mexico. The army paraded its new, European-style uniforms and drills before the public, projecting an image of modern discipline and hierarchy well suited to Porfirian conceptions of the wider social order; official commemorations of the National Guard faded away.[23] However, it was difficult to make the army a compelling symbol of Porfirian nationalism across class, regional, and ethnic boundaries. The army explicitly demanded lighter complexions of the recruits to Porfirio Díaz's new elite presidential guard.[24] Nevertheless, a career in the federal army was never appealing for educated elites. Among the lower classes, the persistence of the press-gang and the harsh experience of military discipline belied the image of paternal patriotism.[25] Elite men suspected of belonging to the new category of criminals called homosexuals were packed off to the army as punishment; while this confirmed the deviancy of these men, it was less clear whether it implied the respectability of military service, or simply reinforced its penal associations.[26]

Aside from the limited appeal of Porfirian nationalism, the project for the army faced other pressing problems. General Bernardo Reyes had cut his teeth in the National Guard, survived Porfirian professionalization, and became a prominent advocate of military reforms himself; he also became the head of a powerful political and military faction intent on propelling him to the presidency. In 1902, Reyes sought a partial revival of Mexico's militia tradition by organizing the Second Reserve, a new volunteer, civilian, but socially exclusive military force that numbered 30,000 and included many middle-class supporters of Reyes. Díaz intervened to disband the reserve and removed Reyes from the Ministry of War. However, countering Reyes came at the cost of handing control of the army to a competing faction of newer professional officers led by General Manuel Mondragón, whose loyalty was conditional on their being allowed considerable leeway to graft. Such arrangements could be embarrassing when they were exposed in public scandal. They also weakened the army as an effective enforcer of the Porfirian status quo. Padded payrolls and empty arsenals, combined with the army's continued reliance on demoralized soldiers rounded up by press-gangs, ensured that the army was ill prepared to combat popular insurgency.[27]

The Mexican Revolution

Between 1910 and 1920, popular revolution and civil war brought massive military mobilization to Mexico. The rebel forces that sprang up to propel the moderate liberal reformer Francisco Madero to the presidency in 1911 emerged from the north and center of the country but were hastily improvised and relatively small. Madero's ascent to power was more of a political than a military victory, as Díaz decided to cede the presidency to Madero rather than further militarize the conflict, trusting that Madero would keep much of the Porfirian establishment intact.[28] In 1911, for all its logistical problems, the federal army had not yet suffered a crushing defeat, which made many officers resentful of the deal with Madero.[29] As president, Madero pinned his hopes on moderate political reform but proved weak and ineffective. On one side he faced former allies disillusioned with his tepid approach to land and labor reform and angered by his decision to demobilize Maderista forces. On the other side lay the Porfirian old guard, especially the army, on whom Madero relied more and more to pacify the country. In 1913, Porfirian elites, encouraged by U.S. ambassador Henry Lane Wilson, led a counterrevolutionary coup. The regime that emerged, led by General Victoriano Huerta, fully embraced a military solution to Mexico's instability, boosted the military budget and press-gang, and employed an overt and unsubtle political repression. This only succeeded in provoking further regional uprisings and the emergence of larger and more determined revolutionary armies. After crushing defeats, Huerta resigned from power and fled the country. In the summer of 1914, the revolutionary forces took power and dissolved the old federal army. Unity proved fragile though, as revolutionary factions turned against one another and plunged the country into a series of increasingly bloody confrontations in 1915.[30]

Men and women joined the revolutionary armies for many reasons: to regain communal lands, to secure local autonomy, to avoid being drafted by the federal army, to obtain some income during a chaotic time, or simply for the mobility and adventure the revolution promised. However, each revolutionary faction built on earlier traditions of military mobilization in notably different ways. The more middle-class Constitutionalist faction emerged in the northern states of Coahuila and Sonora; drawing on their experience in state government, the Constitutionalists created centrally controlled, paid, and geographically mobile forces that approximated professional armies. The short-lived "Red Battalions," made up of 2,500 workers recruited after a deal between Mexico City's anarcho-syndicalists and the Constitutionalists in 1915, did not alter this basic pattern of military organization. In contrast, the peasant villagers led by Emiliano Zapata in central Mexico saw themselves as inheritors of the National Guard's tradition of decentralized, normally unpaid, local militias. Although Zapatismo was not devoid of an overarching military organization, the commitment to local autonomy and immediate land reform made it difficult for Zapatistas to mobilize beyond their regional base, however formidable they were as guerilla fighters on their own terrain.[31] Sitting somewhere between these types lies Chihuahua-based Villismo, whose army is "extremely difficult" to categorize either as a local, popular movement or a centralized, professional force.[32] At any given time, it contained elements of both. After all, Pancho Villa's Division of the North changed considerably over time; initially a loose coalition of popular forces, it grew into a large, heterogeneous, but well-organized force with paid troops and the support of a veritable war economy in Chihuahua churning out uniforms and supplies.[33]

Ultimately, it was from the nucleus of Constitutionalist forces that a new regular army would be constructed. During a series of decisive battles in the Bajío in the spring of 1915, the well-dug-in Constitutionalist forces of General Álvaro Obregón cut down Villa's repeated cavalry charges in a hail of rifle and machine gun fire; from this point it was clear that national power would fall to the Constitutionalists. After the setbacks of 1915, Villa's army morphed into smaller guerilla forces holding out in the sierras of Chihuahua. Between 1915 and 1920, the Constitutionalists slowly tried to reestablish control of the country, pursued the remnants of Villismo and Zapatismo, and drafted the Constitution of 1917. In 1920, the popular, politically astute, and militarily formidable Obregón ousted the Coahuilan *primer jefe* Venustiano Carranza from national power, placing Obregón's Sonoran faction (very loosely) in control of the country.[34]

Antimilitarism was prominent in Madero's program from the start, and it became a core part of revolutionary ideology. To call a revolutionary a militarist, or compare him to the notorious nineteenth-century caudillo Antonio López de Santa Anna, was one of the most reliable insults of the period.[35] Of course, as the scale of the revolutionary armies and bloodshed increased, it was not difficult for critics to portray this antimilitarism as absurd hypocrisy. In practice, any kind of commitment to limiting the military's role in society faced enormous obstacles. Revolutionary military leaders were powerful, frequently ambitious, and entrepreneurial. The revolutionary military formed the 1915 Convention at Aguascalientes, and the Constitutionalists imposed military "proconsuls" on defeated territories.[36] Mexico's export economy proved remarkably resilient in the 1910s. Income from exports was critical to Constitutionalism, and in many places Constitutionalist officers carved out profitable businesses; traded cattle, grain, and ammunition; and controlled railways, drink, gambling, and prostitution. Once electoral politics began again, officers were hugely influential. In short, *caudillismo* remained strong.[37]

However, things were more complicated than a gulf between revolutionary ideology and practice. The revolutionary rhetoric of antimilitarism, while voluble, ubiquitous, and no doubt deeply felt by many, concealed different emphases and ideological ambiguities. The influence of the nineteenth-century institutional liberalism of José María Luis Mora remained powerful. Few revolutionaries proposed a political system formally dominated by the army. Zapatismo sought local control of the militia forces by the villages. Villismo is a more ambiguous case; Villa's army loomed large in his administration of Chihuahua, although the degree of military or broader popular control varied enormously by locality. However, even Villa felt the need to proclaim some sort of allegiance to the liberal-democratic constitution of 1857 and assert his antimilitarist credentials when attempting to court Zapata.[38] The Constitutionalists imposed military proconsuls as a temporary measure, and in 1917 they drafted a constitution that contained many familiar liberal-democratic provisions: separation of powers; civilian control of the army (article 9); a restriction of the army's duties during peacetime to those "directly connected to military affairs" (article 129). These were routine elements of liberal-democratic constitutions and were barely subject to debate. More controversial was the effort by some to eliminate the military's separate system of justice in peacetime. Citing the demands of military discipline, officers such as Francisco J. Múgica defeated this proposal. The Constitution of 1917 simply followed the liberal precedent of 1857 by restricting military justice to questions connected to "military discipline" (article 13).[39]

Other questions remained about the authority of revolutionary officers within the new system. Civilian-military tensions were endemic within Constitutionalist ranks. These conflicts reflected separate institutional and personal interests and produced distinct interpretations of what antimilitarism should look like in practice. Did not, officers asked, the revolutionary military deserve the right to determine the shape of the final revolutionary settlement before returning to civilian life? And, with the return to constitutional rule, might they not make better delegates, candidates, and rulers than effete civilians who had remained on the sidelines when the going had gotten tough? In turn, many civilians responded in kind, lambasting military leaders as uncouth, uneducated, congenitally authoritarian, and a threat to any democratic system, however much liberal-democratic rhetoric they mouthed.[40]

The question of the balance between the central and local organization of violence, so contentious in the nineteenth century, was hardly settled. As we have seen, the revolution in many ways represented a resurgence of traditions of local, civilian mobilization associated with popular liberalism. Many revolutionary leaders could claim both ideological and literal kinship with earlier leaders of the National Guard.[41] Urban workers also drew on traditions of popular liberalism when they offered to form militias.[42] By 1920, the revolution had produced not only a large Constitutionalist army, but a dizzying array of armed peasants seeking land (*agraristas*) and small self-defense groups (*defensas sociales*).[43]

For some revolutionary leaders, the central issue remained the supremacy of civilians over the military officers at the top of the political system. Others were more concerned with the use of the military as an instrument of state and class power. The press-gang, in particular, emerged as a key popular grievance, a striking example of abusive government that any revolutionary worth his salt would eliminate. Thus, while Madero argued that the attempt to create a centralized system of military conscription was eminently democratic, it enraged many of his allies and followers.[44] Finally, influenced by socialist and anarchist thought, some revolutionaries were also beginning to view the military through the lens of class conflict and capitalism. They were concerned less with civilian control at the *cupular* level per se than with which class interests the military represented and how it was used to protect them during strikes and quotidian social and political struggles.[45]

Military Reform under the Sonorans, 1920–1934

Through the 1920s, the victorious faction of revolutionaries from the northwestern state of Sonora controlled the government, led by presidents Álvaro Obregón and Plutarco Elías Calles. In general, the goals pursued by the Sonorans were far from novel: political stability, capitalist development, national integration, and anticlericalism. However, the Sonorans pursued these aims with a new nationalist, even revolutionary fervor and ambition, although their nationalism mingled with an admiration for what they saw as the material progress and dynamism of the U.S. society that bordered their home state. Sonora's would-be state builders were also forced to employ a new range of institutional and political techniques to achieve these goals, operating as they did in the wake of unprecedented mass mobilization and civil war.[46]

During the 1920s and early 1930s, the stated aim of military policy was to create a politically neutral army, subordinate to democratic civilian powers and dedicated to technical, organizational, even "scientific" perfection.[47] The regime represented militarism primarily as a problem of institutional design or individual morality. In this, the Sonorans drew on the experience of Constitutionalism's relatively centralized, professional (and victorious) army, and the liberal-democratic provisions of the constitution. General Joaquín Amaro, the energetic secretary of war from 1925 to 1931, codified rules on military discipline, pensions, promotions, and uniforms; reopened the Military College; and then oversaw the creation of the Superior School of War in 1932.[48] The same year, the Congress granted President Abelardo Rodríguez eight months of special executive powers to reorganize the army, leading to the creation of the Service of Logistics and a central directorate in control of procuring arms and the appointment of an army inspector general.[49] These policies were portrayed by the regime largely in apolitical terms, as technical endeavors, or as campaigns of stern, individual "moralization" of wayward officers and troops.[50] Even after the founding of the National Revolutionary Party in December 1928, the military's removal from politics and its technical and organizational progress continued as the dominant themes. At the opening of the Superior School of War in 1932, official speeches praised the army's loyalty to civilian powers and its lack of a "caste" mentality; press coverage and propaganda discussed the up-to-date military doctrine and tactics taught to officers.[51] In 1933, President Abelardo Rodríguez congratulated the army for having shaken off its "historical tradition" and left behind "political passions."[52]

Military policy reflected other cultural goals of the Sonorans. During the revolution, numerous Constitutionalist officers carried out a "systematic campaign of profanation" against the Catholic Church: officers imposed fines on priests, quartered soldiers and horses in churches, and mocked the clergy by dressing up in religious vestments; in Nuevo León and Puebla, commanders incinerated confessional booths; in at least one case, the army converted a convent into a brothel.[53] Anticlericalism continued to pervade the officer corps under Calles, and many officers encouraged their soldiers to view the church as an obstacle to national progress. Amaro earned the nickname "The Scourge of God."[54] The Sonorans also inherited older liberal concerns with military vice and dissolution. Military reformers proudly differentiated their army from "aristocratic" armies where military ranks overlapped with rigid markers of social class, or where officers themselves formed a privileged caste.[55] However, many of the military leaders were keen to reform the morals of the great mass of their lower-class soldiery, as well as army officers, whose reputation for gambling, philandering, and corruption was notorious. During the revolution, many people thought of army barracks not as bulwarks of respectability but as epicenters of vice, promiscuity, and prostitution. Aside from their poor and unhealthy construction, barracks were full of enlisted men whose crude manners and proclivity for gambling, alcohol, and marijuana were notorious. *Soldaderas*, the female companions of enlisted men who lived alongside them in the barracks, were considered by many as a kind of prostitute.[56] Army reformers largely agreed with this diagnosis and sought to inculcate new masculine habits of sobriety, self-discipline, cleanliness, and physical fitness.[57] Military officers sometimes acknowledged among themselves the distrust and even "horror" with which respectable society viewed the army due to its moral shortcomings.[58]

Amaro's dream of making the army simply an instrument of central, let alone civilian, authority was difficult. In 1923–24, roughly 40 percent of the army rebelled against the government. Many revolutionary generals resented the Sonorans' consolidation of national power, and particularly Obregón's choice of Calles as his successor to the presidency. Ironically, opposition eventually coalesced loosely around Adolfo de la Huerta, one of the few members of the Sonoran revolutionary elite who did not sport a military rank; de la Huerta resented Obregón's backing of Calles, urged a more conservative policy of land reform, saw Obregón's policy toward the United States as too conciliatory, and was angered by the assassination of Villa, whom he considered a potential ally, in 1923.[59] In 1927, generals Francisco Serrano and Arnulfo Gómez lost the presidential election and began to plan another rebellion along with about 20 percent of the army. The government learned of these plans and crushed the movement by summarily executing its leaders. In 1929, General Gonzalo Escobar led about a third of the army in the last serious military rebellion against the postrevolutionary regime.[60]

The Sonoran regime portrayed these rebellions as apolitical: a continuation of personalistic *caudillismo* or, in Alberto Pani's biological analogy, the result of "healthy elements" fighting "morbid germs" in the body politic.[61] However, like nineteenth-century *pronunciamientos*, revolts were not strictly military affairs, and revolutionary generals sought broader coalitions of civilian supporters. Jorge Prieto Laurens's Cooperativist Party was the largest single party in the legislature in 1923, and it backed the de la Huerta rebellion.[62] Serrano and Gómez also sought political allies, notably Chiapas governor General Carlos Vidal. Vidal headed the Chiapas Socialist Party and tried to build a mass, anti-reelectionist party across Mexico to resist Obregón's bid to have himself re-elected president.[63] The rebellions of the 1920s helped the Sonorans purge some of the more recalcitrant officers, but these rebellions also taught crucial lessons to the victors. While Obregón remained skeptical of political parties, recurrent rebellions and the numerous experiments in provincial party building helped to convince Calles of the need for some kind of national political party to stabilize Mexican politics. By 1928, the Sonorans' suppression of competing parties, and Obregón's assassination, eventually made the creation of a national revolutionary party under Calles's auspices possible.[64]

As an instrument for helping to keep the Sonoran revolutionary leaders in national power, the army, combined with other political strategies, just about served. Obregón and Calles managed to obtain recognition and loans from the U.S. government and negotiate temporary solutions to disputes over oil rights, debt, and damages; they cultivated support among some agrarian and labor groups, particularly the Regional Confederation of Mexican Workers (Confederación Regional Obrera Mexicana, or CROM). However, the army remained crucial in defeating military rebellions, and in crushing the rebellion of the Yaqui in Sonora in 1926–27. To project power outside of the cities into the large and often unknown countryside, the army had to cooperate with the various auxiliary and paramilitary forces bequeathed by the revolution. However, the army remained one of the few institutions of national reach and allowed the government to secure the minimal resources that it needed to perpetuate itself in Mexico City: the main ports, oil fields, transport lines, borders, and cities. The army could not defeat the massive popular rebellion of Cristeros across the center-west states of Jalisco, Aguascalientes, Colima, Durango, Michoacán, and Zacatecas; however, by employing counterinsurgency tactics such as concentration camps and new technologies such as machine guns, it could contain it.[65]

The army's technological and organizational advantages over rebels were not enormous, but they made a difference. Mexico's army was made up largely of men equipped with small arms on foot or horseback. The army had no tanks and little heavy artillery, and it was overwhelmingly reliant on railways for mechanized transport. The army's few aircraft were mainly used for reconnaissance, although a few dropped bombs on the Yaqui in 1927. Although many revolutionary veterans had fought in major set-piece battles in 1914–15, soldiers' experience and skills generally resided in counterinsurgency, small-scale warfare, ambushes, crafty maneuvers, small engagements, and what foreign military observers referred to condescendingly as "the pseudostrategy of the bushwacker."[66] However, by the early 1930s, the army had acquired better rifles, more machine guns, and an improved supply and communication system: most commands were now connected by telephone lines, each battalion and regiment had a radio unit, and the army created resupply stations at strategic points across the country. In the early 1930s, the army's roughly 52,000 troops and officers were dispersed across the country as a de facto federal police force. In 1924, the government created thirty-two military zones, whose boundaries largely mirrored those of the federal states. Each zone was commanded by a general and typically had between two and three infantry or cavalry units stationed in it, headquartered in the main provincial cities. At any one time, roughly two-thirds of the troops were scattered across the states in smaller policing squads.[67]

However, the central government's authority over the army was very much a matter of give and take. Those revolutionary generals who helped prop up the government expected to enjoy a share of political power and opportunities to amass wealth, and they usually did. Counterinsurgency and policing disrupted any elaborate plans for training and for the systematic circulation of commanders. They also provided more opportunities for acquiring land or cattle and for profiteering with supplies and ammunition. Through the 1920s, while less important commands circulated fairly frequently, the large, strategic commands such as Jalisco, Veracruz, and Puebla were usually in the hands of powerful generals for years at a time; much like earlier Constitutionalist commanders, these generals often meddled in state politics and used their connections and coercive powers to mediate agrarian disputes and build up businesses in agriculture, the vice trade, and construction.[68] Military commanders' power did not go uncontested and varied from region to region, depending particularly on the relative strength of organized labor, peasant groups, and civilian-led political machines.[69]

The most powerful commanders met with Calles regularly and were consulted on all important national political questions. Jean Meyer produced a rough hierarchy of generals based on the frequency of their meetings with Calles in the first half of his presidency; General Juan Andreu Almazán led, followed by Gonzalo Escobar, Pedro Almada, Claudio Fox, Eulogio Ortiz, Lázaro Cárdenas, and José María Aguirre. After the rebellions of Escobar and Aguirre in 1929, Almazán, Saturnino Cedillo, Amaro, and Cárdenas were the four leading power brokers in the army, alongside Calles.[70] Lieuwen identified a second rung of political generals beneath this "big five" in the early 1930s, all of whom had been prominent in fighting the 1929 rebellion: Eulogio Ortiz, Miguel Acosta, Alejandro Mange, and Matías Ramos.[71] Amaro's new written rules governing promotions and discipline had something of a phantasmagoric quality then, distorted by what ex-Zapatista General Rodolfo López de Nava called the "internal politics" of "military administrative life" in the late 1920s. Internal military politicking and influence peddling were a game that López de Nava "had to learn to play."[72]

Central authority over the army was fragile and highly negotiated; the other key Sonoran claim, that central authority was itself civilian in nature, appeared questionable to many. To be sure, Sonoran military reform enjoyed some successes. The Sonorans shrank the army from a total of roughly 100,000 in 1920 to about 52,000 in 1934 and eroded the army's share of the federal budget from 65 percent in 1920 to 25 percent in 1934.[73] Amaro's reforms created a basic institutional and legal framework for the army that defined it, in theory, as subordinate to civilian authority. The military schools opened and expanded by Amaro began teaching specialized military knowledge to career officers. Initially dependent on old Porfirian officers, by the early 1930s military schools were run by revolutionary-era officers, usually autodidacts like Amaro himself, and official teaching materials and magazines repeated a relentless mantra of loyalty and obedience to the government.[74] On the other hand, military officers' political power remained imposing and, importantly, was seen to be so. When they occupied political posts, military officers (usually) went to the trouble of formally leaving the army and adopted the persona of a besuited civilian. The Constitution of 1917 demanded that aspiring senators and deputies leave active military service ninety days prior to elections (articles 55, 58); this prohibition was extended to six months for presidential candidates (article 81).

However, the sheer number of military men who moved into political posts was hard to ignore: roughly 35 percent of government posts were held by men with military ranks between 1920 and 1934.[75] In 1931, generals controlled the executive committee of the National Revolutionary Party (Partido Nacional Revolucionario, PNR), occupied half of the governorships, and held key cabinet posts in the departments of war, government, agriculture, and communications. Calles famously insisted on the civilian nature of the revolutionary party and arranged for the civilian Emilio Portes Gil to assume the presidency of Mexico. However, the power of Calles and other military men to shape national politics endured, and backstage military politics soon led to another general occupying the presidency. The Sonoran regime had to ally with precisely the type of semiautonomous military cacique that they vowed to eliminate to shore up their own power, San Luis Potosí's Saturnino Cedillo being the best example.[76]

Claims about the civilian nature of the regime involved different notions of "revolutionary time."[77] For the regime, the contradictions and problems of military policy were temporary glitches on the way to the eventual achievement of civilian ascendancy and a neutral army.[78] Others—victims of generals' primitive accumulation during the Cristiada, whose electoral campaigns were obstructed by local garrisons, or who noticed how Amaro himself accumulated properties and cultivated political cliques among newly educated officers—had good reason to wonder if such contradictions were temporary or augured a permanent divorce of theory and practise.[79] After all, the revolution had not only given rise to a noisy public commitment to military neutrality but also contributed to a colorful and widely understood lexicon that people used to describe the familiar discrepancy between military theory and practice: *cañonazos* (military bribes); *generalazos* (politically important generals); *coronelitos* (inconsequential colonels); *generales de dedo* (dubiously promoted generals); and *generales de banqueta* (generals more skilled at banqueting than fighting).[80] In the early 1930s, opposition groups on the right and left scorned the regime's antimilitarism. In short, the aura of hypocrisy about the Sonorans' antimilitarist credentials proved hard to dispel.[81]

The Sonoran regime also sought to turn the army into a respectable symbol of nationalism that transcended social, ethnic, and political divisions. In the early 1930s, the army remained ill suited to this role. Aside from the obvious problem that its core mission was coercing co-nationals, it remained a powerful but heterogeneous and divided organization. The bulk of the army's 45,000 enlisted men were concentrated in fifty-one infantry battalions and forty cavalry regiments.[82] Troop recruitment was voluntary, although regional commanders were not beyond resorting to the press-gang when confronting regional rebellions. Unsurprisingly, then, desertions remained a major problem. According to figures collected by the U.S. military attaché, 21,214 men deserted the army in 1929, about 45 percent of the total.[83] Recruitment for particular units was also highly concentrated in certain indigenous regions and displayed many continuities with Porfirian patterns. In the late 1920s, for example, six battalions and two regiments came exclusively from the sierras of Juchitán, Ixtepeji, and Juárez in Oaxaca. After the regime used the army to put down the rebellion of Yaqui Indians in Sonora in 1926–27, it gathered Yaqui troops in one cavalry regiment and five battalions of infantry. Northern officers considered these units, along with others from Guerrero's Sierra de Iguala (one battalion, two regiments), the Tarascan regions of Michoacán (four regiments), and the Sierra Norte de Puebla (one battalion), as the best and most reliable troops.[84]

The army's roughly 7,500 officers reflected the social and ethnic diversity of the revolution. Most had cut their teeth in northern Constitutionalism, but others had joined Constitutionalism from other revolutionary factions, many as late as 1920. Most had not completed a high school education. Although most officers self-identified as white or mestizo, a few spoke indigenous languages and identified as indigenous.[85] A shared military rank concealed an enormous range of activities and specializations. Some civilian politicians had been awarded nominal ranks during the revolution. Some officers were viewed as genuine specialists in violence, counterinsurgency, and terror, such as generals Eulogio Ortiz, Claudio Fox, and Alejandro Mange, and were sent by Calles to unruly states with these skills in mind. In 1932, General Mange was sent to quell unrest in Guanajuato because of his "reputation as a terrorist."[86] Other generals built their reputation more on their capacity for political fence-mending and mediation backed by varying degrees of force; Lázaro Cárdenas, whose military record included several calamities but who negotiated successfully with ex-Cristeros in Michoacán, probably falls into this category.[87] Others, such as Abelardo Rodríguez or

Juan Andreu Almazán, cultivated the image above all of a progressive entrepreneur. These officers did not always think much of each other; the military-minded Amaro liked to insult the entrepreneur and politician Aarón Sáenz by suggesting he was a "general among *licenciados* and a *licenciado* among generals."[88] The insult captures something of the slipperiness of military ranks—such categories were not hard and fast, and officers could move from one to the other.

Conclusion

The Mexican Revolution brought unprecedented military mobilization, bloodshed, and politicization. In 1914, the revolutionary forces decisively defeated the old regime and dissolved the federal army. And yet, continuities remained. Each revolutionary army drew in different ways on earlier traditions of localism, *caudillismo*, and professionalism. Revolutionary ideology often looked to the past for inspiration and inherited many concerns of nineteenth-century liberalism and antimilitarism.

Revolutionary antimilitarism contained internal ambiguities and different emphases. Mexico's revolutionaries were exercised by debates about the army familiar to nineteenth-century liberals (localism versus centralism, disagreements over the scope of legal and political rights of military men), along with socialist critiques of the army as an instrument of bourgeois repression. Antimilitarism was often divorced from practice, but it was also politically indispensable. After 1920, the Sonorans sought to consolidate central authority over the fractious, autonomous, and caudillo-ridden army inherited from the upheaval of 1910–20. However, they also claimed to embody the ideals of the revolution and were forced to operate in a society that had been mobilized and politicized to an unprecedented extent, many of whose members used the revolution's multifaceted ideology and the erosion of old forms of social deference to protest perceived military abuses. From this point on, political conflicts over the transformation of the postrevolutionary army were not only about securing the authority of the central government, although this was certainly crucial. They also concerned the new regime's search for some sort of legitimacy—its attempt to define and be seen to live up to one of the central claims of revolutionary ideology.

In the 1920s, official military policy aimed to create clear institutional separations between the soldiers and civilians and to depoliticize and moralize the army. The Sonorans drew heavily on liberal-democratic discourse, but they were far from liberal-democratic in practice. Through the 1920s, the regime successfully used the army to hold onto national power, although state authority over the army remained loose and highly negotiated. The prominence and visibility of military officers' power ensured that the Sonorans' claim to be creating an essentially civilian new order was fragile, as was the army's claim to be a respectable, unified institution representative of the nation. It was very much an open question whether the contradictions and unevenness of military reform were temporary, or whether they augured a permanent divorce between theory and practice. In any case, soon a new president would take power, marginalize the Sonoran faction of Callistas, and experiment with a different interpretation of the military's role in society.

Cardenismo, Revolutionary Citizenship, and the Redefinition of Mexican Militarism, 1934–1940

In 1939, two radical printmakers from Mexico City's Popular Graphic Workshop, Leopoldo Méndez and Alfredo Zalce, made a new flyer to be pasted on the city's walls and street corners. In the center of one panel stands a stern young army officer dressed in a smart but modest uniform. Standing behind him are a humble peasant couple and an industrial worker in overalls. At the officer's feet scamper four small, grotesque figures representing Mexico City's right-wing newspapers, whom the officer is shooing away from the others with the swing of a military boot. The reason for the officer's disdain is clear. Aside from their obviously gaudy and decadent clothing, the figures from the conservative press flaunt the money of foreign oil companies that had recently been expropriated by the state. Moreover, as the cartoon's caption makes clear, they are guilty of pining for the former counterrevolutionary military dictator, General Victoriano Huerta. In short, they appear under the sway of capitalism and its characteristic militarist fantasies.[1]

The cartoon reveals something of the bitter debates between contending notions of the revolutionary army during the Cárdenas administration. Certainly, it shows a distinct change in how the army was represented within the left-wing, often Communist artistic milieu in which the printmakers worked. Like many radical artists during the 1920s and early 1930s, Méndez had used the figure of the decadent "repressive military officer" as a standard part of his repertoire of political symbols to question the achievements of the postrevolutionary regime.[2] In 1934, he produced a print underscoring the class inequalities in the army between officers and troops.[3] By 1939, however, the army's solidarity with the masses appears to have been accomplished, the fruit of a new type of class-conscious officer, keen to defend the Mexican Revolution from capitalist elites and their military stooges.

Although this representational shift was due in part to a new Communist party line after 1935 that emphasized the collaborative politics of the popular front, it also reflected changes in the policy and discourse of the postrevolutionary state. Just as the printmakers of the Popular Graphic Workshop supported other radical policies of the Cárdenas regime, they also found much to admire in Cardenistas' understanding of the military's place in politics and society, which in many respects mirrored their own. The flyer itself was sponsored by Mexico City's Workers' University, closely tied to the regime's official labor confederation.[4] Finally, although the cartoon portrayed the press in rather crude and hyperbolic fashion, it was true enough that the notion of the Mexican army presented in the cartoon—of a class-conscious and openly political institution—faced vociferous opposition, not just from the conservative press but from groups within the government and the army itself.

In this chapter, I tell the story of how Cardenismo tried to impose a new version of revolutionary citizenship on the military, one based on class identity and revolutionary engagement. Historians have often described the transformation of the postrevolutionary army as the result of a continuous project of institutionalization and centralization begun by the Sonorans and implemented progressively from the top down, which prepared the way for stable civilian rule after 1946. Cárdenas's presidency is usually portrayed as a decisive moment in this long-term project.[5] Roderic Camp has used an extensive database of officers' careers to suggest that Cárdenas's success in eliminating political officers has been "exaggerated." However, he still portrays Cardenismo largely as a continuation of Sonoran policies of military professionalization.[6] Moreover, historians have tended to assume the state's capacity to enforce military policy rather than explore its reception in detail.[7]

I argue that Cardenista discourse and policy toward the army in significant respects broke with the past, engendered considerable political conflict, debate, and resistance, and had markedly ambivalent results. The chapter first describes the Cardenista project through an analysis of military texts and ceremonies and well-known policies such as the arming of a reserve peasant militia and the creation of a military sector in the revolutionary party. After sketching a general picture of the obstacles Cardenista policy faced, it tells the story of Cárdenas's new schools for soldiers' children and argues that they exemplify the novelty of Cardenista military reform and many of the problems it faced.

Before Lázaro Cárdenas became president, many in Mexico's revolutionary elite saw him as a loyal military man and a decidedly safe pair of hands. However, the confluence of the crisis in capitalism brought about by the Great Depression, Cárdenas's split from the dominant faction of Callistas in 1935, legal changes that extended the right to unionize into the Mexican countryside, and the collaborative tactics of the Communist Party during the popular front all led to a great upsurge in popular mobilization and a major radicalization of government policy. As a complex movement with national, regional, and local variations, Cardenismo certainly had its share of time servers, "sunflowers and charlatans." However, Cardenismo also espoused a recognizable set of goals aimed at sweeping agrarian and labor reform, economic nationalism, and a commitment to political inclusion and mass mobilization tempered by disciplined organization.[8] Cardenistas increasingly interpreted the Mexican Revolution as the culmination of the struggle of the peasantry and working class for an ambitious range of political, social, and economic rights, whose fulfillment would require the creation of some kind of mixed economy.

Cárdenas continued some of the Sonorans' military policies. His efforts, for example, to further centralize and institutionalize the army are amply demonstrated in the rules and regulations churned out by the Commission of Military Studies on the functioning of zone commands, logistics, military etiquette, and officer training.[9] He also sought to curb some of the military's power by creating a new ministry to separate the navy from the rest of the armed forces in 1939.[10] Most important, Cárdenas continued to rely on many familiar Sonoran strategies to manage and contain rather than eliminate military corruption and factionalism. Cárdenas's lengthy military career had equipped him with an extensive knowledge of the officer corps and the country. One of his major political advantages was that he seemed to enjoy some prestige within all the different military factions.[11] Like the Sonorans, Cárdenas sought to exploit his hard-earned knowledge of the army by carefully selecting and circulating the country's zone commanders. In order to exert "underhand" pressure on recalcitrant Callistas in states such as Sinaloa or Durango in 1935, Cárdenas selected new commanders precisely because they enjoyed political ties to their states independent of Callismo.[12] In addition to his reliance on old military allies such as Francisco J. Múgica and Rafael Cházaro Pérez, Cárdenas also increased the potential pool of such loyalists by bringing back a number of revolutionary generals from the political wilderness, principally old Carrancistas.[13] The government also continued the general expansion of military education facilities, although, as we will see, the content and direction of that education would change markedly.

Military ideology also shifted significantly. The Cárdenas administration now represented soldiers as ideally exercising solidarity with the peasantry and proletarian classes. Such solidarity was often portrayed as the result of soldiers' own view of themselves as the "proletarian class of the army."[14] Rather than representing soldiers as standing decorously outside of politics, Cardenistas portrayed them as active participants in a larger story of political and class struggle. Mexico's problem of militarism was understood, at least in part, as stemming from capitalism and class conflict rather than simply deficient institutional design, a lack of definition between civilian and military spheres, or an absence of military honor and morality. Lieutenant Colonel Juan Carrasco Cuéllar's 1938 primer for "soldiers, workers and peasants," published by the Department of Press and Publicity, along with his numerous public speeches and contributions to military magazines, exemplifies this shift in official discourse. Carrasco explained that the army was principally made up of members of the proletarian and peasant classes, saw himself as a "proletarian officer," and argued that Cárdenas wished to transform the army into a "new social and military organization of workers."[15] He also took it upon himself to guide soldiers and workers through some introductory chapters on Marxist sociology in order to "fortify their class consciousness" and explain the current conjuncture of capitalist crisis and the coming collectivization of sectors of the economy.[16]

Military discourse echoed how Cardenistas in the Department of Public Education (Secretaría de Educación Pública, or SEP) portrayed the revolution as the culmination of a longer history of anonymous class struggle and emphasized social and economic rights.[17] Lieutenant Colonel Carrasco explicitly acknowledged his debt to the new class-centered history of Mexico written by the SEP historian Alfonso Teja Zabre.[18] In 1938, Colonel Alfonso Corona del Rosal, an important political officer who later governed the state of Hidalgo (1957–61) and served as president of the PRI (1958–64) and mayor of Mexico City (1966–70), published the first edition of a key training manual for officers. The manual combined exhortations to military discipline with chapters that interpreted the new postrevolutionary state and army in the context of the history of the class struggle. According to the manual, officers could draw satisfaction from helping to consolidate a socially just order and mixed economy, which was the revolution's ultimate objective.[19] The military magazine *El Soldado*, intended for the army's enlisted men, also confirmed that Mexico stood at a critical juncture in the history of the class struggle, with the revolution poised to fulfill its promise for the masses. Nevertheless, the magazine also struck a note of nationalist caution. Although the Mexican Revolution formed a part of the global "struggle of the proletariat," it "has its own physiognomy . . . and fundamentally Mexican characteristics," which Cárdenas would address without the "influence of exotic doctrines."[20]

Under Cárdenas, the government used the new Day of the Soldier to illustrate the army's closeness to the masses. Some local politicians under President Abelardo Rodríguez had voiced their support for such a celebration in the early 1930s, and Cárdenas had actually organized the first such celebration as secretary of defense in 1933. However, after Cárdenas assumed the presidency it became a major national event on which the press lavished attention.[21] Each year on April 27, the president gave a lengthy speech and performed a carefully orchestrated show of solidarity and rapport with common soldiers, "mixing amongst them" and dining and dancing with their families. By sitting down to dine with a "worker" and a sergeant, Cárdenas could "act as a link to confirm the brotherhood of the soldier and the worker."[22]

Official speeches on the day blended predictable military themes of loyalty, bravery, and sacrifice with a new emphasis on social solidarity. The date was chosen in honor of Damián Carmona, a captain known for his calmness under fire from the French in the nineteenth century. The ceremony was also designed to emphasize lower-class soldiers' respectability and "gentlemanliness." The press reported that civilian visitors to the barracks uttered astonished approval at soldiers' improved manners and decorum. In this respect, the state acknowledged some of the contributions of Sonoran military reforms: "The old legend that the soldier—once a product of the press-gang or the country's prisons—was somebody to fear for the *gente de bien*, was becoming obsolete while General Amaro was Secretary of War. . . . It is now definitively destroyed with the creation of the Day of the Soldier."[23] However, speeches also focused on recovering the image of the revolutionary soldier from the perceived condescension of an ungrateful, elitist public who dismissed the revolutionary army as a collection of criminals and "thieves" and stressed soldiers' support for the social struggles of the masses and their constructive role in society; a 1939 poster marking the day portrays a dark-skinned private happily wielding a pickax.[24] Enlisted men stood to give speeches about how they shared peasants' and workers' hopes for sweeping social reform.[25] Government propaganda also featured a poem reassuring soldiers that the working classes did not "hate" them but considered them "one and same."[26]

The organization of the Day of the Soldier also expressed the army's ties to broader society. Instead of the army organizing public ceremonies for itself, the norm during the 1920s, after 1934 local civilian authorities and the SEP led the organization of events, which included various ceremonies performed for soldiers by civilians.[27] Each day began with a group of local women gathering outside of the barracks and singing the traditional "*mañanitas*."[28] In 1938, the Cardenista Confederation of Mexican Workers (Confederación de Trabajadores de México, or CTM) sent groups of workers to congratulate soldiers in the barracks scattered around the capital.[29] The government instructed provincial teachers to organize ceremonies honoring soldiers either in their local barracks or by inviting soldiers to their schools; children were to leave such ceremonies with a clear understanding of the army as not only a defender of "republican institutions" but also "the main agent of the Revolution, and a promise of triumph in the social struggle."[30]

Cardenista ideology took institutional shape in the regime's creation of a peasant militia of *defensas rurales* armed and trained by the army. The government had used armed reservists of different kinds extensively since 1920, and they were important in defeating military rebellions. During the 1920s, the army tried to distinguish between several different categories of reservists: state police forces; local self-defense forces in towns or villages (*defensas sociales*), and armed peasants either defending or seeking land (*agraristas*). The army's attempts to describe the social background of these forces and their strength were unreliable and involved a good deal of guesswork. In the states of Zacatecas, Guerrero, and Guanajuato, at least, *defensas sociales* tended to consist of propertied conservative groups hostile to agrarian reform, including amnestied Cristeros.[31] After the Cristiada, General Amaro tried to reduce the number of armed *agraristas* and formalize the militias' relationship with the army as ad hoc security forces that could be mobilized by regional commanders against subversives and rebels. In 1929, new army regulations dubbed these forces *defensas rurales* and envisaged their use as "factors of order" for the preservation of "public tranquility." They were to be organized and deployed whenever state governments found it "convenient," although they would be under the direct command of the regional army commander. In addition to functioning as police, they would act as army guides and provide protection from bandits. They were also to provide the army with intelligence and were provided with an exemption from telegraph and postal costs for this purpose.[32]

Cárdenas boosted the number of *defensas rurales*, attempted to create a more institutionalized relationship between these forces and the army, and gave them an explicit social rationale. As governor of Michoacán (1928–32), Cárdenas organized the Confederación Revolucionaria Michoacana del Trabajo, which pledged that all *ejidatarios* (peasant beneficiaries of land reform) would receive "adequate armament."[33] As president, he created a central office at the Department of War to oversee the *defensas rurales*. Cárdenas saw this force as a way of defending the government's redistribution of land and tried to restrict membership to *ejidatarios*; he praised the Agrarian Department along with the Department of War for the spread of the militia.[34] As land reforms accelerated, the militia's numbers reportedly expanded to about 60,000 men by 1939. The image of the *ejidatario* who kept his rifle to defend his rights to land appeared in school textbooks in the 1930s.[35] On his visits to new *ejidos*, Cárdenas was often met by a small corps of armed *ejidatarios* standing to attention.[36]

Many Cardenistas argued that their understanding of the army's place in society marked a rupture with Callismo. After 1934, a new generation of Cardenista politicians associated Callismo with "militarism."[37] Cardenista officers within the army even published histories that questioned the technical achievements of the military reforms of the Sonoran regime and their political inspiration. Second Captain Rosendo Suárez Suárez, a history teacher at the Military College, published a short history of the army in 1938 in which he painted a very mixed picture of the army of the 1920s and early 1930s. According to Suárez, at the end of the revolution the army contained far more "bandits" than "soldiers of honor."[38] Amaro carried out some useful reforms, such as introducing sports to the regiments, Suárez conceded, but the author held the army responsible for the brutal assassination of rebel officers in 1927 at Huitzilac and noted that during the Cristiada numerous federal officers were rumored to be "fraternizing with them [the rebels] to sell them arms and munitions." Although he noted that the country had now thankfully left behind "counterrevolutionary militarism and dictatorial *maximatos*," it was up to the army's youth to end decisively "the traditional vices of the institution."[39] It was obvious to Suárez that his criticism of the Sonoran regime would be controversial: "There will be sanctimonious people [*timoratos*] for whom my work will seem scandalous. . . . My profound love for the army has tempted me in certain passages to shut my mouth; but I know that I make a worthy contribution with the truth."[40]

In some ways, Cárdenas's approach to the officer corps was not particularly novel; in the mid-1930s, he built on Sonoran reforms by creating exacting new professional examination requirements for junior officers.[41] However, he did experiment with trying to break down some of the divisions between enlisted men and career officers. In a much-publicized speech in December 1935, Cárdenas promised to change military regulations to allow more enlisted men into career-officer schools. This represented an attempt to secure enlisted men's loyalty at a time of acute conflict between Cárdenas and a politically suspect officer corps. Amaro's jeremiads on discipline and professionalism had a patchy effect on his newly trained cadets who, in the mid-1930s, "invariably" felt loyal to generals Amaro or Calles, rather than President Cárdenas.[42] Cárdenas also understood this policy as a way of producing officers who would see themselves as "protectors of the poorer classes." Cárdenas promised that any civilian accepted to a military academy would first have to serve a year in a provincial regiment or battalion experiencing the humble "life of the soldier."[43] Cárdenas's collaborators in the army also tried to curb harsher military punishments, making it somewhat easier for subalterns to lodge complaints against superiors.[44] Throughout the twentieth century, the army paid extra allowances to officers depending on their additional training and qualifications, administrative responsibilities, and regional differences in living costs, which makes it difficult to compare incomes across the army. However, base rates of pay provide a rough indication of changes and show how junior officers and enlisted men benefited most from increases in base pay and benefits. In 1937, Cárdenas increased the base pay of all officers under the rank of colonel and created new services for enlisted men, such as the schools for soldiers' children discussed below.[45] During the 1930s, the gap in pay between generals, junior officers, and enlisted men narrowed. For example, whereas lieutenants earned 18 percent of a division general's pay in 1928, by 1940 they earned 28 percent. Enlisted men earned 3.9 percent of a division general's pay in 1928, and 6.1 percent in 1940 (see table 2.1).

There were serious tensions in Cárdenas's project for the army. Most important, while the regime talked of soldiers' solidarity with the masses, it never broke entirely with the idea of military neutrality. This was particularly clear when zone commanders interfered in local politics. The national press, particularly *Excélsior*, frequently criticized the partiality of zone commanders. In its press releases the army defended itself from these accusations by denying that zone commanders had ever been diverted from their professional duty.[46]

In 1938, Cárdenas's creation of a military sector in the new corporate party of "peasants, workers and soldiers" encapsulates the difficulty of recon-

TABLE 2.1 Annual Base Pay in Pesos of Mexican Army Officers and Enlisted Men, 1925–1965

	1925	1928	1936	1937	1940	1941	1943	1944	1965
Division general	13,140	13,176			11,160	11,520	12,045	12,585	67,500
General of brigade	9,198	9,223			9,000	9,360	9,490	10,030	55,050
Brigadier general	6,670	6,588			7,200	7,560	8,030	8,570	42,900
Colonel	4,599	4,612	4,032	4,596	5,316	5,676	5,840	6,380	33,600
Lieutenant colonel	3,283	3,294	2,954	3,288	4,008	4,368	4,380	4,920	28,200
Major	2,530	2,635	2,376	2,628	3,348	3,708	4,198	4,738	25,500
First captain	2,373	2,379	2,136	2,376	3,096	3,456	3,650	4,010	20,100
Second captain	2,009	2,105	1,896	2,100	2,820	3,180	3,285	3,645	
Lieutenant	1,825	1,830	1,644	1,824	2,544	2,904	3,103	3,463	
Sub-lieutenant	1,643	1,647	1,488	1,644	2,364	2,724	2,920	3,280	
1st sergeant	785	787			918	954		1,064	
2nd sergeant	639	641			774	810		920	
Corporal	548	549			720	756		866	
Private	311	512			684	720		830	

Sources: Various military attaché reports, 1925–41, USMIR, reel 7; MA to G-2, February 5, 1943, NARA, MIDRF, box 2555; MA to G-2, December 15, 1943, NARA, MIDRF, box 2553; McAlister, "Mexico," 226.

ciling these divergent interests. In many ways, this arrangement grew quite naturally out of the government's rhetoric in 1935–37, which had stressed soldiers' "solidarity" with the social struggles of the popular classes.[47] Earlier, the Cárdenas administration tried to resolve the tension between the notion of an apolitical and a revolutionary army by portraying soldiers' influence as social or ideological rather than political. The founding of the corporate party seemed to eclipse the notion of a politically neutral army altogether.[48] The army justified the move by citing Cárdenas's insistence that the army should follow "the generous idea that we are not professional soldiers but the friends, the armed and organized auxiliaries of the humble classes and of the people."[49] That the military's compulsory presence in the new party sat uncomfortably with its duty to oversee public order during elections was obvious to all and reflected the contradictions of creating a corporate revolutionary party within Mexico's liberal constitutional framework.

The government addressed these apparent paradoxes by arguing that soldiers would participate in the party not as representatives of the army per se but only in their capacity as individual citizens. The government claimed soldiers would regain their full rights to open political participation granted them in the constitution, while the army as a whole could continue to act as the guardian of national institutions. Perhaps the most convincing argument put forward for the reforms was that they would end the hypocritical situation in which military officers' obvious political influence endured but remained unacknowledged. *El Universal Gráfico* remained skeptical of the military sector but agreed that the unacknowledged influence of the army—one of the "dark forces behind the throne or presidential seat"—represented a harmful "paradox," and that at least in the new party soldiers would be no more than other citizens.[50] The conservative *Excélsior*, which had been concerned about Communist infiltration in the army since 1935, worried about the new party causing a "political virus" to spread through the military.[51]

The government created some complex and rather opaque institutional arrangements to convey the impression that soldiers' participation in the party did not compromise the army's ability to remain neutral during political campaigns and elections. The net result of these arrangements was that, in practice, soldiers' participation in the party was highly circumscribed. A total of thirty-three deputies were elected by the units in each zone command to represent them in the party, while another seven were chosen by the SDN. The exact procedures by which soldiers might elect representatives were never made clear to the public.[52] The secretary of defense, General Manuel Ávila Camacho, announced his intention to leave the details up to the "prudent judgement of the zone and corporation commanders." Manuel Ávila Camacho could overrule any of the "elections" anyway if he saw fit.[53] To further reinforce the image that military participation in the party did not erode discipline or institutional neutrality, army delegates at the new party's constituent assembly were required to wear regulation army uniforms at all times and signed a pact that required them to form a "bloc" that only engaged in political debate in private.[54]

Even with the founding of the party, the Cárdenas administration continued to oscillate uneasily between acknowledging the army's informal powers and revolutionary authority and circumscribing them, depending on the context. Cardenistas tended to argue that this apparent paradox represented a false problem since, under the present government, a commitment to social reform, institutional loyalty, and the demands of Mexico's particular conjuncture of class struggle all happily coexisted and reinforced one another.

Cárdenas avoided either a violent coup or a repeat of the kind of backroom maneuver by the military hierarchy that forced President Ortiz Rubio's resignation in 1932.[55] The one attempt at a military uprising, by San Luis

Potosí's General Saturnino Cedillo, was more of a regional political challenge than a serious military revolt and was contained without too much difficulty.[56] Some officers wrote editorials damning Cardenista radicalism, sparred with labor leader Vicente Lombardo Toledano and the CTM in the press, held academic conferences condemning military reforms, and eventually turned to electoral opposition.[57] Best known is General Juan Andreu Almazán's 1940 campaign for the presidency. In the 1920s, Almazán had used his position as secretary of public works and communications to support a burgeoning construction business. For most of the 1930s, he remained Nuevo León's zone commander, was a key regional power broker, and built close ties to powerful Monterrey business interests.[58] Amaro, chief engineer of the Sonorans' military reforms, also moved from backroom plotting to open, and ultimately futile, electoral opposition.[59] In the course of campaigning, Almazán harnessed a broad range of grievances against the official party, counting on the support of disgruntled unions and peasant groups alienated by the agrarian reform or official corruption. To defeat Almazán's campaign, the regime reinforced carefully planned party corporatism and propaganda with the more prosaic electoral fraud and street fighting.[60]

However, while Cárdenas and the revolutionary party stayed in power, other aspects of the Cardenista project for the army fared less well. Like its Sonoran predecessor, the Cardenista state could not extinguish the political autonomy of military officers. After all, although the army could never hope to police all of Mexico's large and often inhospitable territory, military men were still essential to the state's basic ability to rule and were embedded in policing roles across most of country.[61] Cárdenas certainly exercised considerable skill in appointing military commanders and cultivating the political careers of commanders loyal to him. However, the image of obedient, intensely loyal army commanders simply acting as "the watchdogs of Cárdenas" in the provinces oversimplifies their role and risks exaggerating their efficacy as instruments of Cardenismo.[62] Some commanders fit this image well, notably General Miguel Henríquez Guzmán, who spent the *sexenio* posted to the most troublesome states in the country, helped to ram through agrarian reforms against local opponents, built numerous military and public facilities, and hunted down Cedillo.[63] Similarly, General Félix Ireta used his time as sector and zone commander in Cárdenas's home state of Michoacán (1935–37, 1938–40) to build up his own political base, although he remained closely tied to Cárdenas.[64]

However, other of Cárdenas's zone commanders were blunter instruments of central authority and Cardenista reformism. After all, the army remained an unreliable ideological ally of Cardenismo. While Marxist texts circulated in military schools, and some military cadets caused a public scandal by travelling to Spain to fight for the Republicans, in Mexico City's cafés other officers bitterly complained about the unprecedented power of organized labor.[65] In early 1937, U.S. intelligence employed a Mexican captain to probe the opinions of army officers. The Mexican captain, whose anonymity the U.S. military attaché decided to protect, claimed to have spent two months talking to over 400 officers around the country, and particularly tried to focus on the opinions of junior officers by "listening in" on their conversations with "discretion and extreme caution." He reported widespread discontent with radical policies, and ingrained local obstructionism by both military and civilian authorities. Despite the reduction in desertions and the government's unprecedented efforts to improve conditions in the ranks for everyone from privates to colonels through pay increases, promotions, and new schools,

> no one is satisfied. Everyone considers that what has been done
> for him is very little or nothing—that he deserves a great deal more,
> that the president only concerns himself with the Indians, and with
> laboring men whom he has literally showered with favors. . . . The
> more violent use strong language against the president calling him
> "lazy" and "ungrateful to his own." . . . As to the conversations which I
> have purposely overheard, I can decidedly state that all were absolutely
> against the president; they complain bitterly and criticize him as a
> Communist, ignoramus, etc. . . . Every man in the army, from the zone
> commander to the common soldier who forms part of a detachment
> in the most obscure village, obstructs the president's policy which
> involves decided protection for the workman and peasant. Towards
> these elements the army has declared itself an irreconcilable enemy,
> perhaps jealous of the very substantial favors which they receive from
> the government. This obstruction of military men to the president's
> policy consists in their not furnishing the guarantees that they should
> when troops are called in to put down conflicts between peasants.
> It must be remembered that peasants are always quarrelling among
> themselves, over lands given them by the president. Furthermore, the
> military authorities pay no attention to the peasants' complaints.[66]

Zone commanders' autonomy combined with conservatism (or simple corruptibility) ensured that Cardenismo's military policies were subject to many adaptations. Some commanders discreetly curried favor with local elites, built clienteles, or deflected the impact of social reforms at key junctures. In Yucatán, regional elites successfully bribed zone commander General Ignacio Otero Pablos to help derail Cardenismo.[67] In the 1930s, the strategically crucial Sayula garrison generally remained "an effective instrument of the federation," although individual officers sometimes accepted bribes from local landowners.[68] The story of Puebla's General Maximino Ávila Camacho, to which we will return in more detail in chapter 4, is a particularly telling case of military autonomy. In late 1936, after the country's zone commanders had been moved or replaced dozens of times, Francisco J. Mújica's political agents still considered them to be distinctly unreliable allies in combating provincial opponents of Cardenismo.[69] The government's open encouragement to zone commanders to take the "initiative" in organizing the construction of barracks, roads, schools, sports fields, and airfields probably reflected an acknowledgment of persistent military entrepreneurialism and an attempt to channel it to useful, popular ends.[70] In December 1937, Cárdenas renamed the Department of War and Navy as the Department of National Defense to foster the image of the army as a constructive force rather than an institution that the public, officers complained, associated with "endless warfare."[71] However, by 1939 the army command was trying to subject provincial commanders' rampant construction to some kind of "general plan" and ensure that any public funds were used "with honor."[72]

The *defensas rurales* were also shaped by zone commanders' autonomy and corruptibility, and the military hierarchy's own apparent skepticism of the militia. In 1936, the Department of War issued confidential orders for the disarming of peasant militia in at least Michoacán and Guanajuato; in 1937 zone commander General Alejandro Mange struggled to disarm *agrarista* reserves in Veracruz.[73] In the south of Sinaloa, wracked by agrarian conflict, the army opposed the formation of *defensas rurales* throughout the *sexenio* as military commanders repeatedly struggled—and failed—to pacify the region.[74] The government also struggled to enforce a strict criterion of social class for membership in the militia. In May 1937, the president's office sent several confidential circulars chastising commanders for admitting small-holders, merchants, or various others not defined as proper members of the peasant class. By June 1937, the government seemed to compromise and allowed nonpeasant militia who had already been recruited to remain, and defined an all-*ejidatario* militia as a desirable future aim. The U.S. military attaché's sources in the SDN saw this policy change as evidence that Cárdenas had seen the error of his ways and was gradually allowing the army to curtail the peasant militia while seeking to save face. However, the government continued to try to ban large "landlords" and their tenants and employees from the militia.[75]

Deals with officers and commanders had a cumulative effect on national politics. Many army officers moved within the emerging party-state to counter more radical parts of Cardenismo by backing General Manuel Ávila Camacho's presidential bid. According to Gonzalo N. Santos, General Rodrigo Quevedo and Santos himself encouraged Manuel Ávila Camacho to promote his candidacy after the death of the previous secretary of war, with the explicit aim of moderating land and labor policies.[76] Manuel Ávila Camacho built up a sizable following among army officers, aided by his ability after 1938 to dispense offices in the party as secretary of defense.[77] While building his coalition, he also marginalized some of the more radical Cardenista zone commanders. In late 1938, he mediated a tense dispute between Sonora's powerful conservative governor Román Yocupicio and the pro-labor zone commander General José Tafoya, exonerating the governor and sending Tafoya brooding back to Mexico City.[78] He also relied on his elder brother Maximino Ávila Camacho, Puebla's governor from 1937 to 1941, and his influence over a block of conservative state governors. By late 1938, the three main factions of conservative governors had united behind the candidacy of Manuel Ávila Camacho.[79]

The Escuelas Hijos del Ejército

Postrevolutionary administrations often established with great fanfare specialized schools that could serve as laboratories for, and symbols of, their larger political and social goals. In the 1920s, the Casa del Estudiante Indígena helped illustrate the new regime's policy toward indigenous integration; in 1937, Cárdenas demonstrated his progressive foreign policy by setting up a highly publicized boarding school for orphans of the Spanish Civil War in Morelia.[80] The new Escuelas Hijos del Ejército exemplified the aims and ideology of Cárdenas's military reforms and their contested implementation. The regime set up these boarding schools for the children of soldiers across the country at the height of Cardenismo and presented them as one of the policies "of most importance" to the Cárdenas administration.[81] The students of the schools, "wearing brilliant, new uniforms," took pride of place during the Day of the Soldier and Independence Day parades under Cárdenas, thereby placing "before the eyes of the nation the true condition of the little children of the soldiers."[82]

The schools were to provide a stable education for army children, something that military mobilizations and redeployments had previously made impossible. In August 1935, the first school opened in an old church building in Colonia Del Valle in Mexico City, followed shortly by another in Tacubaya, also in the Federal District. The government aimed to place a school in each of the country's thirty-three military zones, and by 1940 schools had opened in the states of Michoacán, Jalisco, Sonora, Durango, Morelos, San Luis Potosí, Zacatecas, Coahuila, Tlaxcala, Guanajuato, Sinaloa, Puebla, Campeche, and Chiapas. Each school provided primary education for 300 to 400 students between the ages of four and twelve, and vocational training for older children in small industrial "workshops" where students could learn a variety of trades (plumbing, repairing shoes) and operate sewing machines and small printing presses. Other schools focused more on teaching modern agricultural techniques. Estimates varied among reformers of the number of children that might be eligible for the schools. Teacher Gregorio Lara estimated as many as 60,000. In October 1935, while the SEP planned the school in Guadalajara, zone commander General Antonio Guerrero estimated that the 2,000 soldiers in the Jalisco zone would have about 250 eligible children. The latter figure was probably more realistic, suggesting a generous national estimate of around 8,000 army children.[83]

The government also saw the schools, which were run by the SEP from 1935 to 1938, as making a vital contribution to the social and political transformation of the country. The schools were supposed to admit only the children of enlisted men (privates, corporals, and sergeants), and the schools' teachers assumed that troops in the lower ranks formed but another part of the working classes. Indeed, it was on this basis, they argued, that soldiers' children belonged under the auspices of the SEP.[84] Teachers assumed that life in the barracks had prevented children, and their parents, from developing a politicized class consciousness, a failing that teachers intended to rectify. In contrast with life in the barracks, "these schools will be closer to the people, and in great part in its sphere of action, and at its service; the students, therefore, will be in intimate contact with the realities of the outside world and will fully identify with the ideals of their class, in which they have been trained, for the social struggle in which, as adults, they will be protagonists."[85] Military magazines also presented the first school as being at the vanguard of "socialist education," even praising its library stocked with everything from children's literature to up-to-date "Marxist pamphlets."[86]

The vocational printing and sewing workshops in the schools, run as co-operatives, provided training that was as much political as technical. The workshops could form "true laboratories of socialism" and "train individuals so that they know that with class consciousness they are capable of successfully controlling businesses that today exploit the working classes."[87] The schools were also designed to educate an unspecified quota of "peasants' and workers' children" alongside soldiers' children to more effectively spread horizontal ties of fraternity and class solidarity.[88] At the opening ceremony of the first school, attended by the president and government dignitaries, students gathered to sing the "hymn of the *agrarista*" before posing for photographs, taken from the roof, of the student body assembled in the courtyard in the shape of a hammer and sickle; this image later circulated in a set of commemorative postcards produced by the SEP.[89]

Teachers at the schools for army children saw themselves as part of a larger struggle against "militarism," social inequality, and violence that they associated, sometimes explicitly, with Callismo and the federal army institutionalized under Callista auspices. Teachers did acknowledge improvements in the army's organization and discipline since the revolution and constantly paid homage to the army's popular historical roots. However, teachers such as Gregorio Lara clearly remained suspicious of the culture of the federal army. While "forming, orienting, and strengthening the class principles of the proletariat," the schools could also "give the military instruction necessary so that they (children) will know how to defend the conquests of the workers: but they will *not* form new soldiers."[90] In a telling metaphor, reformers presented the schools as converting the army's children into "armies of labor" or "new soldiers of labor."[91] The schools would inculcate physical strength and discipline through sports, assured *El Maestro Rural*, but would not form a "militaristic youth" or a "military caste."[92] Margarita Díaz de Téllez, head of the school in Tacubaya, defended the independence of the schools from the Department of War because the SEP was the only national institution fully trained and organized by "socialist tendencies."[93] By contrast, she believed army control "would certainly be unilateral, highly disciplinarian . . . and lead to tendentious teachings inspired by a purely military education."[94] However, Cárdenas also saw schools as one way in which he could recruit the children of lower-class troops into career officer schools. The army proudly announced that 100 of the 662 graduating military cadets of 1940 had been students at the schools for soldiers' children.[95]

The schools also illustrate some of the tensions in Cardenismo's project for the army, and that project's continuities with Sonoran developmentalism.[96] Official rhetoric combined an emphasis on class with the idea that the schools were a paternal gesture of the president. Cárdenas had pioneered similar institutions while zone commander in the Huasteca region and in Michoacán. Although some other commanders had also experimented with similar schools in the 1920s in their respective zones, the schools were constantly heralded in the press and in state propaganda as the president's particular brainchild.[97] In some ways, the schools continued Sonoran efforts to extend military men's exposure to education and other social services as a way to wean them away from loyalty to individual officers and to reform the vice-ridden barracks. The military's interest in moral reform, self-discipline, sports, sobriety, and cleanliness hardly diminished. Teachers wanted to stop the barracks from producing only "wrong-doers, prostitutes and vagrants."[98] However, the administration's focus on the families of lower-class soldiers as a matter of national policy was genuinely new, as was its implicit recognition that lower-class soldiers' consensual unions actually constituted legitimate families in the first place. Although Amaro expanded basic schooling facilities for troops, Callista reforms and benefits had tended to focus on new batches of young, well-educated career officers, and military rules did not recognize consensual unions for the purposes of army benefits.[99]

The record of the schools also reveals the ideological conflict triggered by Cardenista reformism at different levels of the army. The schools certainly tapped into a genuine enthusiasm for vocational education and do not seem to have had difficulty attracting students. Some commissioned officers demanded the admission of their children into the schools; Cárdenas promptly acceded to this request in at least Guadalajara, although this rather undercut the stated aim of only admitting children of the lower ranks.[100] However, the available correspondence between parents of students and the government suggests that the schools were better at fostering a paternal image of the president as the "dignified protector" and "one true father of the soldiers' children" than at promoting class solidarity or anticlericalism.[101] In their correspondence with Cárdenas, soldiers and their families discarded most of the radical rhetoric surrounding the schools in favor of an older language of paternalism and rights conferred by patriotic military service, bravery, and soldierly suffering. Captain Lauro J. Flores thanked Cárdenas for admitting his children, "who have shared with us the sufferings of campaign and the privations inherent to this life of continual hardship." Flores once served under Cárdenas, and he saw the schools as marking a long-delayed reward for fulfilling his military duty: "I fondly remember that during one long tour of duty where you, as head of the forces that combated the reaction, fell prisoner to the enemy, with your bravery and abnegation you taught us the meaning of the fulfillment of duty, and you told us that one day our situation would improve; we are seeing this now although we thought it would never happen."[102] When Candelaria S. de Arcovedo wrote to claim a military pension and a place for her children in one of the schools, she appealed to Cárdenas's paternal instincts and urged him to "think about your own wife and children if they were in the same sad circumstances as ourselves." She combined this appeal with a pointed argument about the heroic manner of her husband's death as an army captain fighting "bandits" in Guanajuato in 1937, in contrast to the "useless" peasant militia who "ran away like scared geese."[103] In Mexico City, one group of "soldaderas" even visited the Department of National Defense to denounce the schools' "attractive young feminine school teachers" who tried to bamboozle them into joining the Communist Party by talking "'about matters of which soldiers know little.'" Speaking to the press after the visit they insisted that they "loved President Cárdenas" but simply wanted their children to "learn to read and write and not to curse God."[104]

Other right-wing officers had severe misgivings about the school's radical teaching staff. In 1933–34, Brigadier General Carlos Martín del Campo had been chief of staff of the Department of War, and U.S. officers remarked on his influence in the army.[105] Afterward he held several posts in the army's department of education. Several times during his career he had, in his own words, obstructed the spread of Marxist "exotic theories" and "traitorous" activities by elements in the army.[106] In 1933, Martín del Campo had helped to foil a plot by three captains, four lieutenants, and one naval officer; inspired by Fulgencio Batista's movement in Cuba, the officers had planned to demand the removal of officers above the rank of captain and the division of the military budget between those who remained.[107] Martín del Campo was certain that Cárdenas had made the schools for soldiers' children a hotbed of leftist agitation inspired by "exotic theories . . . supported by a flag that is not the national one": "In these schools there is a regular percentage of students who do not come from, or have relatives in the army; they are attended by civilian teachers who feel more antipathy than affection for the army and, as a natural consequence, work in a way that is as contrary to it as possible. . . . Logically, those educated in an atmosphere of constant exploitation, in hunger and misery and having as a norm falsehoods and a lack of respect for the flag, cannot but feel hatred towards the army . . . forming a generation without a sense of their civic duties nor culture, that will be at the vanguard of the those who hate the army. . . . This institution [the school], far from having conquered the sympathy and gratitude of the students and their families, will bear the responsibility for social disintegration."[108]

In early 1938, misgivings by officers such as General Martín del Campo, along with budgetary difficulties and endemic syndical conflict within the SEP, probably persuaded Cárdenas to place the schools under the control of the Department of National Defense. Cárdenas explained that the handover was the result of the army being "more closely linked" to the schools' mission but offered no more details. Oddly, though, the first two schools in Mexico City were controlled directly by the president's office until January 1939.[109] This handover to army control led to simmering tensions between the new authorities, who proposed "militarizing" the schools entirely, and the remaining civilian staff of radical teachers, who accused the new authorities of being "reactionaries" and defended their rights to unionize as civilians.[110] The schools became one of the few institutional locations, along with munitions factories, where the army directly confronted organized labor.[111] Wilebalda Rodríguez Jiménez, who taught in several of the schools in the late 1930s, remembered the army directors' hostility toward teachers' efforts to join CTM-affiliated unions, since this "weakened their authority."[112] In 1939, Margarita Díaz de Téllez, director of the school in Tacubaya, complained that army inspectors were trying to remove her because they argued that it was illegal for a woman to have members of the army "at her orders." Meanwhile, the army authorities expelled the members of the school's cooperative of seamstresses, and an unnamed army representative blocked Díaz's control over the school's budget of 8,000 pesos, despite a presidential order that she was to administer it.[113] The tone of the teaching and public image of the schools moderated under military control; the numbers of nonmilitary children in the schools dwindled, officers' children were admitted to their own particular schools, and self-identified "Cardenista" teachers complained about clerical influence in the school in Guadalajara. Teachers in Mexico City complained at harsher discipline in the schools and "a complete ignorance of workers' rights."[114]

Under President Manuel Ávila Camacho, this uneasy compromise gave way to a full assertion of military control and a purge of the remaining leftist teachers who had responded to army control with "passive resistance" toward the "orders of the directors."[115] Some Avilacamachistas in the Congress even tried to turn the schools into a public symbol of Cardenista misgovernment and social dissolution. In 1941, the new federal deputy from Durango, Colonel Enrique Carrola Antuna, took the press on a tour of the schools in the capital and pointed out the poor facilities, flea-ridden beds, and ominous daubings of hammers and sickles on the walls.[116] In 1941, General Edmundo Sánchez Cano, the new director of the school in Coyoacán, also conjured a press campaign to facilitate his removal of staff.[117] After the SEP itself had been purged of leftists in 1942–43, the remaining "founding" Cardenista teachers were removed and the schools were quietly absorbed into the SEP's department of primary education.[118] According to the left-wing Cardenista José Muñoz Cota, Manuel Ávila Camacho's policy toward the army schools was part of a general plan to erase from education "the last revolutionary and socialist vestige of Lázaro Cárdenas." Cárdenas disapproved of "these manoeuvres," but decided to "allow them to happen."[119]

The fate of the Escuelas Hijos del Ejército exemplifies how President Manuel Ávila Camacho's election brought a more moderate course in national politics and a rapid return to the Sonoran blueprint of military neutrality. Other controversial Cardenista innovations in military discourse and policy were quietly dissolved or neutered in the early 1940s. Most famously, President Manuel Ávila Camacho effectively dissolved the party's military sector in 1941, only months after Cárdenas had vociferously defended it to the Congress; Cárdenas remained strongly attached to the idea, at least in private.[120] Those officers who held political posts were directed to join the party's popular sector for middle-class bureaucrats. Although military officers took prominent roles within the popular sector of the party in the 1940s, military matters were not a prominent feature of the sector's demands and propaganda.[121] By the end of Cárdenas's term, the government had drifted toward more conventional policies of recruitment. By 1938–39, efforts to recruit enlisted men into the officer corps dissipated. The Military College returned to a policy of only accepting better-educated "young civilians," and the school created for noncommissioned officers to advance their careers was closed due to "innumerable" problems.[122]

During the Second World War, military propaganda returned to the themes of political neutrality and technical improvements, repeated in countless pamphlets, magazines, speeches, and radio programs. Although some of Cárdenas's ceremonial innovations, such as conspicuously dining with lower-ranking soldiers, were sporadically revived by presidents in the 1940s and 1950s, public military ceremonies shifted in tone.[123] After 1950, the Day of the Soldier, so prominent in the 1930s, lost ground to a new Day of the Army on February 19 that focused on the institution as a whole.[124]

Given these reverses, it is not surprising that many thought that Manuel Ávila Camacho's election also spelled the end for the peasant militia. *Excélsior*, sensing a change in priorities, cast the militia as a troublesome anachronism; residents of Mexico City were canvassed for their opinions and tended to agree that the militia belonged, or ought to belong, to the past.[125] In the 1940s and 1950s, as we will see, the *defensas rurales* continued to be a source of debate within the government, along with other proposed solutions to rural policing. State governments experimented with *defensas ganaderas* (cattle-ranchers' militia) in Zacatecas and Chiapas.[126] Despite their troubling associations with radical agrarianism and reportedly poor discipline, Cárdenas's *defensas rurales* nevertheless represented a step toward centralization from which the state was unwilling to retreat even as it turned rightward. However, any ambiguity surrounding their social revolutionary or military rationale was expunged from official discourse. Between 1939 and 1942, several decisions by the Supreme Court and military tribunals confirmed that the militias were subject to military discipline and law while they carried out orders.[127] Under President Miguel Alemán, the justification for the militia shifted to securing agricultural production for the nation, "moralization," discipline, and literacy, emphases more befitting the "constructive phase" of the revolution in which "the time of hate, rancor and opposition" had been left behind.[128] The CTM's worker militia had regularly paraded en masse in 1936–38, although the government never supplied them with arms, and the military hierarchy was resolutely opposed to doing so.[129] In the early 1940s, Vicente Lombardo Toledano agreed to disband them anyway.[130]

Conclusion

Cardenismo's project for the army was at once ambitious and laden with contradictions. When Cardenistas interpreted postrevolutionary society through the lens of class struggle and sought a radical redistribution of power, property, and rights, it seemed to them that the Sonorans' model of an apolitical army was increasingly inadequate to the task and hypocritical. Cardenismo sought to impose a new understanding of what it meant to be revolutionary on the Mexican army, one based on class consciousness, civic action, and revolutionary engagement. To this end, the regime praised soldiers' solidarity with (and origins in) the working and peasant classes, charged the army with organizing a peasant militia made up from the beneficiaries of land grants, and encouraged commanders to build infrastructure for the masses' benefit. It also created a military sector in the new corporate revolutionary party, thereby both acknowledging the army's power and revolutionary authority and insisting that this arrangement was compatible with military neutrality in electoral politics. The establishment of the Escuelas Hijos del Ejército was one of Cárdenas's most prominent policies, as the administration extended benefits to enlisted men and immersed their families in the vanguard of socialist education; they exemplify the novelty of Cardenista military policy and its numerous problems.

This project's legacy was distinctly ambivalent. Cárdenas faced many of the same obstacles of military autonomy as the Sonorans and could not hope to displace Calles or simply govern Mexico's unwieldy provinces without tolerating military influence across the political system. On the other hand, Cárdenas's approach to the army and his careful political management of commanders ultimately encouraged enough officers to work within the system rather than resort to outright defection, albeit at some cost to Cardenismo as a transformative project. Many officers shrugged off much of Cardenismo, or used their influence to push for a shift rightward and a return to more conventional policies of military reform. Less radical aspects of Cardenismo—its tacit acknowledgment of the background political influence of officers, its tolerance of military entrepreneurialism under the guise of civic action, its promise of a more general political stability—were probably palatable enough to many in the military. By the 1940s, the Avilacamachistas abandoned most of Cárdenas's more controversial institutional and discursive innovations or rendered them eminently compatible with the hollow populism of the PRI.

This story challenges traditional treatments of the army's history that have emphasized the continuity and efficacy of postrevolutionary military reform and smoothed over disagreements about military policy. It also questions the idea that Cardenismo marked the culmination of postrevolutionary state building, inaugurating a new era of regime stability and consensus. Conflicts over military policy and power did not cease with Cardenismo but continued apace, part of larger debates over the meaning of revolutionary citizenship and class taking place across Mexico in the 1930s. In subsequent decades, some officers occasionally lamented the army's deviation from what they saw as its heyday as a genuinely popular, revolutionary institution in the 1930s and its conversion into a force of "simple gendarmes" protecting civilian authoritarianism. However, theirs were rather futile and lonely voices, with increasingly tenuous connections to the army itself.[131] In the coming decades, Cárdenas himself would largely remain tactfully silent.

CHAPTER THREE

Heaven Gave You a Soldier for Every Son

Conscription and Resistance in Mexico in the 1940s

In December 1942, the Mexican government tried to implement an ambitious system of military conscription.[1] Conscription was, along with a national literacy program, one of the flagship projects of President Manuel Ávila Camacho. The project responded to concerns about national defense, but advocates assumed conscription would do a lot more than secure Mexico's borders. Just as the new army schools of the 1930s reveal much about Cardenismo, conscription exemplifies many of changes in military policy and broader political goals of the Ávila Camacho administration. The government argued that conscription would improve the morale, efficiency, and respectability of the army and keep the army loyal to the central government and out of electoral politics. However, the government also hoped conscription would bring about changes in society that were, in a broader sense, political. Military service would inculcate patriotism and discipline among Mexico's unruly menfolk and allow the country to leave behind the social divisions and political agitation of the 1930s.

This attempt to reshape the army's relationship with the duties of citizenship met serious obstacles. Local authorities rarely followed the bureaucratic procedures outlined in the law faithfully, and conscription often became a handy opportunity for abuses and extortion. The draft also met with fierce popular opposition and hostility. This hostility could take the form of violent rebellion and riot against the army and authorities charged with carrying out conscription lotteries. More often, especially after the first couple of years of conscription, more underhand ways of frustrating and undermining conscription prevailed. Many people used competing interpretations of revolutionary citizenship to voice dissent. Along with older constitutional arguments, petitioners adopted the government's own wartime rhetoric on agricultural production, insisted on their material needs as campesinos, argued that the draft infringed local autonomy, and supported their arguments with references to patriotic struggles of the past.

First, this chapter discusses the state's project of conscription in the context of the longer history of military recruitment and discusses its ideological underpinnings. It then shows how the implementation of conscription was shaped by the limited capacity of the central state and different forms of popular resistance. The conclusion discusses conscription in light of neo-Gramscian interpretations that have emphasized the hegemonic nature of the postrevolutionary state and argues that it reveals some of the limitations of this approach.

After independence, state and military elites struggled to fill the lower army ranks. Throughout the nineteenth century, the federal army occasionally experimented with conscription lotteries, but they were frequently undermined by political factionalism and regional obstructionism, not to mention peasant recalcitrance; in practice the army relied heavily on the arbitrary press-gang.[2] The militia allowed for a far more consensual relationship between recruiter and recruited to develop. In some regions, service in the National Guard helped to forge ties between rural communities and national politics and spread a popular interpretation of liberalism that stressed local autonomy.[3] Until the eve of the revolution the numerous problems associated with the press-gang (desertion, indifferent or hostile troops, sporadic rebellions) exercised the minds of Porfirian elites, and some, attuned to foreign examples, recommended a new system of national conscription as the solution to the nation's recruiting problems.[4]

The Mexican Revolution can be seen, in as much as it involved protest against state encroachment of local autonomy, as a reaction to the press-gang and as a resurgence of traditions of popular local mobilization. Huerta vigorously expanded military impressments, and they became a common revolutionary grievance and an inspiration to writers of *corridos*.[5] In the nineteenth century, the suffering conscript had become a key political theme and literary trope throughout Latin America, and concern for the conscript's lot "a standard exercise in the display of sensibility."[6] Mexico's revolutionaries inherited these ideas, and the press-gang became a central symbol of the vices of the ancien régime. Revolutionary delegates and congressmen repeatedly condemned the press-gang as a symptom of Porfirian tyranny. However, military conscription also appealed to some revolutionary leaders. Madero had attempted to implement a transparent, national system of conscription based on random lotteries. Such a system, he believed, was consonant with his liberal principles and would fill the army with "a completely healthy contingent of vigourous young men, of much superior morality to those who were recruited under the old system." It could also discipline Mexico's wayward "national character."[7]

During the 1920s and 1930s, the army's system of military recruitment was decentralized, sometimes fell short, and obtained soldiers that many officers and observers deemed to be of dubious quality. Typically, regiment and battalion commanders created small recruiting "commissions" of half a dozen officers as they were needed and sent them to solicit recruits from nearby towns and villages. In 1927, the infantry briefly experimented with a centralized commission that was based in Mexico City and toured various states recruiting for whichever unit currently needed men, but it only lasted a few years. Recruitment was voluntary, although during the Cristiada it was sometimes necessary to turn to the press-gang.[8] Mexican military officers and foreign observers were concerned about what they saw as the inferior moral and physical quality of the soldiers obtained through this system. In addition to putting up posters, placing advertisements in the local press, or simply posting a large sign outside of the barracks, recruiters typically targeted "*pulquerías*, low canteens and vice dens." The U.S. military attaché's various contacts in the Mexican army complained "with a degree of bitterness" about the "low types" obtained by this system.[9]

It was not surprising, then, that some officers turned to conscription as a possible solution to the perceived shortcomings of the army. Conscription had been a staple part of doctrines of military professionalism imported to Latin American in the late nineteenth century.[10] Conscription has taken a wide variety of forms, sometimes serving the disciplinary, hierarchical aims of conservative regimes, at others exerting an appeal because of its egalitarian and democratic character.[11] By the 1920s, systems of conscription had been introduced in many other Latin American countries, and some Mexican officers clearly thought that their nation lagged behind in the "latest achievement in the field of military organization."[12] As secretary of war, Amaro dispatched dozens of military attachés to survey armies in the rest of the Americas and Europe, and some wrote glowing reviews of the systems of conscription they observed. Conscription's advocates, writing in the press and military publications, provided a familiar range of arguments about its capacity to strengthen national defense, spread national sentiment, and inculcate discipline along with a sense of egalitarian citizenship in the masses.[13] At the same time, it was hoped that conscription would erode the powers of military commanders by stripping their powers to recruit, solve chronic problems of desertion by delivering a disinterested soldiery motivated by patriotic duty, and, not least, finally remove the "immoral" influence of *soldaderas*. All this would help earn the army the respect of a grateful public.[14]

While some rising generals such as Amaro and Cárdenas were attracted to conscription, the revolutionary military elite also contained influential skeptics.[15] In June 1925, General Francisco Serrano, Obregón's secretary of war, wrote an open letter to the head of the presidential general staff in which he equated conscription with wasteful and unproductive "militarist plans," sparking a debate in the press.[16] In a revealing private letter from August 1925, Obregón, the revolution's most prestigious military strategist, objected to conscription on two scores. First, it was simply impracticable at the present time since the army's dirty, dilapidated barracks and the crude habits of the army's "poor *juanes*" would mean that, far from integrating society, conscription would simply antagonize and corrupt "the few men of good manners and learning" that Mexico had. However, Obregón was also suspicious of conscription in principle, arguing that it ultimately represented an urge to reconstruct Mexico on the basis of "brute force" rather than "moral force," which the experience of the revolution had shown to be futile.[17] General Abelardo Rodríguez would remain a strong supporter of conscription into the 1960s; in 1933, as president, he used state propaganda agencies to probe public opinion on the subject.[18] The government held a two-day academic conference at Mexico City's Teatro Principal to discuss conscription, but critics of the regime hijacked the event with speeches condemning generals as "social parasites" and the army's suppression of political and civil rights; on the second day scuffles broke out in the street after police barred critics from the event. After holding this conference and releasing propaganda, a state commission reported, rather sheepishly, that it would be "inopportune" to introduce conscription at present because of the "state of mistrust in the actual collective conscience." All of Mexico's "social classes" thought of the army as a collection of self-interested, predatory generals and consequently considered military service a "tribute of blood, for fratricidal purposes."[19]

By the 1940s, the time was ripe for another attempt at a national system of conscription. The outbreak of the Second World War certainly gave the project a new impetus. Since the Russo-Japanese war of 1904–5, Mexican officials had pondered the rise of Japan, and some had considered an alliance with Japan as a counterweight to U.S. influence.[20] In the 1930s, the Mexican army's high command considered an alliance with Japan unrealistic and planned how best to prosper from an inevitable alliance with the United States.[21] Indeed, in the 1940s, some in the Mexican government worried that the U.S. government's intrusive plans for hemispheric defense might threaten Mexican sovereignty. It is questionable whether the Mexican government ever considered sending conscripts abroad to fight in Europe or Asia; diplomats reported that Manuel Ávila Camacho may have been open to the idea, while Cárdenas was opposed. However, Cárdenas was convinced that strengthening the army through conscription would help Mexico gain more leverage in defense negotiations, resist U.S. plans to post troops on Mexican territory, and extract credit, training, and equipment from the United States to update its armed forces.[22] In 1944, Mexico eventually sent the famous Squadron 201, made up of 300 U.S.-trained fighter pilots and crewmen, to fly sorties in the Philippines.

As important as these strategic arguments was the idea that conscription could help further tame the army, cement internal order against "revolutionaries and saboteurs," and provide a school of discipline, sobriety, cleanliness, and patriotism.[23] The government argued that it was precisely the army's involvement in national defense and conscription that would focus its attention on purely technical matters and distance it from electoral politics. In his public speeches, Manuel Ávila Camacho described how conscription could foster citizenship, national unity, and the necessary discipline required by workers for the competitive "combat" of modern life. Conscripts would make responsible workers since "the lessons of order, valor, prudence, foresight, punctuality and discipline . . . are not only indispensable for combat. They are equally necessary for life. Because life . . . is combat, although not violent."[24]

By the 1940s, various political factions could agree on conscription's disciplinary and nation-building potential. General Rubén García was a popular and influential figure in Mexico's military elite in the early 1930s, closely tied to Amaro. He had long been one of the leading public advocates of conscription and had organized conferences and written newspaper articles and pamphlets on the topic.[25] Under Cárdenas, he fell out of favor with the government and joined the Almazanista opposition in 1940. However, García heartily agreed with Manuel Ávila Camacho on the benefits of conscription for Mexican society. García's earlier writing envisaged conscription as a genuine "melting pot" in which the process of acculturation and "moulding" would act on all social classes to form an ideal group of balanced, self-disciplined middle-class men: "The relationship of the son of the rich and opulent magnate with the offspring of the peasant and the worker, will mean that the latter will acquire many of the good manners of the former, while the former makes the softness of his manners much more manly through his contact with the coarseness and sobriety of the latter."[26]

Despite these earlier criticisms of upper-class decadence, it became increasingly clear that, for García, the working classes were more in need of discipline and patriotism than other social groups. After being defeated as the Almazanista senatorial candidate in Manuel Ávila Camacho's home state of Puebla in 1940, García turned his attention once again to promoting conscription in the press. By 1941, García had updated his arguments, ably adopting President Manuel Ávila Camacho's stress on "National Unity" and the drive for industrialization. He argued that the military's teaching of the virtues of "solidarity and hierarchy, so indispensable in modern times," would help prepare men for the industrial work that he assumed most conscripts would turn to upon leaving the ranks.[27]

Indeed, there is some evidence that conscription's promise to discipline without mobilizing the masses enjoyed some popularity among Mexico's educated middle classes by the late 1930s. Some nominally left-wing groups endorsed conscription's "civilizing mission" and its egalitarian promise. In Morelos, members of the revolutionary party's popular sector praised conscription's universal scope, "without distinctions between classes," and claimed that it would promote "the restriction of vices, the literacy of the people, and the general well-being of all Mexicans."[28] However, many other endorsements of conscription's nation-building potential came in a more right-wing vein, focusing particularly on the army's relationship with its peasant reservists. Pedro Rocha urged Cárdenas to adopt conscription "to prevent the abuses of the *agraristas* in the Republic . . . and therefore not have in our Republic battalions of savage people."[29] Others praised the policy because "obligatory military service will correct many of the problems originating in the revolution; such as indiscipline and the relaxation of the law and respect for authorities."[30] Lieutenant Colonel Rafael Mondragón, writing in the army's *Boletín Jurídico Militar*, argued that conscription would discipline workers that had been led astray in the 1930s by irresponsible leadership and "the diffusion of Marxist doctrines," teaching them to subordinate their interests to those of the nation as a whole. In July 1938, well-to-do students at the National University organized the Military Pentathlon, a right-wing group that aimed to train reserve officers and supported conscription as a way of teaching obedience and patriotism to unruly students; the Cárdenas administration initially kept its distance from the group but recognized it officially in September 1939.[31]

The idea that conscription could speed the integration of indigenous men into the larger mestizo nation was also appealing. In a private letter to President Ávila Camacho, Rubén García reached for well-worn metaphors of racial *mestizaje* to convey the contribution that conscription could make to national integration, albeit by means of vague cultural or psychological processes rather than biological mixture: "We must take advantage of the opportunity that the North Americans have given us to mix the race culturally and mentally, to create strong ties of cohesion between ourselves, incorporating the Indian into Mexican sentiments and ideology."[32] Lieutenant Colonel Mondragón went one step further and argued that conscription would aid *mestizaje* because it would remove "melancholic," "atavistic" indigenous men from their tribes and encourage them to marry white or mestiza women, improving the biological stock of the nation. Mondragón also argued that conscription could integrate elite white men into the nation by teaching them to respect indigenous people and the sacrifices of lowly soldiers.[33] Notably, some urged the conscription of indigenous people not only because of what Indians allegedly lacked (literacy, patriotism, and self-discipline) but also because of what they supposedly possessed, namely, positive racial characteristics that made them particularly suited to military life. The writer Carlos Marín Foucher argued that Indians would make particularly good conscripts since they were "almost perfect biologically speaking" and possessed "a power of intellectual assimilation much greater, without comparison, than that of the white man." Military service could channel the Indian's natural aggression, since "when he hates, (the Indian) hates with all the force conferred by his perfect organic constitution."[34] During the 1940 election, Almazanistas supported the introduction of some form of conscription but emphasized that it would be targeted particularly at the indigenous poor, who were most in need of it. Almazán claimed that indigenous men would form half of the army under his presidency, and that he would remove them and their families to unfamiliar parts of the country, train them in brand-new military facilities, and release them to civilian life with a new work ethic. However, the beneficial effects of conscription for the indigenous were also a feature of official publications and propaganda.[35]

Arguments for conscription based on its democratic, egalitarian character coexisted with ideas about national integration and uplift. On the one hand, conscription was based on an assumption of more or less universal eligibility for the lottery and was praised as "the most democratic form of recruitment."[36] Although conscription was still ultimately coercive, it was contrasted with the arbitrary, unfair, and disorganized coercion of the past. Characteristically, Cárdenas was particularly keen on this egalitarian emphasis, arguing that conscription would remedy "the unjust existing practices where only the proletariat contribute their quota of blood [*contingente de sangre*]."[37] However, if in practice conscription was to live up to its blueprint as a thoroughly democratic form of recruitment, a random lottery could not be expected necessarily to target the illiterate, ignorant, disobedient, or indeed any particular social or ethnic group. Thus, Mexicans qualified for conscription because they were modern, equal citizens chosen in an impartial lottery, but they would only become true citizens once they had received national values and an amorphous "discipline" thanks to conscription. Clearly this presented a fairly serious paradox, although neither an unfamiliar nor intolerable one. It was occasionally recognized, but the issue was rarely dwelt on. Rubén García urged President Ávila Camacho to adopt conscription as soon as possible, "in order to *mexicanizar* . . . (although it seems paradoxical) the Mexicans."[38]

Cárdenas introduced the new law on military service during the last months of his presidency in September 1940, based on article five in the constitution, which obliged all Mexicans to bear arms to defend the nation. There followed nearly two years of discussion within the government and the army about how to implement the law. Officers debated the ideal age of recruits, and whether public school teachers should be subject to the law; some officials urged the government to conscript at least 100,000 men; Sonora's military zone commander was so enthused at the prospect that he instituted "pre-military" training for civilians nearly two years before this was enacted in federal law; other officials fretted about the public hostility they were sure the law would provoke.[39] Eventually the new law was put into effect in August 1942, two months after German submarines sunk two Mexican merchant ships in the Gulf of Mexico and Mexico declared itself in a state of war with the Axis powers. The first round of lotteries was held in December. The law stated that all able-bodied eighteen-year-olds were to receive military training within their municipality each Sunday morning and, where possible, twice during the week. A select number were required to enter the federal army for one year: roughly 10,000 in 1943, 15,000 in 1944, and 20,000 each subsequent year until 1950. These conscripts were to be chosen by public lotteries presided over by a municipal recruitment committee, headed by each municipal president. Black and white balls were placed in a large closed container, while a child "of no more than 10 years of age" was selected to draw them out.[40] In Mexico City and large cities such as Monterrey, the first lotteries were major public events. Lotteries were held in sports stadiums in front of crowds of hundreds and were attended by public officials, military commanders, union leaders, and business representatives. Before the lots were drawn, soldiers marched, brass bands played, and schoolchildren and sports teams performed athletics.[41] In Monterrey, after each conscript was chosen, a brass band played a salute. After the lottery, each conscript solemnly pledged an oath to the flag and sang the national anthem.[42]

The central state was very far from being able, or even willing, to impose the blueprint for conscription outlined in the law. Incomplete birth records impaired registration, as did increased internal migration and emigration.[43] The government also lacked personnel to oversee military drills and relied on hastily trained rural schoolteachers in many isolated areas.[44] The SDN provided a total number of conscripts required of each state, after which state governments enjoyed a good deal of flexibility in allocating these across municipalities. In some places, army commanders used census data to calculate the approximate number of eighteen-year-olds who should register in each town, but it was up to municipal recruitment committees to organize lotteries and decide who was eligible for the lottery.[45] Peter Beattie has argued that, in Brazil, conscription helped centralize power, "breaking down traditional practices that had given *coronéis* a virtual monopoly in the patriarchal 'protection' market."[46] In Mexico, although commanders no longer recruited for themselves, conscription was still quite decentralized. Whether intended or not, this probably helped limit any friction between municipality, state, and federal government over recruitment and may have been the price the central state was willing to pay for a modest and imperfect increase in the supervision and organization of recruitment.

The conscription lotteries remained open to all kinds of abuses, as the bureaucratic procedures and egalitarian view of citizenship underpinning the conscription lottery dissolved in the acid of local *cacical* political cultures. Some youths were simply pressed into the army, or recruitment committees ensured that the only youths eligible for the lottery were those who had already been picked to be sent to the army anyway.[47] Complaints about graft and extortion were legion, particularly in rural areas, as local authorities exploited widespread confusion about the new law. In Puebla, people complained that state authorities made little effort to inform villagers of the new procedures.[48] In Yucatán, "some misunderstanding" of the military service law "had caused the people of Chan Kom to believe" that the law banned the civil registry of marriages of men between eighteen and twenty-five years.[49] A petition of 180 signatories from Xatepuztla, Puebla, complained that their gun-toting local police chief and assistant municipal president extorted them by threatening to take fifty conscripts from the village. The petitioners warned that the two men had continued on a tour of all the surrounding villages to extort more payments.[50] In Michoacán, locals complained about extortion by gangs impersonating military officials.[51]

Military and civilian authorities happily subjected the laws on military service to their own interpretation. Some local authorities simply seized on the laws as an opportunity to get the central state to equip local brass bands.[52] In 1942, another law was passed that created municipal "civil defense" committees, manned by municipal and local military authorities, to oversee wartime propaganda and "voluntary" military drilling of all men between eighteen and forty-five. Many committees, eager to impress superiors with the patriotism and organization exhibited by their districts and, according to critics, "with their eyes fixed on a higher political post," happily conflated this training with army conscription and forced men of all ages to attend military drills.[53] Sometimes this was done fairly brazenly, with published threats of fines and punishments. For months, President Ávila Camacho vacillated on the question of whether the army could force attendance at these drills. The SDN sent the president two different proposals for how civilian drills could be regulated. The first project was based on the army's own system of justice; the second placed fines and punishment in the hands of civilian authorities. The president rejected the first proposal and reviewed the other for months without making a decision. In February 1943, after dozens of protests from Monterrey were covered in the Mexico City press and a crowd of discontented trainees approached Manuel Ávila Camacho during a visit to Veracruz, the government announced in a national radio broadcast that military training of men not subject to conscription was purely voluntary.[54]

Some authorities used conscription to harass recalcitrant unions and troublesome individuals and communities. In Tulancingo, Hidalgo, workers at a factory protested that their manager refused to raise wages and had sacked unionized employees. They had been on strike for most of 1942, and dozens of other trade unions in and outside of the state held strikes in support of workers at the plant. Eventually José Lugo Guerrero, governor of Hidalgo, announced that he had to "intervene . . . in the difficulties arising from the worker organizations in the region, with Gen. Miguel Flores Villar . . . in respect to Military Instruction."[55] When the union at the factory had previously requested that General Flores Villar send a military instructor to train them on Sundays, they claimed to have received only "insults and threats." In different circumstances Flores Villar found the pretext of military instruction a useful way of intimidating striking workers and demanding that they send him a list of all their members of military age.[56] The inhabitants of Tepejillo, Puebla, argued that conscription "is used for reprisals or revenge to blackmail or harm particular people." They were particularly concerned about abuses by the neighboring municipal authorities of Petlalcingo, "because they sympathise with the landlords who are still hostile towards us because we received our grant of an *ejido*."[57]

Popular resistance to conscription was widespread and took different forms. In late 1942 and 1943, the law provoked violent conflict and armed rebellion to the cry of "down with military service!"[58] The most serious uprisings took place in the old Zapatista strongholds of central Mexico and in the ex-Cristero regions of Durango and Zacatecas. From late 1942 to the end of 1943, four or five armed groups of around one hundred men roamed the states of Morelos, Puebla, México, and Tlaxcala.[59] At the end of December 1942, dozens of armed men stormed the towns of Riogrande, Miguel Auza, and Nieves in Zacatecas while the municipalities attempted to drill conscripts in their town squares.[60]

These rebellions involved leaders or movements with broader political and social concerns beyond conscription. The attacks in Zacatecas clearly built on political Catholic networks; ex-Cristeros were prominent in leading the attacks, while agents reported that they received the support of some local priests. Sinarquismo, a Catholic integralist movement that modeled itself on General Franco's Spanish Falange, was founded in Mexico in 1937 and boasted 900,000 (mainly rural) members by 1944.[61] Rebels reportedly shouted Sinarquista slogans during the attack on Nieves. Government agents also reported ties between the Zacatecas rebels and urban Sinarquista leaders in the neighboring state of Durango.[62]

The Sinarquistas also had links to some of the armed groups roaming through central Mexico.[63] For example, the rebel "Plan of Puxtla," pasted on walls across Morelos in the spring of 1943 and found by a military patrol at Jonacatepec, is a transparently Sinarquista document and exemplifies how the issue of conscription could be subordinated to larger political struggles. The plan started by censuring Cárdenas as "the bad leader of the past government, imposing exotic theories, bringing undesirable people to our country, taking funds from the national treasury," who "with his soviet theories, killed industry, commerce and agriculture." Conscription was not explicitly mentioned but implied in the denunciation of Manuel Ávila Camacho as "a puppet of the jew Roosevelt, doing whatever he orders, such as breaking relations with Germany, Italy and Japan, declaring war on these nations, and cooperating with people from the Allied Nations." Finally, the plan demanded the reestablishment of diplomatic relations with all nations except the Soviet Union.[64] In Tlalnepantla, Morelos, José Inclán led a group of right-wing "nationalist" rebels; another leader from Morelos, Magdaleno Contreras, dubbed his rebels the "Forces of the Liberators of the South"; the men joined forces, made contact with Sinarquistas, and began to plan a major rebellion for September 1943. However, Contreras was shot during a skirmish with the cavalry in Morelos, and Inclán was apprehended after a shootout in the streets of Mexico City.[65]

At the other end of the ideological spectrum, the Morelense peasant leader Rubén Jaramillo took to the hills with one hundred armed men hoping to avoid assassination, topple the state government, and defend popular control at the sugar refinery at Zacatepec, but he also opposed the draft.[66] Jaramillo rebuffed offers to join forces with right-wing groups, since they aimed to create "a purely religious order that would return Mexico to the colonial era."[67] Although the rebellion against conscription in Zacualpan, Morelos, was certainly fueled by popular hostility to conscription within the whole municipality, the leader of the *"bola chiquita,"* "Don Cecilio," ultimately seemed more interested in toppling the new governor of Morelos, Jesús Castillo López, than in preventing conscription. Don Cecilio eventually made peace with the governor, albeit under considerable military pressure (and having received the government's offer of a new road passing through the town), and to the great surprise of inhabitants even presided over the first conscription lottery held in Zacualpan.[68]

The government portrayed these rebellions as isolated, ridiculous episodes. Admittedly, it was not difficult to discredit Inclán, who had joined the revolution from law school, reached the rank of colonel, and directed the military prison of Tlatelolco in 1923 before leaving the army and taking up a career teaching mathematics. Once Inclán was jailed in August 1943, the government encouraged the press to portray him in a "comic form" and allowed journalist Armando González Tejeda to visit him in his cell in Mexico City and interview him.[69] From jail, Inclán repeatedly claimed to be the author of the screenplay for the hit film *María Candelaria*, although "no one paid any attention."[70] One of Inclán's collaborators in the city of Puebla, an octogenarian lawyer named Felipe B. Ramírez, had given out ranks of general of division to other allies and even awarded his elderly cook the rank of *capitana*.[71]

However, rebellions drew sustenance from the larger population. Military officers expressed continued frustration at what they saw as the open complicity of many of the local population and municipal authorities throughout Morelos and the state of México with those arming to resist the draft: "If the municipal authorities and *vecinos* in general are not in collusion with these individuals, they certainly display much complacency and help them in different ways, be it with money or provisions."[72] In addition to the larger groups of rebels pursued by the military, in late 1942 and 1943 intelligence agents from Mexico's Department of the Interior reported "innumerable" other smaller armed groups in Morelos, Puebla, and the state of México incensed with the draft; such groups could not carry out "important assaults" but could easily stymie municipal efforts at enlistment and military training.[73] After his son had been conscripted, the municipal president of Tepoztlán, Morelos, arranged for his son to be "'kidnapped'" while taking the bus to report to the barracks.[74] Perhaps the most serious reported incident in Puebla involved the army laying siege to three or four hundred "rebels" in the town of Izúcar de Matamoros, Puebla. To ease the situation Cárdenas visited the town in order to reassure the inhabitants that conscripts would never be sent to fight abroad under any circumstances.[75] Likewise, in Zacatecas intelligence agents and the army also complained about state and municipal authorities protecting those opposing the draft, particularly in the south of the state. They also reported that, aside from the more organized rebellions, there existed a "great number of individual thugs actively agitating against military service" in southern Zacatecas and Durango.[76] Later, the government's investigation of unrest in Zacatecas exonerated the Sinarquista leadership of responsibility and confirmed broad local support for protests.[77]

Supporters of the revolutionary regime, or at least its pro-allied stance, could lend conscription enthusiastic support. The major unions, at least officially, offered no resistance to conscription, associating it with the defeat of "the totalitarian powers."[78] Beneath official union solidarity, some workers complained about drills and practices interrupting already long and unpredictable working hours, but these cases remained rare.[79] In Guerrero, members of the revolutionary party saw their support for conscription as a continuation of their struggles against local political "reactionaries" and "Almazanistas."[80] Complaints about military service from businesses were also rare. In July 1942, Juan Macías, the wealthy owner of "the refineries of Roble and Guayabo, and the mill of Walamo" in Sinaloa, complained about disruptions to work that he imagined conscription would bring.[81] However, it soon became clear that military drills would invariably be demanded in workers' free time rather than during working hours. Far more important to all sectors of business in the 1940s was the threat of increased labor militancy. Businesses were probably unwilling to antagonize the Ávila Camacho administration by confronting it over what were still relatively mild military measures, while the government sought to tame labor militancy and bring about a pact of national unity.[82]

Women were prominent in antidraft protests, just as they had been in the past.[83] In Zacatecas, protesters carefully chose when and how women might participate. In July 1943, the widow of a schoolteacher shot during an earlier skirmish in Nieves reported hearing of new plans to take up arms and prevent the lottery scheduled for the end of July 1943. If the federal army was present, she added, the local protesters had decided to change plans and stage "a protest of women."[84] There are several examples from other states of violent confrontations over conscription in which women played a leading role. Reports told of women hurling stones and trying to lynch military inspectors and the local recruitment committee in Tuxtepec, Oaxaca, in an (apparently successful) attempt to disrupt the first conscription lottery held there in December 1942.[85] Sometimes violent confrontations were fueled by rumors of conscripts being sent abroad.[86] In Pabellón, Aguascalientes, local women claiming the government was set to send conscripts north to fight for the U.S. government led a mob armed with sticks, spades, and knives. The mob attacked the local garrison, resulting in a clash with the army and the defensas rurales.[87]

The 1940s also saw newer understandings of women's relationship with military service emerge. Prominent feminists from Michoacán and Mexico City wrote to the government arguing that, in the interests of gender equality, women ought to receive military training alongside men.[88] These ideas did not prosper. Indeed, one of the attractions of conscription to military reformers had been its promise of finally ridding the barracks of soldaderas, who were blamed for fostering insubordination, promiscuity, and disease.

In 1942 and 1943, the government did decide to mobilize women in civil-defense organizations, although they were restricted to learning first aid or cooking for large patriotic ceremonies.[89]

Although the army was "extremely careful not to allow any information regarding failures to report for service to become public," the government did obtain most of the conscripts that it aimed to recruit. The government inducted 10,212 conscripts into the army in 1943 in two groups, one arriving in January and the other in June. The government fell short of its conscription goals by about 25 percent. About 15 percent of the shortfall was due to the army refusing to induct some of the conscripts it received, deeming them inferior or ineligible. A further 10 percent of conscripts refused to appear for initial training.[90] Many conscripts in this first class had been obtained through procedural "anomalies": some were too old, some were too young, some were not registered, and some had been pressed into service and arrived at the barracks "chained together."[91] All of the conscripts sent from Michoacán and Guanajuato were "indians recruited by the press-gang"; the army still accepted many of these forced recruits.[92] In a tacit acknowledgment of these problems, the army cut the service time of this first class in half and released them after six months.[93] After 1943, the army adjusted its recruiting targets and assumed that about 20 percent of those selected by recruitment lotteries would later be rejected as ineligible. According to the U.S. military attaché, this policy allowed the army to obtain more conscripts, although he noted that the government still refused to provide reliable figures.[94]

Many eighteen-year-olds stopped short of rebellion and employed the "weapons of the weak."[95] Local authorities sold medical exemptions or took bribes to omit names from registration lists.[96] Some men just refused to appear to be registered, photographed, and have their fingerprints taken and, in time-honored fashion, took to the hills for the duration of the conscription lottery. Military commanders issued vague threats against those dodging registration but took no practical measures, fearing trouble if they did.[97] At the end of 1943, only about 25 percent of eligible men had registered for the lotteries.[98]

It is difficult to trace regional patterns of resistance, given the fragmentary nature of much of the evidence (community petitions and individual letters) and the great efforts the government made to conceal shortfalls in enlistment. In an unusually candid conversation with U.S. officials, a Mexican officer in the SDN argued that the northern states of Sonora, Chihuahua, Tamaulipas, and Nuevo León along with Mexico City displayed the most enthusiasm for military training and conscription. The general excluded Sinaloa from this list of northern enthusiasts and recounted how the zone command had recently raided Mazatlán's "most important club" during a ball in order to make an example of the well-to-do young men and spur registration. The south and center of the country were "more indifferent." While the officer's explanation for resistance (Catholic propaganda and ignorance) was simplistic, this regional picture seems broadly accurate.[99] The U.S. military attaché managed to obtain a list of conscripts from each state in 1944. Although the government generally allocated conscripts to zones according to the 1940 population figures, there are some telling discrepancies. Although the army had originally intended to recruit in Sinaloa, Guanajuato, Querétaro, and Quintana Roo in 1944, these zones produced no conscripts the entire year. The northern states of Coahuila and Nuevo León, along with the Federal District, largely made up the numbers (see table 3.1).

In some places, a heavy military presence probably discouraged active resistance; Jalisco was the site of repeated military maneuvers from 1942 to 1944.[100] Most important, state authorities, predicting trouble, did not even try to register or recruit in certain places. In late 1942, the governor of Chiapas, Dr. Rafael Pascacio Gamboa, asked the government to suspend military training and conscription in indigenous communities in his state, pending "orientation work" and an intense program of Spanish instruction for sixteen- to nineteen-year-olds in indigenous areas. The SDN agreed to this proposal "temporarily," and Gamboa promised to implement a special program to this effect.[101] Margarito Rosales, the "governor of the Cora tribe" in Nayarit, also asked Manuel Ávila Camacho for an exemption for the Cora since, although they "loved the Patria," they were ignorant, poor, and "had little capacity," and the majority of the tribe and surrounding villages had decided that they "do not want this to be done." The president promptly and quietly agreed.[102] Although the states of Morelos and Puebla did produce roughly their share of conscripts in 1944, the state governments did not conscript in troublesome areas. In parts of Morelos, the state government effectively ceased trying to conscript people into the regular army and only attempted local drills. Other municipalities in the southwest of Puebla, an old hotbed of Zapatismo, had not produced a single conscript as of 1946.[103]

The government discouraged any debate about conscription in the press or legislature.[104] However, letters and complaints sent to the government illustrate the different ways people justified their hostility to conscription.

TABLE 3.1 1944 Conscripts, by State

State	Total Male Population	% of Male Population	1944 Conscripts	% of Total Conscripts	Conscripts in Excess of Population Share
Aguascalientes	78,591	0.8	160	1	30
Baja California North	41,766	0.4	78	0.5	15
Baja California South	25,542	0.3	51	0.3	0
Campeche	45,055	0.5	71	0.5	0
Chiapas	341,270	3.5	505	3.6	15
Chihuahua	313,225	3.2	613	4	124
Coahuila	277,417	2.9	670	4.3	217
Colima	38,048	0.4	76	0.5	15
Distrito Federal	807,575	8.3	1,820	11.7	527
Durango	243,667	2.5	340	2.2	−45
Guanajuato	520,886	5.4	0	0	−834
Guerrero	361,884	3.7	515	3.3	−60
Hidalgo	383,193	4	750	4.8	124
Jalisco	686,897	7	1,128	7.3	45
México	571,877	5.9	505	3.3	−410
Michoacán	584,238	6	1,150	7.4	217
Morelos	91,054	0.9	130	0.8	−15
Nayarit	107,681	1.1	175	1.1	0
Nuevo León	271,068	2.8	620	4	186
Oaxaca	586,147	6	984	6.3	45
Puebla	635,792	6.6	1,000	6.5	−15
Querétaro	121,656	1.3	0	0	−202
Quintana Roo	10,453	0.1	0	0	−15
San Luis Potosí	339,914	3.5	679	4.4	135
Sinaloa	242,724	2.5	0	0	−386
Sonora	181,232	1.9	351	2.3	60
Tabasco	142,476	1.5	262	1.7	30
Tamaulipas	231,298	2.4	390	2.5	15
Tlaxcala	112,876	1.2	220	1.4	30
Veracruz	806,505	8.3	1,410	9.1	124
Yucatán	210,711	2.2	400	2.6	60
Zacatecas	283,069	2.9	400	2.6	−45

Sources: *Sexto censo general de población*; MA to G-2, NARA, MIDRF, July 15, 1943, box 2551; MA to G-2, December 6, 1943, and May 18, 1944, NARA, MIDRF, box 2553.

A few complaints questioned the legitimacy of the revolutionary regime. For example, the Catholic women of Senguio, Michoacán, saw conscription as yet another abuse by a tyrannical, atheistic regime and complained to the president, "You treat us worse everyday and make us serve you like slaves."[105] However, most complaints appealed to the same legal, patriotic, and revolutionary sources of legitimacy claimed by the government. The Jaramillistas were only the thin end of a larger wedge of people who used the revolutionary regime's own rhetoric to resist conscription. Some people argued that conscription infringed on their constitutional rights. By the 1930s, the old revolutionary intellectual Luis Cabrera had become a fierce critic of the postrevolutionary regime. In 1940, he argued that a permanent system of conscription violated the constitution, since article five, obliging Mexicans to defend the nation, only applied while the country was under threat from a foreign power.[106] Although many people included a request for legal guarantees in their petitions, constitutional arguments usually blended with others.

Rural petitioners often used the official rhetoric of increased agricultural production for the war effort (and national development more generally) against conscription and military drills. Government propaganda efforts were extensive, involved direct collaboration with U.S. agencies (film, radio, and print media), and happily blended calls for patriotic unity against Axis powers with calls for domestic stability.[107] In San Andrés Tuxtla, one local enthusiast composed a *Corrido del Servicio Militar Obligatorio* to spur interest.[108] The emphasis on increased rural productivity trumped the controversial issue of military service in government propaganda and the official speeches now booming out from the loudspeakers newly installed in public plazas across the country. Communities could safely voice their hostility to conscription and onerous military drills by parroting the president's own rhetoric and insisting that military training and increased production were at cross-purposes.[109] Rural producers appropriated the state's own patriotic language to counter unwanted army interference: "We remember very precisely one of your speeches announcing that the battle would not be fought in the trenches, but in the ploughed fields, in the workshops and in the factories."[110]

Some argued that their rural campesino identity was inimical to obligatory military service. This was usually expressed in terms of economic pursuits. All that these "peaceful *campesinos*" wanted was to plough the soil, sow seed, clear irrigation canals, and tend their "miniscule plots."[111] Petitions from campesinos sometimes stressed their poverty relative to other social groups: "Our sector is completely opposed to the prerogatives that other sectors have, like the workers, with their days of rest and better salaries, five or six times better than ours."[112] Recalcitrant *ejidatarios* from Puebla, all "*campesinos* . . . brothers in work," complained about disruption to their farming.[113] However, the idea that campesinos formed a distinct class with their own autonomous interests was also used by opponents of land reform. Some small-holders from Guanajuato wrote in the name of the "humble *campesino* without a union" and suggested that the government should leave them alone and instead conscript *ejidatarios* and unions "who hold lands and bear rifles and . . . in their dealings charge whatever price they want."[114] Sometimes petitioners argued that the "*campesino* class" possessed a parochial outlook that was incompatible with conscription: "Because we belong to the *campesino* class, our sons are not accustomed to another life, moreover . . . the separation of a son from our side, will cause a lot of pain for us."[115]

Conscription also infringed on a commitment to local control over the means of violence. The government was all too aware of this problem and downplayed themes of spontaneous local mobilization in propaganda. In 1943, the Mexican film industry, in collaboration with U.S. propaganda agencies, made the film *Mexicanos al grito de guerra* to tell the story of the origin of Mexico's national anthem during the wars against the French Intervention (1862–67). However, the film carefully stressed themes of national integration and *mestizaje* and made no mention of the 1910 revolution.[116]

The long legacy of local mobilization in Mexico proved hard to shake off, however. The Jaramillistas were the most forceful example of this revolutionary localism, and Jaramillo's demand that military training only be conducted locally was apparently successful in parts of Morelos.[117] But revolutionary and patriotic localism extended beyond the Jaramillistas. Typical was a petition from the villagers of Matías Romero, Oaxaca, who complained at the disruption and practical difficulties posed by conscription but promised to fight "from where we are rooted" and "when the moment arrives . . . as sons of the Madre Patria."[118] Another group of peasants from Tlaquiltenango, Morelos, argued that they would fight to defend the government from any foreign aggression or domestic "reactionaries" but insisted that army training was unnecessary, since "we already know very well how to use a mauser."[119] Other petitioners were more enthused by wartime mobilization but nevertheless insisted that it maintain a local character. Promises of small, local mobilizations are also suggestive of older understandings of state-society relations and the kind of personal ties that facilitated mobilization during the civil wars and revolution. For example, Gerardo Ramírez hinted that his offer to arm and form a "battalion" from the employees in his printing and bag-making plant in Mexico City was conditional on the president forcing his brother Maximino Ávila Camacho to complete the paving of the highway between Tehuacán, Puebla, and Tecomavaca, Oaxaca. He also explained his pedigree for leadership of such an armed group, being the son of a "close friend of Benito Juárez."[120] Saúl Peralta promised to form a patriotic armed group that would be loyal to the president alone.[121]

People supported these calls for local mobilization by appealing to earlier revolutionary experiences and rhetoric. *Ejidatarios* from Chiapas refused to be conscripted, although they suggested that a military instructor could be sent to train them because it would enable them to "better defend our *ejidal* as much as our patriotic rights."[122] The members of the *defensa rural* of Cuautempan, Puebla, justified their request to form an armed band to train local men and "defend the Patria" by stressing their service under the revolutionary general Juan Francisco Lucas. Although keen to fight for the nation and "defend the Ávila Camacho government," they argued that, as members of the "popular sector," they had a right to arm and that, rather than the army or government, it was "society that judges us."[123]

Others praised an even older tradition of local mobilization for national goals. Juan Gómez, from Guadalajara, explained to the president that conscription was unnecessary: "When the Priest Hidalgo gave the cry of independence, all the people, without being compelled, and without having any military instruction, united themselves and triumphed: the people triumphed over the foreign invasion, and finally in the Revolution of 1910, they also triumphed."[124] Celerino Estrada, a Oaxacan delegate of the Liga General de Communidades Agrarias, made the "*campesino* class" the central protagonist in an otherwise very similar reading of history: "Throughout the history of the people the leaders have not been those who have overcome the situation whenever the Patria has needed the effective cooperation of the People. It is the campesino class that has always been ready to give its blood for the Patria, and given this fact, those aforementioned leaders should be made aware that they should be more restrained, and that this is not the way to *hacer* Patria."[125]

The postrevolutionary regime had itself celebrated Mexico's tradition of local mobilization. In his discussion of nationalist iconographies in Mexico,

Miguel Angel Centeno suggests that, of all the Latin American countries, Mexican nationalism comes closest to the European ideal of the "nation in arms," containing as it does "non-elite heroes (the *niños héroes*), the inclusion of civil and international wars, and a variety of icons and media."[126] However, Mexico's tradition of localism ensured that these bellicose elements rarely encouraged centralized conscription. Despite the famous *niños héroes de Chapultepec*, many people associated the federal army with the pretensions of Iturbide and Santa Anna and the infamous Porfirian press-gang. It was not surprising that people explicitly saw conscription as a reprise of the "press-gang of the Porfirian era."[127] This was a widespread sentiment in regions as diverse as Morelos and Tamaulipas.[128] In the 1920s and 1930s, popular memories of the press-gang had been echoed in official propaganda. In the late 1920s, the regime's own history textbooks had portrayed forced military recruitment as a quintessential Porfirian abuse against which the revolution defined itself.[129]

Conscription also involved competing definitions of the boundary between public and private spheres. Many Mexicans felt that conscription involved a confrontation between the claims of the state and those of the Mexican family. Petitioners often identified themselves as members of "Mexican families," rather than as individual citizens.[130] As was the case during debates over conscription in Brazil, some defended the private, domestic realm using the language of family honor and respectability and associated military service with dishonor, vice, and even penal servitude.[131] Angela Pérez, from Playa Vicente, Veracruz, heard about conscription on the radio and assumed that it would merely be for "the *rateros* and assassins that abound in this region."[132] Some people simply found the idea of conscription and widespread military training ridiculous. After returning from a year in the barracks as a conscript, Felipe Neri Roblero tried to drill some reserves to "impart my discipline in my people." He suffered so many "jeering and obscene phrases" from youths gathered around the public plaza that he was forced to remove to a smaller side street with his "platoon."[133] In addition to his constitutional arguments, Luis Cabrera also ridiculed the idea that military service could help educate and integrate Mexico. For Cabrera, while conscription might work in relatively well-educated and ethnically and socially homogenous societies, it was ridiculous to expect Mexicans to mix in the barracks: "While beggars and vagrants share the barracks with the children of the well-to-do and the bourgeoisie, how are they going to learn about equality amidst the filth and marijuana?"[134] Some, if initially seduced by the new rhetoric about the Mexican army, were rudely surprised by actual conditions and reverted back to older associations and images of poverty and vice. Juvenal Aceves and Juan B. Rodríguez, of La Piedad, Michoacán, had allowed their sons to be drafted to serve in a military hospital. Having visited them, both expressed their disappointment: "We thought that they would receive an education and decent food, but they are in the military hospital surrounded by *soldaderas* and recruits from the *ínfima clase* (the lowest of the low)."[135] Hermelindo Velázquez, from Pijijiapan, Chiapas, complained about the decivilizing effects of the army: "Young men are forced to leave the power of their fathers to be taken to the barracks where they will learn vices and where afterwards they will become accustomed to laziness, which will be extremely dangerous because they will abandon the love of work and . . . will return as thieves, which will be disastrous for the nation."[136]

On the whole, however, the language of family honor and respectability in defense of the private, domestic sphere was rather muted. Conscription's advocates saw it as way to create a new, more respectable army possessed of "a higher sense of honor," and among some urban, middle-class enthusiasts this image took hold.[137] In 1942, the government asked for families in the Federal District to house the first batch of conscripts for a couple of days and succeeded in finding homes for them all. Occasionally the doors of the family home were literally flung open: "The conscripts have come to form the most effective link between the army and society because they are representatives of youth from all social classes. Therefore, upon hearing in the press of the opportunity . . . I gladly offer my home to receive a representative of the *New* Mexican Army."[138]

By the 1940s, several factors began to improve the image of military service. During the Second World War, the state aggressively promoted the image of an apolitical, technically up-to-date, and respectable army to the public. The SDN organized press tours of military facilities, flying dozens of journalists from base to base; the press reported that for the first time new military equipment allowed journalists to submit their copy while airborne.[139] The army also circulated tens of thousands of free military magazines and held lavish military parades and war games in front of large crowds, both in Mexico City and in the provinces. A new "military hour" was compulsory broadcasting for all commercial radio stations.[140] The effect of such propaganda is hard to gauge but was reinforced by genuine improvements in service conditions. Many conscripts still complained about the food, shelter, and harsh discipline in the army, and very few of them were converted to a military career by their experience. Throughout the 1940s conscript units suffered desertions. However, conditions did improve after the first year of the program and were superior to those experienced by the remaining regular troops, something that was obvious to conscripts, regulars, and the public. Conscript units were also free of the *soldaderas* who enjoyed such a poor reputation in middle-class society. The Military College tried to reverse the old association of military service in the lower ranks with punishment by ending its policy of sending underachieving or insubordinate military cadets to serve for a term in regular units.[141]

The 1940s also saw a gradual rapprochement between the army and the Catholic Church, although it did not proceed altogether smoothly. The church hierarchy, along with the leaders of Acción Nacional supported the war effort in 1942, and the government allowed priests into military hospitals after a public controversy.[142] That many political Catholics associated soldiering with debauchery, gambling, and visits to "houses of prostitution" is clear in the elaborate measures taken by Catholic groups to prevent conscripts falling into vice. Shortly after conscription was introduced, the group Catholic Action, with the approval of the archbishop of Mexico, organized for groups of respectable young women to invite conscripts to attend mass. The group also set up a "conscript club" near Mexico City's barracks in which conscripts could safely socialize, eat, and receive religious lectures on the weekends; the club in the Federal District had 127 official members. Other such clubs were established elsewhere and were even attended by priests in Guadalajara. While some Mexican intelligence agents were concerned about these activities, they also learned that the subsecretary of war, General Francisco Urquizo, had given permission to Catholic Action.[143] However, in 1944, these moves appeared to backfire spectacularly when José Antonio de la Lama y Rojas, a junior officer who had attended some of these Catholic meetings, tried unsuccessfully to shoot Manuel Ávila Camacho in the yard of the presidential palace, apparently incensed at the army's 1943 ban on officers wearing uniforms to religious ceremonies.[144] A few months later, another young officer and reported friend of Lama y Rojas tried to incite a revolt in Mexico City's main barracks but was promptly disarmed.[145] Nevertheless, the bishop of the city of Puebla wrote pamphlets urging people to stop taking up arms against conscription; thousands of pamphlets were dropped by the air force across Puebla and Morelos. In 1945, Mexico City's archbishop featured prominently in public ceremonies honoring Squadron 201.[146]

Rather than dwell on the disreputability of military service, most complaints defended the private, domestic sphere in economic terms. Along with complaints about food scarcities and steep inflation, the disruption to agricultural work posed by drills and by the loss of working hands was a staple feature of petitions. Conscription could also disrupt work in towns, and conscripts struggled to be reinstated in their old jobs after their year of service.[147] The law on conscription itself encouraged this focus on the economic value of sons' labor by defining the family as a collection of economic dependents. There were several ways of applying for a postponement of military service, but the most important and popular provisions were for young men who acted as the sole provider of dependents. Married men were not automatically exempted from service but received a postponement only if they could prove that they were the sole provider for their wife or children. In some ways the law invited requests for such postponements, and the rule applied to almost every conceivable category of dependent, from parents, children, grandparents, siblings, nephews, and nieces to unofficially adopted children who could be proven to have been under the applicant's care since they were under ten years of age.[148] Increasingly people took advantage of these provisions, and by mid-1943 claims began to flow into the offices of the president and the secretary of defense.[149]

Following a Supreme Court ruling in 1949 that avoidance of military service was not to be treated as a "criminal offence" but only as a sign of a "lack of good citizenship," the law on conscription was changed in 1950. Rather than join the army, each class of conscripts needed only to attend training on Sunday mornings at any of the "Centres of Instruction," which could be a local army base, nearby factory, or football pitch. Although this shift was announced by the secretary of defense with great fanfare as an "intensification" of military service, since the numbers who registered went up, it clearly represented a shrinking of state-building ambition. Military training became a much less serious and less onerous affair whose main objective was the registration and bureaucratic oversight of the male population and the staging of patriotic ceremonies.[150] In 1963, the government gathered tens of thousands of men undergoing national military service for ceremonies commemorating the defeat of the French at the Battle of Puebla.[151]

The state's loss of faith in conscription as a tool of national integration stemmed from several factors. First, conscription continued to be difficult to implement and unpopular in many places. The government urged authorities to carry out the letter of the law and issued thinly veiled threats to expose negligent authorities to public censure, and the functioning of lotteries probably improved in larger cities.[152] However, in the later 1940s conscription could still trigger recurrent low-level violence. In Puebla, lotteries continued to provoke friction, brawls, and occasional shootings, while complaints about corrupt procedures maintained a steady if somewhat-reduced flow into the president's mailbox.[153]

Violent resistance to the draft became much harder after the end of 1943, particularly after the government deployed army units to "convince with their presence."[154] However, people continued to avoid registration and used bureaucratic channels to appeal for exemptions. An official amnesty was announced in 1944 that allowed men from the previous two years who had still not registered for military service to register with the class of 1926, thereby avoiding any legal sanctions and considerably improving their odds of staying out of the barracks. In the hope of obtaining more registrants the government announced in 1944 that it would no longer grant exemptions for students; in 1943 the military commander of Tuxtla Gutiérrez, Chiapas, claimed to have received orders to conscript nineteen- and twenty-year-olds if necessary. The government reintroduced an amnesty to try to spur registration in 1947–48, as conscription remained unpopular.[155]

The civilian president Miguel Alemán (1946–52) also had little enthusiasm for such state-led social engineering in general, particularly as overseen by the army. During the Alemán administration older military men on the right and the left urged the government to retain the original version of conscription, despite its difficulties, for reasons of national defense and as part of a general plan to remove the army from internal policing.[156] However, Alemán's mass transfusion of new civilian blood into the body politic slowly dispelled any lingering notions of the revolutionary army's possible role in social integration, even as it confirmed what, in the view of Alemanista modernizers, was to be the military's main contribution to the rule of the PRI: an obedient political police for the regime.

Conclusion

The government had long worried about its capacity to implement conscription in the face of institutional weaknesses and public hostility. In many ways, the experience of the 1940s confirmed these concerns. Corruption by state authorities produced a considerable gap between the law's theory and practice, and conscription also met different types of resistance. Violent confrontations over conscription were fairly common during the first couple of years of the policy, although rebellion tended to require other social and political grievances. More commonly people exploited the law's provisions for exemptions or simply avoided registration. Through the 1940s, popular resistance and civil disobedience could be effective at the local level; they stymied attempts to register and conscript young men and persuaded some authorities not to risk implementing the law. In order for these problems to result in an alteration of law, they had to be combined with a new political leadership that was more skeptical of conscription's supposed benefits for the army and society.

Popular protest offers a useful way to assess neo-Gramscian approaches to the postrevolutionary state of the 1940s. To some extent resistance to conscription reveals the existence of some sort of shared "mutual language for consent and dissent" and certain "institutional channels" through which to use it.[157] While the Jaramillistas drew on their understanding of revolutionary citizenship to resist the draft, many other people who wrote to the government used official discourse and nationalism to justify their hostility to the new law. Alongside older constitutional arguments, petitioners appropriated the government's rhetoric on economic development and proposed their own interpretations of campesino identity. They also drew on versions of history that celebrated local mobilization and that echoed the stories the postrevolutionary state told about itself. The law's definition of the family as a collection of economic dependents encouraged conscripts to pursue claims for exemptions.

However, the history of conscription also reveals the problems of interpreting post-1940 Mexico in terms of a hegemonic compact between state and society. Revolutionary discourse was indeed pervasive but coexisted with multiple forms of social and political conflict and violence: riots, rebellions, counterinsurgencies, petty fines, and official harassment. Moreover, during the fraught implementation of conscription, any such hegemonic mutual language allowed a bewildering range of interpretations and facilitated as much as impeded resistance to conscription. Some people also combined loyal language with active opposition to conscription (or at least hinted at the threat of it), and many others avoided institutional channels altogether and simply avoided registration. Moreover, some Catholic groups clearly stood well outside the boundaries of this hegemonic language, however broadly it is defined.

A focus on the state's and the ruling elite's hegemonic projects also runs the risk of downplaying conflicts within the political elite itself.[158] In the case of conscription, this problem does not seem so relevant for much of the 1940s. Although state authorities often corrupted the law, few people in the government openly criticized or sought to change it; the central axis of conflict was between the state and society. However, the change in the law in the late-1940s exposed some of the differences between older officers and a new civilian leadership less interested in using conscription as an engine of social integration and military reform. When it came to recruitment, military officers and civilian political elites could disagree about exactly how the army should fit into society. However, disagreements about recruitment paled in comparison to the fierce conflicts over officers' political power that riddled the postrevolutionary state.

CHAPTER FOUR

Civilianism and Its Discontents

Officers, Politics, and the PRI

After he became president in 1946, the civilian Miguel Alemán received a peculiar anonymous letter from a group of army officers complaining about their new uniforms. During the Second World War, the army had designed unfussy, khaki uniforms to help express the idea of soldiering as a respectable but modest, practical profession.[1] The officers complained to Alemán that such inexpensive, deliberately drab uniforms eroded the profession's prestige and "have taken away the posture and nobleness that have characterized military officers in another time."[2]

Such touchiness was understandable. Mexico's large, factionalized, but powerful group of military officers stood at the center of conflicts over military reform, and their grievances went far beyond sartorial concerns. After 1946, Mexico would have a civilian president, and Alemán oversaw a decisive shift in political office holding toward a new generation of civilian bureaucrats and away from the army. The number of military officers in the cabinet (excluding the secretaries of defense and navy) declined from 12 percent in 1940–46 to 0 percent in 1946–52; the figure grew slightly to 2 percent in 1952–58, before returning to 0 percent in 1958–64.[3] By the mid-1950s, military officers no longer seriously challenged the ruling party by contesting elections. In 1961, General Celestino Gasca led an abortive insurrection, recruiting campesinos who had supported the dissident presidential campaign of General Miguel Henríquez Guzmán in 1952. Gasca tapped into widespread peasant discontent, but precious little military support; the army suppressed the movement, although not without bloody engagements in Veracruz, Chiapas, Oaxaca, Puebla, México, Coahuila, and Guanajuato.[4] The idea that, after 1946, Mexico had entered a new era of "civilianism" and consensual politics that distinguished it from the rest of Latin America became an important theme in government propaganda and was echoed by a docile national press. Zone commander General Miguel Molinar Simondy's boast from 1949 was typical: "While officers in the countries of Central and South

America stain their reputations with dishonorable acts, the Mexican Army shows itself before the eyes of Mexicans and foreigners . . . to be a bastion of loyalty and respect for the commander in chief."[5] This chapter argues that, despite these changes, officers retained the power to lobby, graft, politic, and resist policies of military institutionalization, particularly in the provinces, through a combination of informal pacts and bold assertions of power.

As we have seen, in the late 1930s many military officers backed Manuel Ávila Camacho to restore the rhetoric of military neutrality against Cardenista radicalism. This chapter begins with an overview of Mexico's officer corps in the early 1940s. Presidents Ávila Camacho and Alemán let zone commanders and their troops linger longer in garrisons than did Cárdenas, and officers challenged central political control, grafted, and sometimes embarrassed the government. I then tell the story of how the Alemán administration defeated key groups of dissident officers between 1948 and 1952 who sought to arrest the drift toward the civilian dominance of national politics. Finally, the chapter describes officers' continued prerogatives that survived the turn to civilianism and argues that these were crucial to the pact that emerged between officers and the PRI; I illustrate these prerogatives by showing how a faction of officers helped to build the Avilacamachista political machine in the state of Puebla from the 1930s to the 1950s.

Officers' role in national politics is one of the few aspects of the army's history to have received sustained scholarly attention. Studies have often seen the advent of civilianism as the culmination of long-term policies of institutionalization and military education begun by Amaro in the 1920s. More recently, studies by Elisa Servín and Aaron Navarro have made it clear that factions of military officers did not disappear from politics in the 1940s but continued to contest presidential elections until 1952.[6] These valuable studies show how officers were still learning the rules of the political game in the 1940s and early 1950s, not simply from their military textbooks but from the broader political environment. However, they do not explore in detail the relationship between national and provincial military politics, or between officer politics and the army's changing organization and institutional roles. Without these levels of analysis we cannot understand the ways that the PRI did affect the "removal of the military from politics" and, crucially, the ways it did not.[7]

The military was secretive, and systematic analysis of officers' independence is difficult. To address these problems this chapter draws particularly on underused diplomatic sources, particularly reports from military observers and the reports of Mexico's own civilian intelligence services, along with petitions sent to the government. Diplomatic sources certainly have their biases and blind spots. Most foreign observers were based in Mexico City, and their grasp of provincial politics was shaky. Military attachés gathered very useful information about military organization, factions, and gossip, but they knew far less about nonmilitary topics. U.S. observers sometimes pondered Mexicans' supposed "racial inclination to follow certain personal leaders."[8] Similarly, British observers bemoaned how Mexico's "predominant Indian strain, and consequent apathy, are probably guarantees that she will never produce an army of the efficiency and energy of the great nations."[9] Indeed, some Mexican officers also used crude national stereotypes; in 1941, General Roberto Fierro, head of the Mexican air force, treated the U.S. military attaché to his thoughts on Mexicans' characteristic "lack of regard for human life," which Fierro argued would help the government crack down on political agitation during the Ávila Camacho administration.[10] However, such biases are often so predictable and clear that they are relatively easy to identify and discount. While the main institutional records of Mexico's army remain sealed, the advantages of diplomatic and intelligence records as a source of information on military politics far outweigh their limitations, especially when read alongside other sources.

Military Officers in the 1940s

In the 1940s, the image of an apolitical army disseminated by the government was not simply for public consumption. In military publications, Cardenistas' talk of soldiers' class identity and solidarity evaporated; in its place troop magazines and manuals emphasized familial metaphors, personal morality, self-discipline, and vague national unity. In 1943, an article in El Soldado pointed out that, although the revolutionary army had been made up mainly of workers and peasants, it was led by "idealists of the middle class." Since the formally "nebulous" revolutionary ideology had "crystallized" by the 1940s, soldiers should aim to spread sincerity, honor, and virtue and act like "an elder brother of the Mexican family."[11] A similar turn away from social topics occurred in Corona del Rosal's textbook for officers; whereas the 1938 edition had discussed the army's role in Mexico's larger class structure, the 1952 edition stuck to themes of military obedience and honor.[12] After 1946, education at the Military College tended to focus narrowly on technical, military topics and eschew broader social and economic analysis. In practice, this ensured that officer education began to lag behind civilian degrees in perceived prestige and status; some officers complained bitterly about this change, but to no avail.[13] However, officers' formal education about acceptable political behavior had shifted abruptly; as recently as the 1930s, officers had regularly attended party meetings in uniform. In any case, compelling sources of political education existed for officers besides military magazines and classrooms; the political and factional conflicts of the 1940s and early 1950s eventually taught officers about the risks of dissent, but also about some of the possible benefits of loyalty.

Mexico's army still contained a great many officers. During Cárdenas's presidency, the total number of generals in the army changed little. The available data suggest that, from the 1940s to the 1960s, the pay ratios between different ranks established by Cárdenas continued (see table 2.1). However, President Ávila Camacho increased the number of generals by about one hundred, and the officer corps grew yet more top heavy; division generals grew from 9 percent to 12 percent of the total (see table 4.1). Most generals and colonels traced their military careers back to the revolution, and consequently a large number hailed from the northern states of Sonora, Coahuila, and Chihuahua. Generals who backed Obregón's rebellion against Carranza in 1920 dominated, making up 75 percent of the total. The remainder had remained loyal to Carranza (15 percent), rejoined the army after 1920, or had been members of the old federal army.[14] The army also contained about 8,000 colonels, majors, captains, and lieutenants. These officers had either joined the revolutionary forces and worked their way up (so-called *tropero* officers), or were the products of the postrevolutionary Military College and, after 1932, the Superior School of War. Some officers, such as generals Marcelino García Barragán, Bonifacio Salinas Leal, and Adrián Castrejón, had fought in the revolution and then attended the first classes at the Military College in the 1920s.[15] By the 1950s, cadet officers came disproportionately from the Federal District, had a relatively high level of education, and were more likely than revolutionary officers to come from a middle-class background; troops were less educated and tended to come from rural areas.[16]

Several hundred of the most able, best-connected, and powerful officers served in the army's elite units based in Mexico City: the general staff of the army, the president's own general staff, and the units assigned to guard the president. From 1925 to 1930, the presidential guard was commanded by officers who were "friends of President Calles" and ranged in strength from

TABLE 4.1 Number of Mexican Generals in the Army, 1934–1953

	1934	1938	1941	1942	1945[a]	1953[b]
Division generals	31	36	54	54	—	107
Generals of brigade	124	127	124	152	—	198
Brigadier generals	230	226	258	234	—	247
Total	385	389	436	440	504	552

Sources: MA to G-2, January 1, 1934, and November 1938, USMIR, reel 7; MA to G-2, "Who's Who Army Lists," March 25, 1942, NARA, MIDRF, 2555, "5990.03"; MA to G-2, April 16, 1942, NARA, MIDRF, 2551, "March–April"; Bateman to FO, July 6, 1945, NA, FO 371/44476 (1945), AN2267; "Escalafón de la Plana Mayor del Ejército" of 1953, AGN, ARC, 556.1/105.

Note: Unfortunately, the available figures do not show how many generals had a commission and how many had no commission but were receiving full pay.

[a] Only the total number of generals is available for this year.

[b] The total does not include 39 generals whose retirement was being processed: 7 division generals, 4 generals of brigade, and 28 brigadier generals.

about 1,000 to 2,000 men. After 1930, guard duty continued but rotated between different battalions and regiments. In 1946, just before taking office as president, Alemán re-created a dedicated unit of presidential guards numbering 4,000 officers and men.[17] About 60 percent of Mexico's officers were attached to the infantry and cavalry, whose units were still scattered across the country; the remainder were assigned to administration, military justice, logistics, engineering, artillery, and the air force.[18] Their central responsibility was domestic policing. Of course, from a broad sociological perspective this police work was necessarily political, whether or not it was perceived as such (which it often was). These roles ensured that officers' judicial autonomy—their say in where and how policing was done—could be sweeping, as we will see in chapter 5. However, our focus here is how officers also enjoyed political autonomy in the narrower sense of interfering in elections, government appointments, and policy, and in using their military posts to make money.

The army's system of zone commands ill fitted the regime's rhetoric of military neutrality. This had long been obvious to more candid members of the army, and reform-minded officers had periodically suggested that the system be changed.[19] Nearly all of Mexico's military zones were federal states, and zone commanders and state governors were expected to provide effective political counterweights to each other. In 1945, the SDN announced that it planned to discontinue "many" zones that were strategically unnecessary, but these plans were never carried out.[20]

TABLE 4.2 Total Changes in Zone Command, Average Months in Command, and New Zone Commanders in Each Presidential Term, 1935–1952

	Jan. 1935–Dec. 1940	Jan. 1941–Dec. 1946	Jan. 1947–Dec. 1952
Total changes in zone command	181	118	82
Average months per command post	13	21	29
Total new zone commanders (post-1934)	—	15	28
% of new zone commanders (post-1934)	—	13	34
% of new zone commanders promoted from cavalry regiments	—	47	18
% of new zone commanders promoted from infantry battalions	—	0	43

Sources: Bimonthly reports on military commands, 1934–41, USMIR, reel 7; personnel tables in AGN, MAC, 606.3/91, and AGN, MAV, 298/22349; various reports on military commands, MA to G-2, NARA, MIDRF, 2551-3; *La Prensa*, September 8, 1951.

Since the late nineteenth century, Mexico's politicians had understood that one way to prevent commanders from meddling in local societies—from "*cacique*-ifying" themselves, in Heriberto Jara's phrase—was simply to move them around the country on a regular basis.[21] Postrevolutionary state builders regularly announced their commitment to the bureaucratic circulation of commanders. Contemporary observers and historical accounts have tended to take these announcements at face value. Cárdenas did move his zone commanders around more than Calles (1924–34). On average Cárdenas's zone commanders remained in their posts for just over thirteen months (see table 4.2). However, infantry and cavalry units changed less frequently. On average, Cárdenas moved his regiments and battalions to different states once every twenty-two and twenty-four months, respectively. Cárdenas's officers could expect to remain in command of a battalion for an average of forty-one months and a regiment for thirty-six months. However, the circulation was not bureaucratic but political, and these averages conceal huge variations; command changes spiked at moments of political crisis such as during Cárdenas's break with Calles and Cedillo's rebellion in the summer of 1938.[22]

Manuel Ávila Camacho changed his zone commanders less frequently. Commanders remained in their posts for an average of twenty-one months between January 1941 and December 1946. The change was palpable in some states: under Cárdenas, only one commander remained in his post for the entire *sexenio*, General José Amarillas in Tlaxcala. Ávila Camacho allowed his generals to stay in the same zone command for all but a couple of months in Morelos (Pablo Díaz), Veracruz (Alejandro Mange), Puebla (Anacleto López), Michoacán (José Tafoya), and the Federal District (Rodrigo Quevedo).

Mexican intelligence agents and foreign observers usually understood military politics as a factional struggle between officers loyal to one of the two remaining revolutionary generals with national political clout: Manuel Ávila Camacho and ex-president Cárdenas. Another ex-president, Abelardo Rodríguez, was also often credited with influence over an amorphous group of old Callista officers. There is more than a grain of truth to this image. Cárdenas, in particular, was still a powerful figure. Although many of the changes in the army's organization during the early 1940s reflected strategic concerns, they were also informed by factional military politics. In 1941, President Ávila Camacho created three powerful regional commands that controlled land, air, and sea forces in their regions. These commands made some military sense in terms of defensive planning, but they were also used to accommodate three of the most powerful, and mutually hostile, generals: Joaquín Amaro, Abelardo Rodríguez, and Cárdenas. They have sometimes been seen as a political "masterstroke" by the president that allowed him to subject rivals to "military discipline."[23] However, while in command of the Pacific Region in 1941, Cárdenas stonewalled instructions from Mexico City and negotiated with the U.S. army over the installation of radar stations and construction of new airfields. U.S. general Stanley Embick noted that "everything Cárdenas does is on a personal basis," and that he "deliberately" ignored orders from Mexico City that "the Mexican government does not feel strong enough to make him obey . . . and I think he knows it."[24] By late 1942, Cárdenas was appointed secretary of defense, removed the Avilacamachista general Roberto Fierro from the command of the air force, placed allies in key military commands, eroded the influence of the presidential general staff, and discontinued the powerful regional commands at the end of 1943.[25] While secretary of defense, Cárdenas was rumored to have threatened to resign in order to persuade President Ávila Camacho to place his allies in key government posts. These included Cárdenas's former chief of staff, General Tomás Sánchez Hernández, as subsecretary of education, along with other cabinet-level appointments.[26]

Cardenista and Avilacamachista factions carried ideological overtones. Some Cardenista officers, such as generals Francisco Múgica or José Tafoya, or the army captain and journalist Raúl Arias Barraza, were clearly interested in labor politics and social reform.[27] Manuel Ávila Camacho had recruited military officers with the promise of moderating Cardenista reform and favored many officers of moderate or downright conservative views. Some diplomats noted how factions in the army partly followed differences over military doctrine and, particularly, wartime collaboration with the U.S. government. Avilacamachistas were particularly keen on incorporating U.S. army doctrine and organization, while Cardenistas were typically more skeptical and insisted that the Mexican army should retain its traditional emphasis on small-scale, domestic policing and counterinsurgency. However, military doctrine was hardly the main axis of conflict in the army. A few officers who had trained in fascist Italy formed another clique in the early 1940s, headed by the ex-Carrancista general José Luis Amezcua, but they remained negligible politically. General Sánchez Hernández headed a group of officers committed to French military organization and training; however, he remained a political ally of Cárdenas. General Francisco Urquizo (subsecretary of defense, 1942–45; secretary of defense, 1945–46) was reportedly a politically weak "compromise selection," intended to placate all the "cliques" in the officer corps.[28]

Factions were also defined by long-standing networks of patronage and personal loyalty. Consequently, military politics could produce some odd-looking ideological bedfellows. For example, Cárdenas seems to have been adept at cultivating unlikely military allies; in 1941 Colonel Luis Alamillo Flores, the main organizer of Amaro's dissident campaigns of the late 1930s, was placed on Cárdenas's general staff. After a tense start, the two men struck up a close working relationship, after which Alamillo was convinced that Cárdenas had backed his subsequent promotion.[29] Along with the ties forged during the political conflicts of the 1920s and 1930s, military networks also encompassed a new generation of officers who had graduated from army schools and been promoted in the 1930s. In 1937, Cárdenas had worked out a deal whereby he would control 30 percent of officer promotions in the army, while the Department of War, under Manuel Ávila Camacho, would control 70 percent; officers doubtless remained aware of who had sponsored their ascent.[30]

However, military factions were loose, changing entities. It is relatively easy to identify officers at the core of these groups. For example, any list of Cardenistas would reliably include Cárdenas's carefully selected military aides and public mouthpieces such as Captain Jerónimo Gomar Suástegui, known in the army for his "hero worship" of Cárdenas; commanders such as General Henríquez Guzmán, on whom Cárdenas had relied in moments of crisis and with whom his family went into business; and personal friends and relatives such as General Cristóbal Guzmán Cárdenas.[31] It would also include officers who had held prominent political offices during Cárdenas's presidency and whom Cárdenas subsequently endeavored to readmit into the army, such as Colonel Enrique Calderón, ex-governor of Durango. In 1941, Calderón moved to Ensenada to serve under Cárdenas despite neither having formally rejoined the military nor having his rank ratified. Despite Cárdenas's recommendations, Calderón's repeated requests to rejoin the army as a colonel were rebuffed by secretaries of defense Manuel Ávila Camacho and Agustín Castro in the late 1930s, and in 1941 by the Avilacamachista senate. Calderón was later sent to the Soviet Union as a military attaché since this posting did not require senate approval of his rank.[32] As we will see below, a similar core of Avilacamachista officers can be identified, many of whom were posted to Puebla. However, outside of these nuclei were many officers who were relatively independent and harder to categorize.

Few officers had the national political power of Cárdenas or, for that matter, his acute sense of the need to maintain an apolitical public image.[33] However, other commanders meddled in state and local politics, often, but not always, with a view to obtaining a political post. Some zones offered more political leverage and prestige for their commander than others. In the 1920s, the strategic Jalisco command was seen by officers as a powerful, and highly profitable, "prize *jefatura*"; in the 1940s, it was widely seen as the equivalent of "almost a sub-department of state."[34] In Veracruz, General Alejandro Mange established a powerful and profitable *cacicazgo* from his position as commander, which endured into the 1950s.[35] At an altogether lower level of command, local army commander Major Jesús Monroy's interference in municipal affairs across Guerrero's Costa Chica was, according to intelligence agents, extensive, embarrassingly overt, and possibly counterproductive; Monroy's nickname, "Major Disaster," was appropriate.[36]

The government's appointment of military men to political posts reflected President Ávila Camacho's reported trust in them as agents of national unity, but it also responded to officers' independent politicking. Although General Blas Corral Martínez boasted of the president's support for him to become governor of Durango in 1943, he had been pressing his case along with local allies for years. He was known in the army as an independent figure who had managed to get along reasonably well with each of the main military factions.[37] The public viewed Corral with cautious optimism, noting that, unusually, the general had served as "undersecretary of national defense, and is yet a poor man."[38] However, the general not only used his army command in the state to prepare the way for his governorship, but did so "publicly," holding political banquets and making speeches, to the obvious distaste of intelligence agents sent by the central government. The government was embarrassed by this, and eventually moved Corral to the command of the neighboring state of Zacatecas for a few months before he formally announced his candidacy; by this point Corral had already appointed his "political kin" to other military commands in Durango.[39] Once he began campaigning he arranged for another "friend," General Simón Díaz Estrada, to take over the Durango command.[40] General Bonifacio Salinas Leal arrived to the governorship of Nuevo León in 1939 having been one the army's longest-serving cavalry commanders in the 1930s. If Salinas initially enjoyed the reputation of being a pliable servant of the central government, he promptly shed it. Salinas built up an independent political base, imposed his own man as gubernatorial successor in 1943 in the face of resistance by the central government, rejoined the army, and, as we will see shortly, continued as a political figure who was far from a compliant instrument of central authority.[41]

Political infighting was less ideologically polarized than in the 1930s, but it could still surface in very public and embarrassing ways. General Pablo Macías Valenzuela, who was secretary of defense from 1940 to 1942, had coveted the governorship of Sinaloa since the early 1930s.[42] In 1944, from his position in the Mazatlán zone command, Macías was initially discreet; his personal secretary circulated propaganda on his behalf. However, after Sinaloa's sitting governor Rodolfo T. Loaiza was shot dead in 1944, Macías was widely suspected of planning the murder. In Sinaloa, it was an "open secret" that the killer, Roberto Valdés (alias "El Gitano"), was one of Macías's pistoleros.[43] Macías was a well-known conservative and political enemy of Cárdenas, and the murder triggered infighting within the army; according to the British minister's informants the case "was being used as a touchstone to ascertain the political allegiance of army officers, who were expected to say whether they were for or against the accused general."[44] Cárdenas, as secretary of defense, tried to charge Macías in a military court for the crime, on the basis that when it was commissioned he had not yet become governor and did not enjoy gubernatorial immunity.

The military hearings dredged up many embarrassing details. Military lawyers referred to Macías's military aide and driver as his "pistolero," and El Gitano revealed that the zone command had routinely farmed out counter-insurgency tasks to him.[45] The court also read out accusations that General Rafael Cerón Medina, commander of Mazatlán's garrison in 1944, had previously protected El Gitano from criminal proceedings, and had even intervened with a local family to help him procure a wife. At this point in the trial, according to the military record, "El Gitano lowered his face and smiled maliciously, perhaps satisfied that two Generalisimos, one an ex-Minister of War, had descended to the level of obtaining a woman for a disgusting bandit like him." As an example of the force of military justice the trial proved disappointing. Macías left the capital before testifying, military hearings were discontinued after Ávila Camacho sent the case to the Supreme Court, and Macías served out his full term as governor of Sinaloa.[46]

Some states were largely insulated from commanders' politicking because they were under the sway of political leaders or *camarillas* that were relatively independent of the army. Under the leadership of Isidro Fabela, the state of México escaped the military autonomy so visible elsewhere.[47] Gonzalo N. Santos was an extremely well-connected and powerful politician, leading Avilacamachista, and governor of San Luis Potosí (1943–49). After he consolidated his *cacicazgo* in San Luis Potosí in the early 1940s, military commanders could still be a nuisance—they might require bribes or promises to appoint their relatives to political office—but they did not threaten his regional control.[48]

Officers' political autonomy went hand in hand with entrepreneurialism. Some simply grafted on the military or state budget, drew pay for fictitious soldiers, or appropriated equipment and provisions outright. More subtly, some in the military high command used inside information and influence to set up private monopolies supplying military equipment and materials or obtain construction contracts.[49] General Gilberto Limón, secretary of defense from 1946 to 1952, speculated with lands for a new military college.[50] During the war, the army announced that it would gather dozens of generals to attend regular "information sessions" at the SDN for their professional improvement; the generals, when not bristling with indignation at having to listen to lectures by subordinate officers, spent much of their time discussing ways in which they could profit from military construction and state lands.[51] Attendees included generals Juan Barragán Rodríguez, Pascual Cornejo Brun, Federico Montes, Joaquín Amaro, Miguel Acosta, Antonio Ríos Zertuche, and Blas Corral Martínez. When the group began to discuss gubernatorial elections, Manuel Ávila Camacho launched a brief campaign of negative publicity against them.[52] Top-level corruption among officers was not always subtle. After seeing the new airplanes acquired from the U.S. government parked at Mexico City airport, secretary of communications General Maximino Ávila Camacho requisitioned one for his own use, plastering his name on the side. Members of the presidential general staff also took one, and Maximino and General Heriberto Jara later took another two. The head of the Mexican air force objected "furiously and unsuccessfully."[53]

More covertly, commanders in the field made money by selling protection or extorting from vulnerable groups, directly taking over land and commerce, or taking a cut when subordinates did the same. Officers' control of militia units was a particularly reliable source of income.[54] In 1943, Zacatecas's commanders demanded a going rate of 300 pesos for admission to the *defensas rurales*.[55] Other military officers exploited troop labor, sold protection, and covertly built up businesses. The *cacical* practices of General Agustín Olachea Avilés, zone commander in Nayarit (1940–44) and Jalisco (1944–46), were later recalled by a soldier who served under him in some detail. These included taking bribes to station troops in distant regions in Jalisco and using soldiers to crack down on competitors to his liquor-smuggling business in Nayarit. Under Olachea's protection, his "henchmen" in local commands also extorted from local populations, although they were apparently careful not to report all of their activities back to the general.[56] By the late 1940s, General Macías Valenzuela was widely and plausibly rumored to be embroiled in Sinaloa's growing opium trade, as were other commanders in the state.[57]

The central government followed a logic of divide and rule, and it preferred to tolerate the entrepreneurialism of individual officers rather than that of the army as an institution or of powerful blocks within it. For example, Manuel Ávila Camacho balked when a consortium of powerful generals proposed a takeover of lands expropriated from German nationals in Chiapas during the war.[58] However, several of the military colonies created in the 1940s were run by individual generals for their own benefit.[59] In the Sierra Norte de Puebla, General Salinas Leal simply seized some disputed land for the purpose, despite protests from the Agrarian Department and villagers who complained about Salinas and his "hound-pack of soldiers."[60] For some officers entrepreneurial autonomy acted as a trade-off for political meddling. General Pablo Díaz Davila generally kept a low profile in gubernatorial and national politics; he briefly considered running for the governorship of Zacatecas in 1943, but Manuel Ávila Camacho persuaded him to step aside. From 1936 to 1939, and again from 1940 until 1953, Díaz remained ensconced in Morelos's zone command; according to critics, he steadily accumulated lands and business interests in Morelos, some acquired legally and some "by force."[61] However, for other officers such as Corral and Salinas, entrepreneurialism was an indistinguishable part of politics, not a substitute for it.[62]

For most of the 1940s, the rules of the political game for officers were rather lax, amenable to improvisation and sometimes diverging to an embarrassing extent from the state's official discourse. Moreover, even if it had been politically possible, the government could not simply insist that the military follow its formal rules, since this would interfere with the careful management of elections that was desired by the leadership of the PRI. In 1946, President Ávila Camacho publicly ordered the army to help guarantee fair presidential elections. In San Luis Potosí, a naive officer followed presidential orders to guard ballot boxes to the letter and tried to prevent the necessary electoral chicanery from proceeding, earning himself a sarcastic rebuke from Gonzalo Santos.[63] General Agustín Castro, while trying to build support for his own abortive presidential bid in 1946, seized on Manuel Ávila Camacho's comments and took out a large newspaper advertisement urging soldiers not to acquiesce in electoral fraud and suggested that military discipline in such matters should be tempered by "reasoned discipline." The secretary of defense, General Francisco Urquizo, published a stern rebuke of Castro, who had himself been secretary of defense only five years earlier.[64] It was only after a period of tense military politics between 1948 and 1952 that clearer, unspoken rules for the army's political game emerged.

The Defeat of Dissident Officers, 1948–1952

After he became president in 1946, Miguel Alemán echoed the language of postwar democracy elsewhere in Latin America and presented his civilian identity as the culmination of Mexico's modern destiny, a guarantee of consensual government and administrative efficiency against the radicalism of the left and the far right.[65] Alemán himself was not so impolitic as to directly criticize the policies of earlier general-presidents; such an approach would hardly have been convincing given his own political debt to Manuel Ávila Camacho. After the scandal over the army's killing of about seventy political protesters in the town of León, Guanajuato, in January 1946, Manuel Ávila

Camacho and Alemán tried to foster the idea that a civilian candidate would mark a break with the past.[66] Although the government never criticized the army as an institution, it portrayed the party's new reforms and civilian presidential candidate as allowing the country to close the book on "a chapter in Mexican life marked by violence, and begin another in which our politics have been dignified and ennobled."[67] Assorted Alemanistas and press allies were less coy about arguing for the superiority of civilians to army officers who governed with an incongruous military "spirit of discipline."[68] When Alemanistas equated civilian rule with a new "constructive phase" of the revolution, they implied a vague critique of the destructive radicalism of earlier regimes and a loose association of radical politics with military abuses. For some of Alemán's intelligence agents, it was obvious that many leftists were "militarists by custom."[69] Later in Alemán's term, the government went beyond its vague praise for the merits of civilian rule and argued that the next president should necessarily be a civilian, preferably a young one, thereby consolidating Mexico's achievement of political maturity.[70]

During the political crisis of 1948 and the dissident presidential campaign of General Miguel Henríquez Guzmán in 1952, officers again openly contested the power of president and party. In August 1948, following the devaluation of the peso, the press reported that two groups of powerful generals began to meet to plot the formation of a new military party and push Alemán from office. The first was led by Antonio Ríos Zertuche and included other northern generals such as Salinas Leal, Miguel Z. Martínez, and Maurilio Rodríguez. In response to press reports of this group's machinations, a second group started to meet, led by General Alamillo Flores, who was rumored to be allied again with his old patron General Amaro. Alamillo enjoyed support in the central institutions of the army, including among students and recent graduates of the Superior School of War and the Military College, of which Flores was director in 1948, and the officers of the general staff and artillery regiments.[71] In addition to these two main groups, anxious government agents reported generalized discontent among officers in August 1948; Mexico City's bars and brothels hosted shady meetings and "insidious subterranean politics" in which other generals such as Agustín Castro, various ex-Carrancista officers, and "pseudo-revolutionaries" drank, caroused, and hurled lewd insults at the president; Avilacamachista officers serving in the senate were well aware of discontent in the army and applied more polite pressure of their own; and Alfonso Corona del Rosal suggested to Alemán that he carry out moral education among officers with "greater intensity" but also urged him to improve his administration's image, adopt price controls, freeze salaries, encourage people to buy Mexican manufactures, and repave Mexico City's streets.[72]

Military groups were secretive, and it is difficult to assess their plans. However, the political pressure which Alemán faced stemmed as much from a general shift in political power toward a new generation of civilian bureaucrats as from the incessant bureaucratic modernization of the army per se. Historians have often interpreted Manuel Ávila Camacho's announced retirement of 550 generals in July 1945 as an indication of the tightening bureaucratic grip on the army and a major source of army discontent under Alemán.[73] However, military retirements proceeded far more slowly and unevenly than suggested by official pronouncements. The SDN's plans to reduce the total number of generals to eighty-four proved wildly exaggerated, and the speech probably served as a vague threat and an assertion of presidential power rather than a realistic goal. The speech also likely served to impress hemispheric public opinion. The *New York Times* reported the "drastic shake-up" of the army high command approvingly.[74] Between July 1945 and the end of 1952, the army probably retired around 206 generals, which meant that 69 percent (346) of the army's generals in 1945 remained seven years later, although they had come to form a slightly lower proportion of the total at 63 percent.[75] Moreover, the government's 1953 table of serving generals suggests that Manuel Ávila Camacho's threat to retire officers after twenty-five years of service was, at most, enforced in a highly uneven manner; all but seven of the ninety-four division generals of 1953 had served more than thirty years in 1945.[76] Army retirements probably fed into the military plots of 1948; agents reported shady meetings of retired officers, one of which was reportedly organized by the head of the army's department of pensions himself.[77] However, many of the key figures pressuring Alemán in 1948 were still prominently in active service. Or, if they were out of active service, this was because of presidential displeasure rather than because they were too old or unqualified. The retirement age mandated for division generals was sixty-five. In 1948, Salinas Leal was a remarkably young division general, at only forty-eight; Miguel Z. Martínez was sixty. Ríos Zertuche was fifty-four in 1948, and was in active service but without commission (*en disponibilidad*); he and Maurilio Rodríguez ran the Military Agricultural and Ranching Colony at Palma Sola, Veracruz, and enjoyed logging rights on lands that had once belonged to the Aguila oil company.[78]

Rather than simply protest at tightening bureaucratic reform, the generals were alarmed that Alemán was weakening their political contacts within the army and loosening their access to state power and patronage. In August 1948, these generals were presented with apparently abundant evidence of Alemán's mismanagement, and a gilt-edged opportunity to apply some swaggering pressure. Before organizing their "military party," Ríos Zertuche first demanded an increase in the number of generals in the cabinet to five; after a meeting with Alemán, intelligence agents reported overhearing Ríos Zertuche, Maurilio Rodríguez, and Salinas bragging that they had referred to Alemán with the informal "tu," caused him to fall into a "panic," and could now pressure the president to "get whatever we want."[79] Ríos Zertuche was reported to have canvassed numerous older politicians and generals including Manuel Ávila Camacho, Abelardo Rodríguez, Anacleto López Morales, and Rodrigo Quevedo; to drum up support, his group intended to send to each state a military delegate "who had previously been a governor of that state."[80] That both groups of generals in 1948 were hostile to organized labor was obvious from the generals' own recorded comments and the manner in which the government chose to respond to them in the press. General Emilio Acosta warned the generals about the consequences of plotting, even as he shared their obvious disdain for organized labor. If a military party was formed "the government, confronting the disloyal flight of its most obliged defenders, would see itself forced to search for support among the nuclei of workers through their leaders and *this would make things infinitely worse*." Some plans may have gone beyond backroom lobbying and party-building: on August 3, rumors spread that the Alamillo Flores group planned to assassinate Alemán, and army pilots admitted to U.S. officials that the air force had been grounded because of fears of a coup; later in August, Mexican spies reported that Alemán was appearing at meetings with a serious injury in one hand and that, when a large group of officers called on him, he had expected them to demand his resignation.[81] Although the generals' plans for toppling Alemán in 1948 came to naught, military politicking continued.

When General Henríquez Guzmán began his presidential campaign in 1950, he attracted widespread military support. He certainly had some genuine support among active officers, including prominent zone and regiment commanders. In June 1951, Mexican intelligence services counted twenty-two generals, fifteen colonels, seven lieutenant colonels, one major, and four captains sympathetic to Henriquismo. However, probably a third of Henríquez's military supporters were veterans rather than serving officers.[82] He was also joined by the remnants of the conservative military groups of 1948 who had not been mollified or paid off by the regime, chief among them General Ríos Zertuche. In 1950, Ríos Zertuche was removed from his post at the Palma Sola military colony after a public scandal over his profiteering with logging contracts.[83] His alliance with Henríquez was anomalous and was recognized as such. Henríquez was strongly associated with his long-time mentor in the army, Cárdenas, while Ríos Zertuche had always been distant from the Cardenistas as a group and was fond of lambasting worker agitation and leftist influence in Mexico.[84]

Henríquez's supporters in the army argued that military officers' influence on presidential politics was inevitable and legitimate. In 1952, Henriquistas propagandized among officers intensely, arguing that the circumstances of the Korean War demanded that a military officer be in the presidency and that it was best for officers to stick together and support each other.[85] In his party program, in many respects similar to that of the PRI itself, Henríquez appealed to older officers by promising to end policies of "forced" retirements.[86] In August 1951, the SDN declared it would now demand that soldiers who wanted to be involved in electoral politics retire completely from the army rather than simply acquire a temporary license.[87] Henriquistas, along with other military officers involved in dissident politics, criticized the government's hypocrisy by highlighting the PRI's politicization of the army and argued that soldiers had the right as citizens to participate in free elections.[88] They also evoked a version of recent history that differed from official civilianism; the postrevolutionary military was less a primitive scourge that had finally been tamed and more an organized conduit for popular, nationalist aspirations. At a Henriquista rally in Jalisco, a railway worker spoke to congratulate Henríquez for his conduct as zone commander during a railway strike in Jalisco in 1942; the general "gave us all his support and for that reason we won."[89] Official "civilianism" was, they argued, an unconstitutional doctrine "invented" by Alemán in order to "monopolize power."[90] Henriquismo grew into far more than simply a military movement, though, and drew the support of a heterogeneous mix of ex-Cardenistas, dissident peasant groups and unions, and various recalcitrant regional camarillas.[91]

Henriquismo failed to derail the PRI partly due to its own limitations as a movement, which were numerous. Lázaro Cárdenas's decision to withhold public support was crucial, a belief shared by many supporters, observers, and opponents as well as the movement's leadership. The issue rankled with Henríquez and his brother and campaign manager, Jorge, for years afterward.[92] Government repression and machine politics were important, although in some places Henriquismo simply lacked enthusiasts. In Guerrero, hardly a bastion of PRIísta loyalty, it was tainted by association with the unpopular camarilla of General Alberto Berber. As Elisa Servín has argued, organized mass peasant support was lacking in all but a few regions. Conversely, some popular social movements that joined with Henríquez had their own independent regional momentum and, indeed, continued long after 1952.[93] Denied the support of Cárdenas, Henríquez had only limited appeal as a military man of the people, and even this was no doubt diminished for many by his well-earned reputation as a military entrepreneur. Henríquez himself toned down talk of his military credentials as the campaign wore on.[94] As was the case during the crisis of 1948, the prospect of military officers in government was probably viewed by the populace with ambivalence. By 1948, Alemán's early popularity had faded and he was seen by many as a playboy; rumors of spectacular corruption among his inner circle were rife. However, when intelligence agents fanned out to Mexico City's markets to monitor public opinion in July and August 1948, they recorded a lot of grumbling about inflation but little faith in the competence of the army to address it. One group of vendors declared that corruption in the Alemán administration was "even worse" than that of the notoriously venal General Maximino Ávila Camacho during his tenure as secretary of communications, hardly a ringing endorsement of military officers. In September 1948, two generals were prosecuted for racketeering in the Mexico City meat market. After reading about military plots in the press, another group of vendors supported sweeping changes in the government but agreed that "at this time of economic crisis, we do not need generals, but hard-working men, who will preserve the nation's money and cultivate the land."[95]

Henríquez and the military dissidents of 1948 also failed because the regime defused tensions in the army with a hastily improvised blend of professional incentives, political deals, and patronage. Like previous presidents, Alemán improved military benefits, housing, and access to credit.[96] In 1947, Alemán initially conceded pay raises only to officers in command of troops. After the government received numerous complaints and "unrest began to grow," he extended these across the army. By September 1949, Alemán had conceded pay raises of 53 percent to enlisted men, 43 percent to captains and lieutenants, 55 percent to majors and colonels, and 34 percent to generals. He also raised cadets' allowances at the Military College.[97] As we will see in chapter 6, Alemán also tried to mollify revolutionary veterans by promising new benefits. Aaron Navarro has recently argued that Alemán's recruitment of military cadets into a new intelligence agency controlled by the presidency, the Federal Security Directorate (Dirección Federal de Seguridad, DFS) in 1947, provided an important new incentive for younger officers to remain loyal to the regime and gave the army an expanded role in the kind of political intelligence work that would underpin the PRI regime.[98] Although Navarro is surely correct that the SDN requested that Alemán recruit cadets to the DFS, and that the DFS represented an appealing opportunity for the cadets chosen, it is unclear that the episode marked a decisive shift in the incentives offered to officers or in the army's institutional roles. Ten cadets were recruited in 1947; the remaining thirty-two original agents and staff received military ranks simply to bolster their pay, a policy that, if anything, antagonized the military establishment.[99] The DFS was controlled strictly by the president's office from 1947 to 1952 before passing to the civilian agency that traditionally controlled intelligence, the Department of the Interior, and only a "handful" of the agents employed by Alemán continued after 1952.[100] Some military officers continued to work with the DFS in the 1950s, although it is not clear that they did so in greater numbers, or with greater influence, than had the many officers who had collaborated with other civilian intelligence agencies such as the General Directorate of Political and Social Investigation (Dirección General de Investigaciones Políticas y Sociales, DGIPS) prior to 1946. In the 1950s, the DFS, according to Sergio Aguayo, was an overstretched and rather shambolic operation; agents were concentrated in Mexico City; in 1952–57, the agency's director "'sold credentials all over the place'" to honorary agents who were to act as part-time informers.[101] According to a 1955 sample of seventy honorary agents obtained by Aguayo, probably around 15 percent were military officers.[102] In any case, throughout the 1940s and 50s, most of the army was still expected to police the countryside, repress dissent, and provide their own intelligence on political and social disturbances to the SDN; as we will see in chapter 5, they remained busy.[103]

Alemán carefully cultivated political allies and ideological sympathizers in the army. The Presidential Guard was commanded by Alemán's uncle, General Juan Valdés. Alemán's secretary of defense, General Limón, came from a suitably conservative wing of the revolutionary elite. After heading Calles's Presidential Guard and the army's Department of War Materials (1931–34), he had fallen out with Cárdenas and been marginalized before returning under Ávila Camacho to direct the Military College (1942–45). Limón was also a "close friend" of Abelardo Rodríguez, and it was widely rumored that he owed his position to him.[104] Intelligence reports also reveal numerous self-identified "Alemanistas" serving in the army who were happy to rail against the leftism of the Cardenistas and support "Alemanista" candidates in the provinces. General Manuel Solís, head of the SDN archive, wrote a note to Alemán assuring him of the army's support, since officers well remembered that Cárdenas, "through misunderstanding, error or weakness," had allowed the SEP to attempt the "sovietization of Mexican children."[105] Several Alemanista political clubs sprang up among officers; some even supported Alemán's reelection.[106] In Tamaulipas, Alemán tried to displace the followers of Emilio Portes Gil and appointed his subsecretary of national defense, General Raúl Gárate Legleu, provisional governor. Gárate in turn packed local police forces and state administration with military allies; the move also probably served to counter the influence of the state's zone commander, General Salinas.[107] Some political conversions were rather abrupt and surprising. The officer whom Alemán appointed to head his presidential general staff, General Santiago Piña Soria, while certainly a young product of postrevolutionary military education, was politically ambitious. Before embracing Alemanismo, Piña Soria wrote for numerous military publications and for the CTM's *El Popular*; he had been known as a protégé of the labor leader Vicente Lombardo Toledano; before 1946, Lombardo was rumored to have sponsored Piña's rapid military promotions in exchange for the officer feeding the CTM a steady flow of information about military politics.[108]

However, military graft could trump previous ideological and political ties. Under Alemán, both Piña Soria and the secretary of defense, General Limón, used their discretionary powers over promotions to graft on an unprecedented scale. These competing sources of patronage were a source of tension between the presidency and the SDN. However, they allowed for the cultivation of new political clienteles within the armed forces. After Alemán left office, the government received an anonymous note from a group of officers with a list of 177 generals promoted by Alemán who had not completed the required five years in their earlier status. Most were promoted in the years after the 1948 crisis, with a heavy concentration in 1952. Of these, 147 were generals promoted while in command of troops: 11 division generals (2 before 1948); 42 brigade generals (5 before 1948); and 94 general brigadiers (4 before 1948).[109] Conversely, the government cut off dissidents' access to government contracts and lucrative posts and sent them large invoices for unpaid taxes.[110]

For powerful senior officers mere ideological appeals or the promise of an early promotion were unlikely to suffice. Alemán weathered 1948's initial storm of military plotting in part because he temporized skillfully. He promised to sack some of the most unpopular and venal members of his administration but argued that he could not make changes immediately and be seen to be bowing to military pressure. This was an argument that apparently appealed to Cárdenas and Manuel Ávila Camacho, who used their backstage power to council against more drastic action. By the end of August 1948, the DFS reported that Amaro had been persuaded to put his political efforts on hold.[111] By mid-September 1948, Alemán was aided by the public support of unions, and defused popular outrage over inflation with an increased supply of affordable food in the cities. One press report from November 1948 even suggested that the plotters were discouraged by a Democratic victory in the U.S. presidential election.[112]

However, Alemán also came to terms with key troublemakers. To hold the line in 1948, Alemán had to cede some influence on the army back to Manuel Ávila Camacho, whose house was "constantly teeming with generals" during August 1948, and to officers associated with the Avilacamachistas. While Alemán removed Amaro from his zone command in Oaxaca, he also funneled payments to other crucial zone commanders from his unaudited discretionary fund.[113] It is naturally difficult to obtain more detailed information about these payments. General Anacleto López's military file reveals that, in addition to his army pay, he received payments from Alemán's office of 2,000 pesos a month throughout 1952 in return for carrying out a "confidential mission."[114] Gonzalo Santos's memoirs are suggestive. In 1950, Alemán was rumored to be considering a bid for reelection. Santos claims that, at this moment, Manuel Ávila Camacho "had control of the army." However, Santos advised the former president that it would be cheaper to intimidate Alemanistas in Congress with paramilitary forces rather than with soldiers since this would bypass the need to "seduce" the army.[115] Whether paid or not Salinas Leal and Miguel Z. Martínez continued in prominent zone commands; Martínez moved into the military zone of Guerrero and faithfully pursued Alemán's regional opponents; Salinas Leal commanded the zone of Tamaulipas from 1946 to 1951.[116] In February 1949, Alemán also disbanded the SDN's General Staff, despite general staff officers' complaints and appeals for a judicial *amparo*. This represented a gain for the president's office but also for the other traditional opponents of a powerful, centralized staff of educated young officers: old provincial commanders.[117] In 1950–51, the government also created ten new powerful regional commands that probably served to sweeten the bitter pill of civilian succession. The army's explanation that the regions marked the long-awaited rationalization of the zone system along purely technical, military lines is unconvincing. The old zone commands based on state boundaries did not disappear, but were simply reorganized in groups of two to three under a new layer of regional commanders. The regions were headed by well-known political, entrepreneurial generals. One, Pablo Macías Valenzuela, was a powerful ex-governor of Sinaloa and known as an Alemanista ally. Another, Leobardo Ruiz, lacked much of a political base outside of the army but was "politically ambitious," considered himself a possible future president, and was loyal to Manuel Ávila Camacho.[118] More striking are the commanders who had previously been at the heart of Alemán's conflicts with the army, such as Rodrigo Quevedo, Miguel Z. Martínez, Alejandro Mange, and Salinas Leal. The latter four men, along with Pablo Macías, retained their commands until 1959 when the government disbanded the regions and continued the old zone command system.[119]

Discreet Continuities

While officers' attempts to wield national power had been defeated, they retained power within the system, provided they used it tactfully. It has long been known that military officers continued in formal political posts—as congressmen, senators, governors, and party chiefs. Indeed, military participation below the cabinet recovered somewhat after 1952. Cárdenas and Manuel Ávila Camacho had appointed military officers to 48 percent and 40 percent of governorships, respectively; Alemán cut the number to a mere 13 percent. From 1952 to 1964, 23 percent of state governors were military officers. In Alemán's term, military officers made up 5 percent of federal senators and 3 percent of deputies; through the 1950s their numbers recovered to 20 percent and 11 percent, respectively, in 1958–64. From 1948 to 1966, the army's share of the federal budget declined slightly overall, but remained quite stable; it ranged from 9 percent to 14 percent and averaged 11.3 percent.[120] We still know little about the historical trajectories of what Roderic Camp calls the PRI's "political-military" officers, still less about zone, regional, and garrison commanders in the provinces.[121] However, as historians move into this period, we are beginning to get a clearer sense of officers' informal powers that lurked under the waterline of formal politics.

Alemán and Ruiz Cortines did not rotate army commands with anything like the frequency suggested by official policies, and officers successfully resisted retirement. As under Cárdenas, changes in zone commanders spiked at moments of political crisis, such as during the spring and summer of 1948.[122] However, after the crisis abated, command rotations were distinctly sluggish. The available data suggest that, although Alemán did introduce more new zone commanders than Manuel Ávila Camacho and also promoted more infantry commanders to zone commands than his predecessor, zone commanders spent an average of twenty-eight months in each command between 1946 and 1952 (see table 4.2). Manuel Ávila Camacho may have favored cavalry officers to compensate them for the declining importance of the cavalry in the early 1940s, or simply because of his background as a cavalry officer and fondness for polo and horsemanship.[123] Alemán left Pablo Díaz in Morelos and Alejandro Mange in Veracruz. In the 1960s, officers still complained, in private, about the "pernicious practise" of leaving zone commanders unchanged for years at a time.[124] Other durable political generals would include Félix Ireta, zone commander in Michoacán from 1954 until 1969, and Anacleto López, Zacatecas's zone commander from 1953 until 1966, both of whom had amassed lands and built up clienteles among state militia in the 1930s and exerted influence over a succession of PRI governors.[125] After commanding the Tamaulipas zone for most of Alemán's *sexenio*, Salinas Leal retained his position as commander of the fifth military region based in Guadalajara from 1951 to 1958. Salinas was a friend to other seasoned zone commanders like Ireta; in reports to the SDN, Salinas credited Michoacán's stability to Ireta's long knowledge of the state and political connections, although he offered few details. Salinas in turn reasserted himself as powerbroker in Nuevo León after 1951, and was recurrently alleged to be meddling in national politics well into the 1970s.[126] Moreover, a focus only on zone and regional commands is probably misleading. Some zone commanders such as Ireta had long been prominent in their home states as regiment and battalion commanders.

Military entrepreneurialism also continued, now more firmly established as compensation for the military's retreat from national power. Ruiz Cortines tried to rein in the previous administration's selling of promotions. In 1953, this provoked an unusually critical and lively senate debate and investigation, after which the senate refused to confirm several promotions. Such moves earned Ruiz Cortines some praise from "older soldiers."[127] However, the general pattern of the government restricting the military's budget while tolerating individual officers' corruption held. The army's construction of nonmilitary infrastructure probably declined. By the 1950s, the government tried to discourage the army from working on construction projects that were unconnected to its military duties and thus "contrary to its nature and dignity." In contrast to the dozens of public construction projects the army reported each year in the 1930s, in 1952 the army only reported eleven construction projects in the whole country, including six roads, two airfields, two schools, and a bank.[128] Although General Limón and some other senior officers were very interested in building up Mexico's military industry, these plans did not prosper. They could count on little support from the rest of the government or from the U.S. government, especially after Mexico refused to sign on to a series of continental defense treaties. What remained of the Cardenista faction sought to decrease Mexico's dependence on U.S. arms but opposed any formal strategic alliance with the U.S. government.[129]

However, there is plenty of evidence that officers continued earlier entrepreneurial practices and that these were commonly understood within political society. It was well known that, given their poor pay, as many as a third of army officers moonlighted in other jobs and activities, some licit, others less so. Diplomats described how, although the "blatant" corruption of the Alemán years had been driven "underground," military corruption formed part of a routine system comparable to that in other government departments. At the top of the military hierarchy, officers in the SDN developed a well-known system of bribes and kickbacks for all contracts with suppliers; 15 percent was standard for the SDN and 25 percent for the army's Department of Military Industry. This was understood as "standard practice" and "the only way business can be done."[130] In 1955, the SDN's chief of communications was "eased out of his job after having made a modest fortune of eight million pesos out of public funds." Although his replacement was known to diplomats as a "friendly, honest man with an excellent military record," after a month in the position he had continued in the same vein.[131] Rodrigo Quevedo returned to Chihuahua as regional commander from 1951 to 1958; in 1954, the army reported that he used his military connections to support business allies in their struggle to control a mining enterprise.[132] Lower down, provincial commanders skimmed budgets and supplies; threats and intimidation usually secured compliance from other officers.[133] According to detailed, signed complaints from the 1950s, military commanders speculated with urban military lands in Mexico City; came to profitable alliances with expanding logging interests in Chihuahua, Jalisco, and the state of México; organized cattle rustling in Puebla and Veracruz; and took a cut from contraband crossing the Guatemalan border.[134] By the 1960s, ex-president Cárdenas complained that garrisons in Mexico City were integrated into a citywide system of kickbacks and extortion that paid 500,000 pesos a month to the army officer who headed the city's police.[135] DFS agents sent to report on zone commanders in the 1960s found few cases of open conflict with the party. However, Nayarit's zone commander, General Alberto Cárdenas (1963–67), protected political allies, controlled a smuggling operation, and selectively refused to cooperate with the state government.[136] In the late 1960s and early 1970s, Jalisco's zone commander, General Amaya Rodríguez, recruited "confidential agents" to repress dissident student groups in Guadalajara while gaining a foothold in drug trafficking.[137]

Facing these uncomfortable continuities in substance, the regime engineered changes in the military's style and public image. Officers in politics no longer challenged the PRI ideologically and submerged their political agency in the rhetoric of presidential authority. For example, when General López de Nava received the party's nomination for the governorship of Morelos in 1951, he presented it effectively as a presidential order, rather than something for which he and his political allies in Morelos had been working for years. Officers knew that the secretary of defense was carefully chosen to balance the power of different military factions: Matías Ramos (1952–58) was an "archenemy of Cárdenas"; Agustín Olachea was also hostile to the Cardenistas and tied to Abelardo Rodríguez; the ex-Henriquista Marcelino García Barragán (1964–70) had long been associated with Cárdenas. However, they did not discuss such things openly or, when they did, insisted that their comments not be published until after their death.[138] Cárdenas's public behavior during the Second World War, during which he "barely made a public utterance," became the model for commanders by the 1950s. The government discouraged officers from making even the most anodyne public statements about the army and militia's maintenance of rural order, censored disagreeable films, and fostered self-censorship in the press.[139]

The government's response to a planned speech in March 1953 by secretary of defense General Matías Ramos provides a rare glimpse of how the government carefully restricted officers' public statements to purely technical matters. Ramos submitted a proposed speech to the president's office in which he called on the army's rural militia to maintain their loyalty to the government and the army, avoid the temptations of leftist "professional agitators," guarantee political stability, and therefore cooperate with the government's policy of lowering prices through increasing agricultural productivity. The presidential secretary, after congratulating the general on his good intentions, asked him not to give the speech. The prospect of a general making statements about issues not directly related to security and order, he explained, could "from a psychological point of view cause some surprise" and expose civilian authorities to accusations of weakness and ineptitude: "some sectors of public opinion could believe in a twisted way that the civilian authorities have not been successful and that this has caused the intervention of the highest military authority, a belief that some disorientated or dissident anti-revolutionary groups with interested ends would perhaps start to propagate."[140] The result was a significant narrowing of what could be known or said publicly about the army, which profoundly shaped the public sphere.

Avilacamachismo, Officers, and Politics in Puebla

The state of Puebla provides one example of the ways officers preserved political and economic powers in the provinces. Puebla had long been a conflictive state. During the revolution, a formidable array of armed groups surrounded the city of Puebla's conservative elite: Zapatistas in the south, ex-federal officers such as Higineo Aguilar and Juan Andreu Almazán in the southeast near Tehuacán, the followers of Domingo Arenas in the northwest of the state, and, in the Sierra, contending forces led by the Márquez brothers and Juan Francisco Lucas. The Constitutionalists took the city of Puebla in 1914, but officers only brought a measure of peace to the state by slowly forging alliances with revolutionary caciques.[141] In the 1920s and early 1930s, the state of Puebla was justly renowned as violent and unstable; state governors struggled to remain in office and subdue unions who battled one another for control of textile workers; the government's control of the countryside was disputed among semiautonomous caciques, the state's *agraristas*, bandits, and a highly independent and entrepreneurial military. Through the 1920s, *agraristas* generally ignored the state governor and clogged up the corridors of the army headquarters, eager to petition the commander.[142] By the mid-1950s, politics were much changed; the state government was controlled by an Avilacamachista political machine that had gradually and fitfully extended its control over state politics from the late 1930s. A faction of military officers led by the Ávila Camacho brothers played an integral, if not a leading, part in this transition.

The bases for the Avilacamachista political machine, or *cacicazgo*, were laid by General Maximino Ávila Camacho, governor of Puebla from 1937 to 1941. During a lengthy military career, Maximino had learned the considerable benefits that could accrue to military commanders by not overtly challenging the central government; the wealth Maximino accumulated by stealing cattle in Zacatecas during the Cristiada was well known by the political elite and is amply attested to by the dozens of complaints in his military file.[143] After being overlooked for the governorship of Puebla in 1933, Maximino eventually obtained Cárdenas's unspoken acquiescence to build a formidable political machine there in exchange for loyalty to the regime. Maximino began constructing his *cacicazgo* as zone commander (January–September 1935). He expanded the authority of his military command over the entire state, including the Sierra Norte de Puebla, which had previously been part of the Tlaxcala zone. From a strictly strategic point of view the absorption of the Sierra was questionable; to an aspiring governor it was eminently rational.[144] He built an alliance with the CROM through his power to intervene in agrarian and labor disputes and even started his own state newspaper to support his gubernatorial bid.[145] Maximino's use of the zone command to extend his control over state politics was more or less an open secret.[146]

The general story of Maximino's governorship has been well told by several historians. In 1935, the state was torn by violent inter-*sindicato* labor conflicts centered in Atlixco, and the countryside was ruled by a patchwork of highly autonomous rural bosses. By the late 1930s, Maximino had constructed a broad, multiclass political alliance in the state, obtained a rapprochement with the state's business and Catholic elites, and decisively shifted the state's politics rightward. The rising tide of federal interventionism and mass organizations of the corporate revolutionary party, often seen by historians as flooding irresistibly into the provinces under Cárdenas, broke on the rocks of Maximino's regional power base. Maximino oversaw the organization of these national entities in Puebla more or less on his own terms and similarly resisted the interference of radical federal teachers. For example, Maximino founded a state peasant league in 1938 to tie Puebla's many competing peasant organizations to the official party. It was most important in Puebla's central valley between the city of Puebla and Tehuacán; in other areas, such as around Teziutlán, Maximino supported local elites' efforts to prevent peasants organizing.[147] Federal government intelligence agents also faced obstacles; one agent complained that he could not even obtain a record of the debates of the local congress "due to the obstacles put in my way."[148] The Avilacamachista machine was one of the few *cacicazgos* of national reach; its influence extended to surrounding states, and Maximino Ávila Camacho's power base in Puebla helped his younger brother, General Manuel Ávila Camacho, become president in 1940. Until the 1960s, the governors of Puebla would all come from Maximino's political circle.

Less familiar is how the rise of Avilacamachismo affected the army in the state. Puebla well illustrates how Cardenismo's reforms of the army were shaped by officers' political independence and conservatism. As zone commander, Maximino fostered ties with rural powerbrokers through his authority to arm and select the state's *defensas rurales*.[149] The CTM's grand parades of "workers' militia" in Mexico City were echoed in Puebla in 1942, but there they consisted of Maximino Ávila Camacho's allies in the rival CROM, along with other non-CTM unions, all "uniformed and militarized."[150] Conversely, military officers' organization of paramilitary forces did not necessarily proceed through these new institutional channels. In 1940, Avilacamachista ally General Donato Bravo Izquierdo returned to Tehuacán and took it upon himself to drum up several "battalions of peasants" to help in the campaign against Almazanismo in the state.[151]

Cardenismo's rhetoric about the army was also subject to idiosyncratic local interpretation. In 1936, an ex-Zapatista from Teziutlán complained that the town's cavalry commander, Colonel Edmundo Sánchez Cano, had "betrayed" the idea of the Day of the Soldier by celebrating it with a dinner offered by the town's priest and Catholic organizations, which were allied to armed groups that had attacked federal teachers.[152] In the late 1930s, the zone commander's chief of staff supported Catholic groups' efforts to celebrate the anniversary of the conservative General Iturbide's declaration of independence, rather than Hidalgo's *grito*.[153] Avilacamachista rhetoric emphasized order, hierarchy, and stability, and the military was portrayed very much as a disciplinary antidote to agitation, rather than a mobilizing revolutionary force. As governor, Maximino Ávila Camacho liked to wear his military uniform in public at events such as the commercial fair he organized in 1939. During meetings with recalcitrant students or local powerbrokers, Maximino Ávila Camacho often brandished a riding crop, a commonly understood trope of harsh military discipline.[154] In 1939, another of Maximino's younger brothers, Colonel Rafael Ávila Camacho, was mayor of the city of Puebla; he, too, sometimes wore his army uniform, and he created a "militarized" sports club for employees of the city government. In addition to playing baseball and basketball, employees took part in "military exercises and marches, for purely disciplinary purposes," all paid for by contributions from employees' wages.[155]

Once the Avilacamachistas had consolidated their hold on the state government, military officers continued to be important to politics in several ways. From 1937 to 1964, civilians outnumbered those sporting military ranks among Puebla's federal deputies and senators roughly eight to one. The number of officers serving as federal deputies peaked at three from 1940 to 1943 and two from 1946 to 1949. The rest of the time, only one officer served as a deputy or, from 1949 to 1955, none at all. An officer occupied one of Puebla's two seats in the senate from 1934 to 1940 and from 1958 to 1964.[156] However, military officers still occupied key political and administrative posts in Puebla, not least the governorship, with Rafael Ávila Camacho filling the post from 1951 to 1957 and General Antonio Nava Castillo, a star polo player, political conservative, and "very close friend" of the Ávila Camacho brothers, serving first as federal deputy from 1940 to 1943 and then as governor from 1963 to 1964.[157] Avilacamachista state governments appointed military officers to civilian administrative posts at the head of the Atencingo sugar mill complex in the 1950s, in municipal town councils whose elections the state government annulled on a regular basis, and even in the state university. The army took it for granted that political and military elites would be intertwined in Puebla. In the 1940s and early 1950s, General Felipe Vallejo Contreras served in the general staff of Puebla's military zone and commanded several battalions; from 1955 to 1957, he was a key local deputy for Ciudad Serdán, who ran a propaganda drive for the state government; in 1957, he returned to the zone command, despite having served in the army for thirty-nine years; according to his military record, he technically remained in active service throughout this period.[158]

Building a political machine necessarily involved reigning in Puebla's centrifugal political forces, and this included the state's military commanders. In the 1940s, officers who tried to intervene in local political disputes on their own initiative were quickly reprimanded. In 1941, this was the fate of Captain José Nuñez Valdez, commander of the military squad stationed at the Atencingo sugar mill. Nuñez had been asked to intervene in a local political dispute by some of the villagers of Calmeca, and had done so aggressively. He detained three gunmen connected to the faction who ran the municipality and marched them to the town of Izúcar de Matamoros in chains before presenting them to the local judge, who promptly released the men. Although he insisted in a letter to the federal government that his response to the petition was legitimate because the situation in Calmeca threatened to descend into violence, the state government had him transferred out of the state.[159]

At the same time, because the Avilacamachistas derived much of their original power from political networks in the army, it made little sense for them to eliminate informal military powers altogether. After Maximino stepped down as zone commander, the Ávila Camacho brothers used their military connections to arrange for well-known allies to be posted to the state. For example, General Anacleto López, who commanded Puebla's military zone in 1935–37 and 1940–46, was a good friend of the Ávila Camacho brothers; Maximino Ávila Camacho had served under López in Zacatecas during the Cristiada, and López had cleared Maximino of numerous accusations of profiteering and arbitrary violence during the campaign.[160] In 1936, López was frequently accused of supporting Maximino Ávila Camacho's gubernatorial campaign.[161] During the 1940s and 1950s, military officers generally limited themselves to low-level graft and extortion; they sold protection from land invasions, loaned soldiers to landlords to help intimidate *ejidatarios* petitioning for land, or took a cut from harvests, stolen cattle, or illegal logging; they did not build independent bases of political power.[162]

Prominent among Avilacamachista officers were several ex-Callistas who recovered from the trials of Cardenismo thanks to an alliance with the Ávila Camacho brothers in the late 1930s. Several such officers were posted to Puebla after 1935. General Rodrigo Quevedo (zone commander, 1937–38), along with his brothers, enjoyed a profitable term as governor of Chihuahua in 1932–36. Afterward, the Quevedo machine was put on the defensive by competing local groups and the Cardenista central government. After his term, Rodrigo Quevedo even found himself subject to an internal military investigation for homicide, a very rare occurrence for a revolutionary general.[163] Quevedo was also one of the first officers to approach Manuel Ávila Camacho to suggest a presidential bid, and the 1940s saw Quevedo mount something of a comeback; after the army dropped the homicide investigation at the end of 1939, he commanded the crucial Federal District zone from 1941 to 1948.[164] While Quevedo was close to Manuel Ávila Camacho, his relations with Maximino were sometimes rather strained. When Quevedo was posted to the zone command in July 1937, Maximino Ávila Camacho cut off the command's supply of petrol from the state government, and the two men had a fierce argument on Puebla's streets.[165] General José María Tapia (zone commander, 1952–55) was one of the conservative officers whom

Cárdenas removed from the army in 1935 for plotting with Calles. Early in the 1940s, Manuel Ávila Camacho readmitted the general to the army. Maximino Ávila Camacho appointed him to the powerful position of postmaster general, and he busied himself intercepting Sinarquista communications and "watching the mail of the Cárdenas faction."[166]

Donato Bravo Izquierdo (infantry commander in the city of Puebla, 1943–46; zone commander, 1946–48 and 1955–58) had a similar trajectory, although he had been involved in *poblano* politics long before the ascent of the Ávila Camacho brothers. After working in textile factories in Veracruz, Bravo Izquierdo had risen to prominence as a moderate revolutionary general based in the region around Tehuacán, in the southeast of Puebla. In 1927, Calles appointed Bravo—a "staunch Callista"—to the provisional governorship of Puebla, with instructions to curtail the power of the state's *agraristas*.[167] He did so ably, planning the murder of *agrarista* leader Manuel Montes. In 1931, Governor Leonides Almazán—brother of General Juan Andreu Almazán—was ambushed on an isolated road and his car riddled with bullets. The governor escaped with his life, but Bravo was widely suspected of planning the attack.[168] During the Cárdenas administration, Bravo, like Quevedo, found himself on the defensive; some 12,800 hectares of his lands in Puebla were expropriated, and the military began to reinvestigate two accusations of homicide made against him in the 1920s. However, by 1939, the military had concluded that the accusations lacked sufficient evidence, and Manuel Ávila Camacho appointed Bravo to head his electoral committee. In any showdown with Puebla's Almazanistas, Bravo would be a very useful, if not indispensable, ally. In 1939, Bravo even complained to the SDN that he saw no reason why he should take a leave of absence from the army while campaigning for Manuel Ávila Camacho, since he and other serving officers had been promoting his candidacy for over a year. After the 1940 election, Bravo persuaded the army to cancel the political leave he had received and restore the wages of which he had been deprived.[169]

Below the zone command, numerous battalion and regimental commanders were tied to the Avilacamachistas. Maximino Ávila Camacho was a political patron to Edmundo Sánchez Cano, Teziutlán's cavalry commander from 1935 to 1937.[170] In 1947, Colonel Antonio Nava Castillo was posted to the Atlixco cavalry command; intelligence agents reported that he owed his placement to Manuel Ávila Camacho's backstage influence.[171] The indigenous *serrano* General Demetrio Barrios was another ally who commanded the units guarding President Manuel Ávila Camacho in 1944 and remained in command of the 37th battalion of infantry in Puebla into the 1950s; though based in the city of Puebla, Barrios had detachments from his battalion placed in towns across the Sierra Norte de Puebla.[172] Colonel Ricardo Jiménez Nava was another officer stationed in Puebla who enjoyed close ties to the Avilacamachistas. In his letters we can see how officers blended personal appeals with the language of military modernization and youthful regeneration. Jiménez wrote to thank Manuel Ávila Camacho for the commission commanding the regiment of cavalry that the president "gave to me," reporting that he had reorganized the regiment so that it was made up of "men who are young, and committed to order [de orden], with a low proportion of men rendered useless by age, whose retirements are already being processed." In this and subsequent letters he then asked the president for a range of favors, including uniforms, new horses, and a scholarship for a major under his orders. In January 1946, while stationed in Atlixco, Jiménez received money from the president for new horses and parade equipment.[173]

The Avilacamachistas dominated state politics in the 1940s and 1950s, although they never quite approached the seamless unity that Maximino Ávila Camacho liked to portray himself as having bequeathed to the state. After Maximino Ávila Camacho's unexpected death after a lavish banquet at Atlixco in 1945, the Avilacamachista coalition fragmented. Carlos Betancourt, Maximino Ávila Camacho's choice as next governor, was unexpectedly deprived of his political patron and found himself in a greatly weakened position.[174] As Betancourt tried to appease the Alemán administration and build up his own machine, he confronted public scandals over his clumsy and violent attempts to impose municipal slates and fell out with his own federal deputies, and with many other former Avilacamachistas. Under Betancourt some local Avilacamachista stalwarts such as General José Martínez Castro in Tecamachalco were almost displaced from local office. By the end of the 1940s, ex-governor Gonzalo Bautista had even thrown his lot in with Henriquismo and was campaigning across the state.[175] The army was also affected by the political instability of Betancourt's governorship. Avilacamachista control of the military briefly loosened. In March 1948, President Alemán removed General Bravo from the zone command; Bravo objected and wrote to ask Alemán for an explanation since Bravo felt that he had been "the victim of some intrigue."[176] In 1950, the military zone commander General Gabriel Leyva Velázquez intervened to mediate a long-festering agrarian dispute at Soltepec, and intelligence agents reported that Atlixco's cavalry commander,

Colonel Nava Castillo, "openly sympathizes with Henriquismo." By July 1951, however, Nava Castillo had joined a secret group of self-identified "Aleman-ista" officers.[177] Other relatives of the Avilacamachistas were more notable as political embarrassments than useful allies; into this category falls another younger brother, Captain Gabriel Ávila Camacho, who was even more adept than Maximino at embarrassing the famously dour Manuel Ávila Camacho. After serving as the city of Puebla's police chief in 1937–41, Gabriel Ávila Camacho was briefly arrested for shooting the son of a rich jeweler in Mexico City. In 1946, he was again briefly arrested for the attempted murder of the fiancé of Maximino Ávila Camacho's widow during a gunfight in Mexico City's streets in a dispute over the family fortune.[178] In 1947, Gabriel Ávila Camacho's efforts to have himself elected senator were vetoed by the rest of the Avilacamachista group, and he returned to Teziutlán to manage the family's lands.[179]

However, General Rafael Ávila Camacho, state governor from 1951 to 1957, largely brought an end to infighting among Puebla's political elite. In 1949, Alemán had removed the scheming General Alamillo from the head of the Military College and, at Manuel Ávila Camacho's recommendation, appointed Rafael Ávila Camacho in his place. This appointment was greeted with skepticism by many cadets and officers, who questioned Rafael Ávila Camacho's military credentials, associated him with the corrupt Maximino Ávila Camacho, and saw him as "a somewhat uncouth 'pistolero' type." However, he won over some of the cadets by improving food and facilities at the college, sometimes with funds from his own (ample) fortune.[180] After he stepped down from his post at the Military College, Rafael Ávila Camacho ran unopposed for Puebla's governorship in 1951. Rafael's backing from his elder brother, ex-president Manuel, his enduring support among the Avilacamachistas whom Maximino had placed on the regional and local committees of the PRI, and his brokering of labor and municipal disputes in Atlixco, Atencingo, and Matamoros all allowed him to reconcentrate power in the governorship. Under Rafael Ávila Camacho, the Avilacamachistas' hybrid alliance of military officers, state government, and local elites enjoyed considerable autonomy from the federal government.[181] Critics increasingly viewed the state's military commanders as being under the governor's control, or under the control of Rafael's friend and longtime ally General Bravo, who returned to command the zone in 1955 before becoming state senator in 1959.[182]

Conclusion

Officers' retreat from political power in the 1940s was bitterly contested and consequently incomplete. After 1940, military education and propaganda espoused an apolitical identity for the army. However, officers' politicking, factionalism, and entrepreneurialism belied this image, challenging and sometimes embarrassing the central government. By the mid-1950s, the government had managed to shunt political reality closer to the discourse of civilian rule that it preached. However, demilitarizing politics was a conflictive, messy, and incomplete process. The military politics of the 1940s and early 1950s eventually taught army officers several things. It taught them that entering the electoral opposition risked political repression and economic reprisals. It revealed some of the limits of public enthusiasm for government by military officers. However, it also showed that, in exchange for national loyalty, officers could expect to enjoy some political and entrepreneurial autonomy within the PRIísta system. Casting their eyes to Puebla, officers would have observed a compelling case of the uneven demilitarization of politics, as a small faction of officers moved between military and political posts and used their military networks to help build the Avilacamachista machine that dominated state politics from the late 1930s into the 1960s. This is not to say that the government's civilian image was irrelevant. Officers had to learn to reproduce official rhetoric as part of the PRI's new modus operandi. The political struggles of the 1940s and 1950s produced a new, durable set of unspoken political rules for the army and a potent political myth about the army's unity and clean divorce from civil government.

When contemporaries acknowledged or complained about officers after the 1940s, as they sometimes did, they usually portrayed officers' entrepreneurialism and political meddling as anachronistic, the persistence of immoral habits among older officers. This was a useful way to frame complaints to the government, or for the military hierarchy to try to deflect institutional responsibility. In 1953, secretary of defense General Ramos wrote to President Ruiz Cortines to inform him of the continuing "lack of moral solvency" among many commanders, but blamed this on the persistence of habits among older officers.[183] Although more research is needed to understand its precise contours, it is clear that officers' residual autonomy was not inimical to the PRIísta state but a fundamental part and condition of it. As we will see in chapter 5, there was nothing anachronistic about the army's enduring policing role, upon which officers' residual power was ultimately based.

CHAPTER FIVE

Military Policing and Society in Mexico, 1940–1960

In the previous chapter, we saw how a faction of military officers led by the Ávila Camacho brothers helped to build the *cacicazgo* Avilacamachista. The Avilacamachistas were generally successful in getting political allies or cooperative officers posted to the state. These officers were vital not only because they did not build competing political networks. They, and their soldiers, also provided a good measure of the organized force that allowed the Avilacamachista political machine to function. These roles, and how society responded to them, are the subject of this chapter.

There is a dearth of scholarship on military policing in Mexico. Those who have tackled the topic have tended to focus on the large-scale counterinsurgency of the Cristiada in the 1920s, or the repression of Mexico's new student and guerilla movements after 1965. The middle decades of the twentieth century—the crucial years in which the PRIísta state took shape—do not much register in scholarship or public discussion of military policing. However, a focus on military policing, and the ways that people responded to the army with praise or with complaints and protest, can illuminate the profound continuities in the army's institutional roles that survived the more famous changes in *cupular* officer politics and provide broader insights into politics and state-society relations during what is usually seen as the PRI's heyday of stability and legitimacy. Under the PRI, the river of national politics appeared to run smoothly on the surface; underneath were churning currents of local conflict, military and paramilitary violence, and competing interpretations of revolutionary discourse.

To contextualize the case of Puebla, the chapter first provides a national overview of the army's organization from the late 1930s to the 1950s. It then explores the ways that soldiers—largely at the behest of Puebla's Avilacamachista political and military faction—performed many of the tasks of social and political control typical elsewhere, along with some more unusual innovations. Finally, by using military service records, the press, intelligence reports, memoirs, and roughly 250 petitions and complaints, the chapter analyzes protests and criticism of the army. It argues that attempts to limit military policing, while risky, tenuous, and generally unsuccessful, were not completely quixotic. The conclusion then considers how typical the case of Puebla was.

The Army and Domestic Policing, 1930s–1950s

Although Puebla's experience of military policing had some distinctive features, in its basic institutional outlines it was typical of the development of the army in these years. In the 1940s, the government slightly expanded the army and reorganized it. It grew in strength from 50,000 in 1940 to around 57,000 in 1960. During the Second World War, the army acquired some elite, mechanized units of infantry and cavalry. The air force, which had 25 functioning aircraft in 1941, had around 200 in 1945, and the army reorganized and expanded its logistics and communications branches.[1] Between 1942 and 1945, the army created four large mixed divisions, each under a unified command, made up of infantry, artillery, and cavalry units. These divisions were based in Mexico City, Monterrey, and the city of Puebla. The SDN hoped this change would extricate the army from police work and allow for sustained training with new equipment. Some officers hoped that these divisions would also allow for deployment overseas. In 1942, the army created new second-line regular units called Regional Guards, made up of older troops, to manage the remainder of domestic policing tasks.[2]

However, many of these changes proved temporary. It was not possible to completely extricate the new divisions from police work and counter-insurgency, and the government deployed units from the Puebla division across the state in response to antidraft protests and rebellions.[3] At the end of 1944, the Regional Guards were quietly disbanded, partly because of unusually high rates of desertion, but also because the government realized that "internal order is at times enough of a job to require the attention of the entire Mexican army."[4] By 1950, more ambitious plans for maintaining the mixed divisions were put to one side. It was obvious to foreign diplomats, military officers, and troops alike that the army's basic rationale remained the maintenance of internal order.[5]

Consequently, throughout the 1950s, the army was still dispersed around the country much as it had been in 1940, and its core role was the application of force and sometimes terror against the Mexican population. Four elite units—one infantry division, a mechanized brigade, a regiment of mechanized cavalry, and the presidential guards—inherited the most up-to-date equipment acquired during the war. Their soldiers were generally among the most educated and well paid in the army, and were concentrated in the capital and the city of Puebla.[6] The infantry and cavalry were divided between troops stationed in major provincial towns and those dispersed in isolated, frequently unhealthy and downright dangerous policing squads in the surrounding countryside. In the 1940s, the infantry's rank and file viewed such provincial assignments as only fit for *"los más pendejos"* who could not avoid them through personal contacts.[7] In the early 1950s, the army maintained the same number of infantry units spread across the country as it had in 1940. The cavalry shrank from a total of forty regiments in 1941 to twenty in 1950; however, this was the result of the army's shift toward more mechanized and administrative units and did not lead to a reduction in the army's overall numbers. Although the Federal District lost regular infantry and cavalry troops, this was more than compensated for by the presence of the new elite infantry division, mechanized brigade, and presidential guard units (see table 5.1).[8] In 1953, the army stationed 650 squads of approximately fourteen troops in smaller towns and villages, an average of about twenty squads for each state, or one in every fifth municipality. In 1953, the president's secretary informed the SDN that it should cease to categorize these squads as temporary assistance to civilian authorities. The president's secretary argued that policing squads should now be classified as an ongoing, essential part of the army's mission since, he noted vaguely, they were "in accord with national reality."[9]

The *defensas rurales* showed similar continuities. Cárdenas had given the militia a clear institutional relationship to the army and a presence in each state. Between 1938 and 1950, the total numbers of *defensas rurales* and their geographical distribution remained fairly stable. It is difficult to generalize about these forces with any precision: some served as makeshift local policemen; others harbored some residual *agrarista* loyalties and were unreliable agents of repression; a great many were simply gangs of pistoleros serving local bosses. However, they were concentrated in areas of old Cristero and revolutionary mobilization, notably Michoacán and Chihuahua, and were an important enough element in social control that the government maintained them in the face of legion complaints about abuses and *caciquismo*.[10] As can be seen in Puebla, the army could shift the geographical focus of militia recruitment within a state while keeping the total numbers fairly stable.

TABLE 5.1 Infantry Battalions and Cavalry Regiments in Each State and Total Change in Troops, 1940 and 1950

State	1940		1950		Total change in number of troops
	Battalions	Regiments	Battalions	Regiments	
Aguascalientes	1	0	1	0	0
Baja California North	1	0	2	0	+601
Baja California South	1	0	1	0	0
Campeche	1	0	1	0	0
Chiapas	2	0	2	0	0
Chihuahua	2	2	1	1	−1041
Coahuila	1	2	1	1	−440
Colima	1	0	1	0	0
Distrito Federal	9	3	4	0	−4,325
Durango	1	1	1	0	−440
Guanajuato	1	3	1	2	−440
Guerrero	1	2	3	0	+322
Hidalgo	2	1	1	1	−601
Jalisco	1	3	1	3	0
México	1	4	1	2	−880
Michoacán	2	2	2	1	−440
Morelos	2	2	2	1	−440
Nayarit	0	1	1	0	+161
Nuevo León	1	1	1	0	−440
Oaxaca	2	0	2	0	0
Puebla	1	2	2	2	+861
Querétaro	1	1	0	1	−601
Quintana Roo	1	0	1	0	0
San Luis Potosí	1	2	2	0	−279
Sinaloa	2	1	1	1	−601
Sonora	2	1	2	1	0
Tabasco	1	0	1	0	0
Tamaulipas	2	3	1	1	−1,481
Tlaxcala	1	0	1	0	0
Veracruz	5	2	7	2	+1,202
Yucatán	1	0	1	0	0
Zacatecas	1	2	1	0	−880

Sources: Personnel tables in AGN, MAC, 606.3/91, and AGN, MAV, 298/22349.

Although precise information about where these forces were stationed within each state is hard to find, army units were probably concentrated in areas of economic and strategic importance (mines, dams, power plants) and flash points of social and ethnic conflict in the countryside.[11] Intensive agrarian capitalism could still trigger dispossession, social conflict, and violent insurrection, whether based on long-established crops such as sugar or newer waves of coffee and logging.[12] The data in table 5.1 suggest that most of the reductions in provincial forces caused by the decline of the cavalry occurred in Mexico's northern states; the states of Puebla, Veracruz, and Guerrero all actually gained troops in this period. In 1953, according to a confidential report, the army was involved in "notable incidents" across the country but particularly in Oaxaca and Guerrero. These included putting down various local "rebellions," pursuing armed groups, and dispersing crowds during riots.[13] Ethnic and social conflict often overlapped. For example, the military was a constant, violent presence among the Triqui in Oaxaca, and even bombed San Juan Copala in 1956.[14] In western Jalisco in 1955 the army sent hundreds of troops to put down a rebellion of Huichol villages that it claimed were trying to create "an Indian republic."[15] Other observers insisted the revolt was triggered by the aggressive expansion of logging by political and military authorities.[16] Henriquismo's disgruntled agrarian leagues also remained active and kept the army busy in several small counterinsurgencies.[17] In 1955, a rebellion by indigenous villagers in the region of La Trinitaria, Chiapas, was driven by a mixture of agrarian and ethnic conflicts, under the leadership of an ex-Henriquista veteran. It was defeated with a display of military terror, mass executions, and beheadings that even the intelligence agent sent to investigate found shocking but which the army insisted were standard (if secretive) practice in such cases.[18] There are fewer examples of such heavy-handed military violence in the old bastions of political Catholicism after 1950, although Benjamin Smith's recent finding of military repression of a rebellion in 1962 in Huajuapam de León, Oaxaca, reveals that religious conflict could still trigger military violence.[19]

In the 1940s, soldiers did a lot of policing but also enjoyed a substantial say in how it was done. The constitution's formal boundaries separating the army's responsibilities for military security from the civilian judicial system were extremely porous in practice. Officers, politicians, and bureaucrats all portrayed the army's police work as upholding public order and security (crowd control, the pursuit of armed groups and bandits), with occasional missions countering smuggling and narcotics or supporting the campaign against foot-and-mouth disease. The army's power to interpret these tasks and carry out everyday policing at the local level could be sweeping. It was particularly important in unstable, fractious states such as Sinaloa, Guerrero, and Oaxaca, or in rural peripheries in general where civilian police were feeble, few, or nonexistent.[20] In the 1940s, Guerrero's zone commander took over the investigation of dozens of criminal cases abandoned by the state government. Although army commanders' formerly sweeping power to mediate agrarian conflicts had declined, it had not disappeared.[21]

Admittedly, by the 1950s the government had developed new civilian agencies with which to manage conflict, which probably reduced the state's reliance on the military in some places. However, the provincial reach of intelligence services remained distinctly limited, certainly compared to that of the federal military. In 1952, the DGIPS had only fifteen agents with which to gather intelligence outside of Mexico City.[22] Through the 1940s and 1950s, some state governments strengthened their judiciaries and police forces, but this trend was fitful and regionally uneven, as the case of Puebla demonstrates well.[23]

The history of how the Mexican police actually functioned is hard to establish, particularly outside of Mexico City, and largely remains to be written; the police's deep institutional connections with the army are clear. Urban areas usually had more policemen and some basic judicial institutions, but even here soldiers remained vital to policing and crowd control. In 1956, the government sent soldiers to occupy Mexico City's National Polytechnic Institute to quell student protests; in 1959, soldiers and police broke a national strike by the railway workers union, rounded up thousands of railwaymen, and held them in military camps across the country for several days before transferring them to civilian penitentiaries.[24] Military officers ran many police departments, including that of the Federal District. Although the government went to the trouble of formally removing officers from active duty in the army before appointing them to civilian police forces, the change was often cosmetic. This was particularly so in the Federal District, where well-connected army officers ran the police, and the government had "militarized" the police force's organization and training in 1939, enhancing hierarchy and impunity. The police force was not simply somewhere the government could place officers to remove them from the army payroll, although this sometimes happened; in the 1940s, key military officers in charge of large police departments continued to receive their army pay in addition to a police salary. In the 1940s, all policemen were expected to salute any military officers they met in the street.[25]

Whatever their institutional berth, when soldiers did police work, it was sometimes conducted in a military style of violently countering a threat rather than accumulating evidence for a legal trial. Army officers could organize or carry out torture and extrajudicial executions with impunity. In 1943, the army responded to draft rebellions in Morelos and México by summarily executing any "bandits" that they encountered; soldiers stationed in Nayarit proceeded in the same fashion.[26] Pursuing bandits and gunmen across the countryside was difficult, dangerous, and not necessarily popular in the army. As one commander stationed in Michoacán remarked, some officers felt that such work was "not really a soldier's job." However, the same reluctant officer still influenced what policing there was in the backwoods of Michoacán. In a common strategy, he usually contracted a "professional bandit hunter" called Huerta, who, rather than bringing bandits and high-waymen to trial, "usually shot them."[27] Not all officers relied on outsourcing violence. General Miguel Z. Martínez was well known within the military as something of a specialist in state violence. At a political meeting in 1948, revolutionary veterans muttered to themselves about his sanguinary reputation.[28] He cut his teeth in counterinsurgency during the Cristiada, moved in and out of political offices and cavalry commands in the 1930s, became Manuel Ávila Camacho's head of police in Mexico City in 1940, and moved back into the army to command several troublesome military zones and regions into the 1950s. Whether the general was in a military or a civilian post, it did not make much difference to his standard modus operandi of harassing, detaining, torturing, and executing groups of petty criminals, bandits, and political dissidents.[29] A captain who served under Martínez remembered how, while a commander in Guadalajara in the 1940s, the general organized a "cleansing [*limpieza*]," during which he ordered soldiers to kill dozens of "*delincuentes*" and dump their bodies on the outskirts of the city:

> General Z. Martínez was in permanent contact with those doing the "cleansing" day and night to give instructions and remove any doubts they may have had about the mission. His high-pitched, childlike voice became well-known among the policemen and soldiers dressed as civilians who constantly talked with him by telephone: "General, we have two *rateros* that we found robbing someone's house, what shall we do with them?" "They die, they die." This little phrase became

very popular among the "commissioned" men and they repeated it with smiles and jokes at any pretext. If someone had a problem with a bus driver or something like that which made his life difficult, his compañeros immediately imitated the womanly voice of the general: "He dies, he dies."[30]

General Jesús Arias Sánchez was another military officer who moved freely between counterinsurgency in Sinaloa and formal police posts in Nuevo León in the 1940s. According to a military doctor who served with him, General Arias Sánchez was happy to bypass legal niceties during the "pacification" of the south of Sinaloa in the early 1940s. Something of the nature of Arias Sánchez's campaign is suggested by an agent's assessment in 1950 that the whole state of Sinaloa respected the general because "he has imposed himself in such a way, since his time here, that it is almost afraid of him."[31]

Indeed, much of this policing was nakedly political, and was viewed as such. When communities viewed army policing as political and illegitimate it sometimes triggered dramatic conflict, as the attempted lynching of an isolated garrison in Nayarit in 1946 and the actual lynching of a foot-and-mouth-disease inspector and military escort in Michoacán in 1947 show.[32] However, beyond these sporadic outbursts, it is much harder to trace the incidence and the popular legitimacy of military policing. To do so, we must move from a national to a regional level of analysis.

The Army in Puebla, 1940–1957

While the Avilacamachistas occasionally squabbled among themselves, they also faced opposition from different groups in *poblano* society. Governors Gonzalo Bautista (1941–44) and Carlos Betancourt (1945–51) faced pressures from peasant movements within the National Peasant Confederation (Confederación Nacional Campesina, or CNC), particularly at the large Atencingo sugar mill in the southwest of the state where a popular movement aimed to bolster cane growers' earning power and autonomy from the mill administration.[33] Maximino Ávila Camacho had increased the state's control of the countryside by cutting deals with powerful caciques, creating a regional peasant confederation, and suppressing bandits and political opponents. However, his successors still faced the frustrated remnants of the state's *agraristas* dotted across the countryside, unable to mount a serious state-wide challenge but capable of organizing around isolated land disputes and seeking allies with independent peasant organizations such as the General Union of Mexican Workers and Peasants (Unión General de Obreros y Campesinos de México, or UGOCM). The state was also the scene of many large Sinarquista rallies and marches in the first half of the 1940s. Union disputes never reached the levels of "intense warfare" of the mid-1930s, but rivalries between the CROM, the CTM, and the Regional Federation of Workers and Peasants (Federación Regional de Obreros y Campesinos, or FROC) continued and generated low-level violence through the 1940s, particularly in the conflictive textile factories around Atlixco.[34]

The Avilacamachistas generally sought to contain these challenges with a familiar mixture of incentives and violence, *pan o palo*. Land reform slowed in the state in the 1940s, although it did not cease altogether; after 1941 most new land grants were concentrated in the isolated sierra region in the northeast of the state, particularly around Huauchinango. The government offered developmental benefits to peasant communities throughout the 1940s: access to seeds and credit, new schools, wells and irrigation, roads, electrification and sanitation projects.[35] However, there were strict limits to the *pan* that was available for distribution. In general, economic growth in Puebla in these years was sluggish, and most of its benefits accrued to a small political and economic elite connected to the Avilacamachistas.[36]

Not all of the *palo* that the state government required was provided by the army. Mexican politicians generally understood that using the army to attack prominent political enemies risked the government's fragile legitimacy and was best avoided if possible. Indeed, soldiers involved in strikebreaking, street fighting to control electoral booths, or harassing *agraristas* sometimes disguised their involvement by dressing as civilians.[37] In Puebla, the army avoided direct implication in the most prominent political murders of the period: journalist Trinidad Mata; former deputy for Tepeaca and Almazanista Telésforo Salas; *agrarista* leaders "Doña Lola," Porfirio Jaramillo, and Adalberto García; dissident FROC leader Fernando Escamilla; and CTM leader Leobardo Coca.[38]

Despite these precautions, the army remained deeply involved in local policing, political and otherwise. Puebla formed Mexico's twenty-fifth military zone, whose commander was based in the city of Puebla and appointed by the SDN. At least four units of cavalry and infantry were based in the urban centers Atlixco, Tehuacán, Teziutlán, and the city of Puebla from the late 1930s to the 1940s. In the late 1940s, the government ceased to station infantry or cavalry in Teziutlán and stationed a larger regiment of mechanized cavalry in the city of Puebla. Army commanders based in Puebla, Atlixco, and Tehuacán typically stationed small detachments of five to fifteen soldiers in nearby villages and railway stations where, in strict constitutional terms, they obeyed the state government, and commanders could also send out squads to sweep their respective sectors. The army always had three commanders in charge of arming, training, and recruiting Puebla's *defensas rurales*. The southwest of the state had long been conflictive, a hotbed of agrarianism and *sindical* conflict in Atlixco's textile factories. By the end of the 1940s, the army stopped trying to recruit militia in this region, relying on regular troops and concentrating the militia in the state's central valley between the city of Puebla and Tehuacán and in the Sierra Norte de Puebla around Zacatlán and Huauchinango.[39]

Soldiers were important and numerous relative to civilian police. In 1942–43, the number of federal troops in Puebla swelled due to wartime reorganization and antidraft protests but generally remained stable over this period. Throughout the 1940s and 1950s, roughly 2,300 regular troops were stationed in Puebla at any one time. Puebla's civilian police forces probably gradually increased between the 1930s and 1950s. In the early 1940s, for example, Governor Gonzalo Bautista reorganized the city of Puebla's police force and created a new unit of traffic police.[40] However, by the 1960s, the state's 2,246 soldiers still outnumbered municipal (929) and judicial (51) policemen by a ratio of 2.3 soldiers for every civilian policeman. If the state's 825 *defensas rurales* are added to the military forces, this ratio climbs to roughly 3:1. By the 1960s, of Puebla's 215 municipalities, 33 percent had civilian police forces, while 32 percent were policed by detachments of militia (15 percent) and regular troops (17 percent).[41] In the 1940s and 1950s, the state's judicial police was itself run by military officers.[42]

The army performed many crucial tasks of social control. In 1943–44, the army sent several thousand troops to fight against antidraft rebellions and harass complicit municipal authorities with fines and beatings. In Xicotepec, the army punished the uncooperative members of the municipal council and the local judge by forcing them to stand to attention for hours on end in the town square.[43] The air force also dropped thousands of leaflets across the state offering amnesty to rebels who put down arms, and threatening to annihilate those who did not. Commanders occasionally sent out "flying columns" to carry out disarmament raids on unsuspecting towns or track down armed groups in peripheral parts of the state, although there is less evidence of these undeclared petty counterinsurgencies after the 1940s.[44] In the late

1940s, the government's campaign to eradicate foot-and-mouth disease by slaughtering cattle was intensely unpopular, and soldiers provided escorts to inspectors; to the extent that the campaign was implemented at all, it was carried out at gunpoint.[45] Throughout the period, the army protected rural properties and combated the remnants of *agrarismo* by harassing dissident *ejidos* and peasants planning to solicit land. Soldiers also broke strikes and prevented the CTM from organizing around Atlixco and Tehuacán.[46] The Avilacamachistas' allies in the CROM largely escaped skirmishes with the army.

The army also performed more directly political tasks. Soldiers protected local authorities during student riots over bus fares in the city of Puebla in 1949 and during numerous protests over the imposition of official candidates in municipal and state elections that spiked during Betancourt's governorship.[47] When the army lacked the men to establish a permanent detachment in a conflictive municipality, "flying columns" were also sent out to secure the election of party slates.[48] Of course, all of these tasks were carried out in the name of public order. Army protocol demanded that all political dissidents be referred to as "bandits" or "*gavilleros*."[49] However, in private meetings officers made their political role abundantly clear. In 1943, some Sinarquista leaders went to Tehuacán's barracks to meet with the regiment commander. The general explicitly told them to stop organizing marches and meetings since these constituted political "agitation." Rather than threaten military detention or a fine, he simply suggested that if they did not desist it was possible they might "die while walking along the road somewhere."[50]

Even more controversial than these roles was the state government's appointment of military officers to civilian posts, at the head of municipal councils (as occurred in Atlixco in 1939, Tehuacán in 1943, Atlixco again in 1945, Chietla and Izúcar de Matamoros in 1948), or even into the state university administration (in 1942–43 and 1952).[51] Although Puebla's constitution gave the governor the power to annul municipal elections with the approval of the state legislature, the appointment of military officers clearly expressed the state government's faith in officers' ability to intimidate and discipline political opponents, and a rather cavalier attitude to the supposedly firm boundaries separating civilians and soldiers. Unlike the fictional village of San Pedro de los Saguaros, whose Alemanista interim municipal president was memorably satirized in the 1999 film *La Ley de Herodes*, the municipalities in which the government appointed military officers were far from being marginal rural backwaters; the list includes the main population centers in the state, excluding Huauchinango and Cholula.[52] Officers in these towns arrogated to themselves the authority to meddle in politics and labor disputes in surrounding municipalities.[53]

Over time, the army managed to distance itself somewhat from bloodshed. While the army carefully avoided implication in major political murders, its collective, low-level policing did sometimes lead to bloodshed. Violence against "humble folk" in the state's peripheries was less visible and embarrassing than that against prominent urban leaders, a point made with some bitterness by Huehuetlán's provisional municipal president after a brutal military raid in March 1943; the army arrived on the outskirts of the village at night, found a guide to take them to the house of a suspected "*maleante*," and then riddled it with bullets, killing two townspeople.[54] According to cases I have culled from 113 complaints sent to the government, from a total of 69 different incidents that involved the army, soldiers were directly implicated in killing 31 civilians in 13 different incidents between 1939 and 1957, and of attempting to kill a further 5. However, allegations are concentrated in the first half of the 1940s: 24 in 1939–45, 10 in 1946–51, and 2 in 1951–57. Moreover, 8 of the 10 accusations from 1946–51 involve officers installed in municipal councils who occupied a hazy institutional no-man's-land between the army and civilian authorities.[55]

It is likely that there was a genuine decrease in military bloodshed, rather than simply in the public's willingness to complain about it. As noted above, after 1951 Rafael Ávila Camacho oversaw a general return to political stability in the state. Moreover, there was no shortage of pistoleros on whom the Avilacamachistas could rely if needed. For the case of Porfirio Jaramillo, the powerful peasant leader from Atencingo assassinated in 1955, available federal intelligence reports (along with oral histories) do not implicate soldiers in his murder; elsewhere, agents reported military bloodshed in some detail.[56] Nevertheless, it was clear, at least to Governor Rafael Ávila Camacho himself, that whatever stability obtained by the mid-1950s was due, in part, to earlier doses of military repression and the continued threat of it. The governor successfully urged the federal government to keep the state's contingent of troops in the 1950s, since Puebla's "historical antecedents" had shown how important the army was in protecting order and property in the countryside.[57]

Soldiers' involvement in police work was not always viewed as political and illegitimate. From 1940 to 1957, in addition to the aforementioned 113 vivid and convincing complaints about the army stationed in Puebla, the central government also received 92 petitions either praising soldiers or requesting their assistance. Most petitions simply asked for a small detachment of troops to be posted to the letter writer's locality (58 percent) or asked that particular military units or personnel not be moved by the SDN (24 percent). The army was necessary, most argued, to counter dangerous armed groups of civilian agitators, pistoleros, or bandits (57 percent), or to enforce rural property rights (20 percent).[58] Individual citizens wrote most of these petitions (45 percent), although unsurprisingly many were sent by municipal authorities (20 percent).[59]

Sometimes the way the army policed and mediated municipal disputes was broadly to the satisfaction of the people involved. In reports to their superiors, local authorities and military officers always portrayed their interventions as apolitical and cautious, intended to mediate disputes, counsel restraint and "moderation," and convince local political factions that "the past is the past."[60] Sometimes, units of the regular army and the staff of the military zone genuinely played this mediating role. In November 1949, the state government deposed a popular municipal president in Acatlán and imposed an outsider from Atlixco; a small group of soldiers had to protect the new administration from dozens of villagers intent on removing them from office. An agent from the governor, the chief of staff of the military zone, and five other military officers promptly arrived to mediate the dispute and settled on a local, compromise candidate for the municipal presidency who was apparently acceptable to local people.[61]

Likewise, when policing coincided with popular justice it could enjoy some legitimacy. In Puebla and elsewhere, where particularly "hardened" robbers, rapists, and pistoleros might face only feeble civilian authorities, some individuals and communities clearly sought out the army, and they were not always disappointed when rough justice was meted out.[62] Filadelfo Gayosso Rios recorded testimony from Tlacuilotepec of a popular lynching in May 1943 of a hated "local delinquent," Vicente Nepomuceno. After an army squad arrived to take the beaten man into custody, Nepomuceno's victims approached the soldiers "to ask for the application of the law." A few days later the "sergeant shot him [Nepomuceno] in the chest with a mauser," before leaving the jail doors open so the townspeople could complete the lynching.[63]

Occasionally, peasant and labor groups requested the protection of the army in their disputes with local opponents and Avilacamachista allies, although they were increasingly disappointed. These requests persisted into the 1950s, although in fewer numbers; some prominent groups, such as the *ejidatarios* of Atencingo, were clearly disabused of the idea that the army might fulfill this role by the mid-1950s.[64] In 1954, the villagers of Hueytamalco, near Teziutlán, asked for the army to protect them from the pistoleros of Ernesto Nuñez Velarde. Nuñez owned the lands that they planned to petition as an *ejido*, and also happened to be Rafael Ávila Camacho's brother-in-law. However, the villagers' allies in the UGOCM were skeptical that the army could perform this role in Ávila Camacho's own bailiwick since, they informed the president, typically "even the troops stationed in this region do not provide any guarantees at all."[65]

The case of Soltepec illustrates that, while the old idea of the revolutionary army as an ally of agrarian reform could still occasionally appear, it was tenuous and increasingly lacked relevance. The *agraristas* of Soltepec were locked in a bitter, decades-long dispute to regain 675 hectares of *ejidal* lands stripped by Maximino Ávila Camacho. Soltepec had long had the reputation of being a particularly combative *agrarista* stronghold.[66] In 1919, the village of Soltepec had been granted an *ejido* from the lands of the hacienda La Rinconada. The landlords, like many others in the Puebla-Tlaxcala Valley, mounted a trenchant defense of their lands, splitting ownership of the property among various members of the Tamariz family and receiving a legal *amparo* from a local judge that was confirmed by the Supreme Court in the late 1920s. However, in 1937 the Cárdenas administration decreed that the lands belonged to the villagers. Nevertheless, in 1939, the judge of Ciudad Serdán ruled that the *ejidatarios'* occupation of the lands was illegal, and the lands were returned to the Tamariz family, with the help of the army. In the process four *ejidatarios* were killed and thirty-two were taken to the city of Puebla, jailed, and then fined. For most of the 1940s, Soltepec's *agraristas* complained that a detachment of soldiers on the lands intimidated, abused, and occasionally shot at them; they also blamed the zone commander for obstructing the Agrarian Department's attempts to restore their lands.[67] However, after General Gabriel Leyva Velázquez took over the zone in 1950, they started to praise the new commander for helping them recover their land (or at least refusing to eject them from it), and focused their ire on the governor and the Tamariz family.

In April 1950, *La Prensa* published an open letter from Soltepec's villagers that makes only a diffident appeal to the army's social revolutionary tradition. After detailing their travails against the landlords of La Rinconada and Governor Betancourt, the *ejidatarios* claimed to have already met with General Leyva. Despite having been recently removed from their lands once more, they showered praise on the general for his earlier interventions and clearly hoped that more might follow.[68] They also exempted the zone commander from any blame for their brutal treatment, preferring to blame the soldiers of the local detachment who had been corrupted by landlords. The letter is laced with a cautious ambivalence, though: after explaining that Leyva's initial help to them was proof of his status as an "authentic social revolutionary" willing to stand up for popular claims against corrupt local agencies, the villagers insisted that the general's subsequent obedience to the governor's orders to remove them from their land was but further proof that he was a truly "honorable military officer."[69] This was a rare outburst however. Puebla's rural bourgeoisie saw Soltepec's open letter as scandalous and shocking. Leyva's intervention was soon reversed and Soltepec's *ejidatarios* were frustrated.[70]

It was always risky to discuss, let alone criticize, the army in public. Disparaging the army, theoretically an obedient instrument under the control of the president, was dangerously close to questioning the legitimacy of the entire regime. Unlike the corporate party, the army offered few obvious institutional channels through which people could either praise or condemn its conduct. Avilacamachismo drastically curtailed public debate, especially about the army. In the mid-1930s, Maximino Ávila Camacho had faced a barrage of criticism. The press, particularly *La Opinión*, which supported the left-wing Gilberto Bosques's bid for the governorship in 1937, condemned his meddling as zone commander in 1935.[71] Maximino Ávila Camacho tried to control coverage through a series of state and commercial publications; while zone commander he launched the *Diario de Puebla* with the journalist Julián Cacho in order to promote his candidacy for the governorship.[72] In the late 1930s, journalists were intimidated and assassinated. In 1937, one journalist poked fun at the violent reputation of the military officer whom Maximino Ávila Camacho had placed in charge of the state penitentiary, and appeared the next day "with his head bandaged and his arm in a sling."[73] In April 1939, Maximino Ávila Camacho was accused of planning the murder of journalist Trinidad Mata.[74]

Despite these risks, various groups complained to the government about how the army policed local societies. Most complaints were written by individual citizens with no formal connection to the government (45 percent) or by *ejidal* authorities (17 percent); the remainder are split roughly evenly between *sindicatos* (8 percent), CNC-affiliated peasant leagues (12 percent), independent peasant organizations (8 percent), and municipal (6 percent) and state authorities (3 percent). Less frequently, people wrote to the SDN or the press or held protest meetings in the streets. The Sinarquistas and various peasant groups met and petitioned military officers. While this practice never disappeared, by the late 1940s it entailed some new risks and offered diminishing returns.[75] General José Heredia Aceves, zone commander from 1948 to early 1950, scolded peasant organizations who appealed to him for help, and even embarrassed them by forwarding their correspondence to the federal government. A group called the Confederación Campesina Miguel Alemán saw this as a new and unfair response. Although they asked the general to be "forgiven" for having made "an inopportune request," they explained that their petition "was impelled by the declarations of the Secretary of National Defense who said he would help to combat the *caciquismo* that reigns in the villages, and its fraudulent activities."[76]

As was the case during conscription protests, people complained about the army in ways that drew on the state's own liberal-democratic and revolutionary rhetoric. In the 1940s and 1950s, few people demanded that the army leave Puebla altogether or, conversely, that the army be handed political power. This marked a change from the fraught 1930s, when some unionists called for the army to be removed from the state altogether.[77] Rather, most petitions assumed that the army could perform a legitimate policing role, provided it was controlled by democratic, civilian authorities and used in a way that was proportional to an armed threat. For example, in 1942 María Gregoria wrote to the government to accuse a local squad of soldiers of killing her husband and offered a precise counterfactual detailing the procedures that should have been followed: "I am very well informed and I can affirm that my husband had not committed any crime . . . but supposing, without my conceding it, that he had committed one, Sub-Lieutenant Bernal, in completion of his duty, would be asked by the first civil authority of the municipality, the only one entitled to do this, for the necessary help in his apprehension, and having done this he would have had to put him at the disposition of those who requested him, so that this civil authority would judge him, but not assassinate him in a predatory way, which is what he did."[78]

Most people complained that the army was being used to ram through unpopular and corrupt policies, and was doing so in a heavy-handed, violent way. Most petitions concerned agrarian conflict (53 percent), as people

complained that the army enforced illegitimate rulings over land grants, ha-
rassed peasants who planned to petition for new *ejidal* grants, or protected
corrupt *ejidal* authorities. Others complained about soldiers enforcing the
official party's control of elections (8 percent) or meddling in union disputes
(5 percent). Complaints about officers enriching themselves through extortion or larceny were rarer (5 percent). Others focused more on the army's
sins of omission, as soldiers remained suspiciously inactive in the face of
well-connected local armed groups and gunmen (10 percent).[79] Those villages that asked the army to combat the armed gangs led by General José
Martínez Castro, a powerful cacique in Puebla's central valley, or gangs of
pistoleros around Chietla were disappointed by the meager results.[80]

The army was rarely seen simply as a blameless instrument. Complaints
often condemned army commanders for allying with or being corrupted
by civilian politicians and elites. In 1947, a group of mestizo residents from
Tlacuilotepec complained about General Demetrio Barrios's reassertion of
political influence in the Sierra Norte de Puebla. Their letter was unusually
racist, blamed the general and his brother Gabriel's authoritarian instincts
on their indigenous background and "atavistic" habits, and urged the SDN
to replace them with properly trained white or mestizo officers.[81] However,
they were far from alone in seeing local commanders as being suspended
in webs of political and economic allies. Sometimes these complaints seem
rather disingenuous, part of the tradition of blaming lower-level authorities
for abuses rather than the presidency. However, in other cases people were
genuinely confused about exactly whose orders the army was obeying. For
example, villagers petitioning for land at Soltepec and La Junta in the 1940s
were caught between the competing civilian authorities (the federal Agrarian Department and the state government), local army detachments who
stonewalled orders from the federal government, and the president's office,
which vacillated or failed to deliver a clear ruling for years.[82]

However, over time people writing complaints to the government were
less likely to portray army commanders as acting independently and more
likely to see them as colluding with the Avilacamachista state government;
given Rafael Ávila Camacho's control of the state during his governorship,
this perception was astute. Although complaints of outright military political autonomy never disappeared, they declined as a percentage over time,
from 51 percent in 1940–45, to 46 percent in 1946–52, to 21 percent in 1952–
58. The percentage of complaints about soldiers colluding with municipal
authorities also declined over time: from 12 percent in 1940–45, to 11 percent

in 1946–51, to 3 percent in 1951–57. The collusion of soldiers with private actors remained a more stable item in complaints: 33 percent in 1940–45, 26 percent in 1946–51, and 28 percent in 1952–57. Over time, people were more likely to complain that soldiers were either colluding with the state or federal government or simply carrying out military orders. The percentage of complaints about military collusion with the state government was 6 percent in 1940–45, 9 percent in 1946–51, and 21 percent in 1952–57. The percentage of complaints about collusion with federal authorities was 0 percent in 1940–45, 3 percent in 1946–51, and 7 percent in 1952–57. The percentage of complaints that presented soldiers as acting with no autonomy at all was 6 percent in 1940–45, 6 percent in 1946–51, and 24 percent in 1952–57.[83]

While few people appealed to the army as an agent of social reform, those writing complaints did their best to contrast their own experiences with the official version of history that located military abuses firmly in the nation's past. After Captain Flores Moguel, an officer stationed at the Atlixco garrison, started to intervene in local affairs, villagers in the south of the state stressed the sheer anachronism of such "abuses by a Captain of the Federal Army in the middle of a twentieth century in which you impart legal guarantees." After Uvaldo Ramos and Jesús Quiroz were threatened with arbitrary arrests and fines by a local commander, they complained, "We do not think it just that we are living as if we are still under the Dictatorship."[84] Even when petitioners clearly understood that soldiers were controlled by the state government, they likened their actions to a local outbreak of praetorian militarism. After municipal elections in 1942, Senator Noé Lecona visited a number of municipalities that had resisted the governor's slate of candidates, ordered local soldiers to "liquidate" the municipal council of Cuautilulco, and, according to the deposed officials, threatened several others with the same fate. Although the villagers clearly understood that Lecona was coordinating these actions, they sought to tar him with the brush of militarist tradition by accusing him of conducting his own little "barracks revolt [cuartelazo]" in their village.[85]

For all their compelling details and rhetorical flourishes, complaints usually drew a meager response from the government. There is no evidence of soldiers being formally charged for any of the accusations discussed in this chapter; people often expressed rather low expectations of military justice even as they directed complaints to the government.[86] As far as the deployment of soldiers was concerned, Avilacamachismo's allies in the regional bourgeoisie or the CROM, provided they were not allied with competing political factions, largely got their way.[87] On the few occasions the state's chambers of commerce and agriculture criticized the behavior of the army they were very discreet, sending letters and reports to the government rather than seeking public controversy. Their petitions argued that military force was an unfortunate necessity in the state since it would inculcate respect for private property and state authority and permit regional economic development.[88]

However, in some cases the government responded to complaints about military abuses because they received the backing of one group of Avilacamachistas against another. When the army responded to complaints that had the backing of the state government or the CTM by moving soldiers elsewhere, it also absolved soldiers of any wrongdoing.[89] The case of Colonel Maximiliano Ochoa Moreno provides an example of this type of limited response. Ochoa was very much part of the inner circle of Avilacamachista officers. During Manuel Ávila Camacho's tenure as secretary of defense and as president, Ochoa had headed his group of military aides and had been given several politically delicate tasks. In 1938, Ochoa wrote one of the few official reports that criticized political meddling by a Cardenista general. In the 1940s and 1950s, he was known to have managed several of Manuel Ávila Camacho's business interests.[90] He also had the reputation of a tough, even brutal officer. He was held responsible by diplomats and organized labor for the murder of demonstrating workers from munitions factories in 1941. U.S. diplomats investigating the affair reported Ochoa's fascist sympathies and his character, "bordering on barbarity"—he had been Mexico's military attaché to Berlin in the early 1930s. After taking a brief leave of absence, Ochoa was placed in command of a regiment of cavalry at Huauchinango, Puebla, in 1942.[91] Here he had responsibility for policing the district, overseeing military training, and protecting a strategically important electrical power plant. While at Huauchinango, Ochoa and his forces provoked more than a dozen complaints about petty larceny against local shopkeepers, unpaid debts, arbitrary killings by his troops, and political meddling by the colonel in municipal government.[92]

At some point, Ochoa clearly began to antagonize other Avilacamachistas. Local boss General Lindoro Hernández, who had served as a federal deputy in 1937–41, complained about Ochoa's de facto takeover of municipal government in Huauchinango and accused Ochoa of threatening to kill his nephew, Ofir Hernández, auxiliary municipal president of the village of Apapantilla. The secretary of the marine had asked Ofir Hernández to investigate complaints that Ochoa's men had been fishing in a nearby lake with sticks of dynamite.[93] Colonel Nava Castillo, then a federal deputy for Puebla, also forwarded complaints about Ochoa to the president, as did Governor Gonzalo Bautista. In 1943, Ochoa was briefly removed from the state.[94] However, this was very much a temporary reprieve. In 1944, Ochoa returned as a cavalry commander in Atlixco and continued to provoke complaints by villagers about his seizure of crops and his sponsorship of the CROM's pistoleros. In 1945, Puebla's zone commander, Anacleto López, confirmed to the SDN that the accusations of Ochoa seizing crops, intimidating local peasants, and associating with pistoleros were accurate, and claimed to have asked the colonel to moderate his behavior.[95] In 1946, workers affiliated with the FROC blamed Ochoa for organizing the assassination of two union bosses.[96] Ochoa's reputation among workers as a hatchet man for the Avilacamachistas certainly survived intact, and even spread. Locals complained that he had packed the *defensas rurales* with thieves, murderers, and henchmen.[97] In 1946, the villagers of Tochimilco learned about Ochoa's tenure as military attaché in Berlin in the early 1930s after hearing one of his pistoleros boasting about it, and they wondered if Ochoa had not become "accustomed to using the Nazi jackboot" to try to "exterminate the weak."[98] Ochoa eventually left Puebla in 1947 and took another leave of absence; he reentered active service under Ruiz Cortines and, in the late 1950s, commanded the zone of Oaxaca and conducted a bloody counterinsurgency in the Triqui region.[99]

Colonel Salvador Martínez Cairo, installed by Governor Betancourt as head of the municipal council of Izúcar de Matamoros from 1948 to 1951, was another officer who attracted particular criticism but largely remained immune to it. The town had seen a tense struggle to control the municipal government and, with it, the district's electoral apparatus. Since the mid-1940s, cane growers in the nearby *ejidal* cooperative at Atencingo's sugar mill had been organizing with the aid of *morelense* agitators led by Porfirio Jaramillo. They demanded control over the workings of the *ejido*, freeing it from informal control by the mill. In 1946, Jaramillo's group, with help from the CNC and Agrarian Department, took effective control of the *ejido*. In 1946, the mill was also forced to accept the unionization of its workers into Section 77 of the CTM-affiliated National Sugar Workers Union. In the coming years the relationship between the mill administration and the *ejido* became increasingly strained to the point of crisis. In 1949, a report by a federal commission largely blamed the situation on the obstructionism and recalcitrance of the mill, which refused to pay for the harvests of 1947–49, withheld financial documents from the commission, charged the *ejidatarios* very high rates for essential credit, and refused to negotiate a new work contract. One of the problems of the cooperative's managers, from the commission's point of view, was their "custom or vice . . . of backing in the majority of cases the petitions of their compañeros" for higher sugar quotas.[100] The *ejido* retaliated against the mill by starting to grow other crops.[101]

The *ejido* and millworkers also followed the usual practice of Puebla's unions and tried to extend their power into the local municipal and state offices. In 1947, the *ejidatarios* accused the municipal governments of Matamoros and Chietla of intimidating the cooperative and millworkers and of protecting a group of pistoleros under Hilario Ibarra that was forcing workers to abandon the *ejido* and mill. In 1948, they supported Adalberto García as local deputy and Jesus García Pérez for the municipal presidency of Matamoros.[102] Adalberto García was elected, despite being initially denied recognition as the official PRI candidate, while García Pérez also won the municipal presidency. However, the governor immediately intervened to annul the municipal election, as the state's constitution allowed, and appointed Colonel Martínez Cairo to head the municipal council. The colonel's essential task was to halt the electoral insurgency of the *ejido*, instill order, disarm the locals, and ensure that the district elected the CROM's candidates for federal deputies in 1949 and, later, supported the official candidate for governor in 1951.[103]

The colonel's tenure was, by most accounts, corrupt and crudely coercive. Among other things, he was accused of systematically extorting money from inhabitants and businesses, of planning numerous political murders, including that of new deputy Adalberto García and local priest David Morales, and of allowing the police to rape several women.[104] Martínez Cairo provoked so many complaints, including open letters to the local and national press, that the central intelligence services and army investigated his behavior. Both concluded that the colonel had simply been slurred by habitual troublemakers and ne'er-do-wells in the town. The report filed by Colonel Antonio Nava Castillo, then commander of the military sector of nearby Atlixco, was brief and superficial and employed a circular logic common in military reports; rather than investigate complaints against Martínez Cairo in detail, Nava Castillo argued that because the colonel had carried out splendid new material improvements in the town, the complaints could only be attributed to perpetual malcontents rather than genuine discontent.[105] In 1950, an agent from the Department of the Interior produced a somewhat more detailed report.

He found no evidence that Martínez Cairo was responsible for the death of the head of the *defensas rurales* of the nearby village of Santa Ana Necostla. However, he did accept that most people thought that the colonel's head of police was responsible for the extortion and murder of local merchant Guadalupe Ariza Urosa, noting that the police chief had even started to sell off the victim's possessions. The agent stressed that although Martínez Cairo "has the reputation of being an 'energetic' person, and even 'hard,' who has exceeded legal limits during the disarmament campaign" and imposed hefty fines, the complaints were all orchestrated by "a group of powerful people of the place" who head an "Avilacamachista" committee. This group, including Leopoldo Rivera and Graciano López, attacked Martínez Cairo because of his "hardness" and the fact that he did not come from Puebla and took advantage of random crimes to slur him. The agent claimed that the people he talked to did not believe the colonel responsible for the murder of Adalberto García, although he noted that the crime remained unsolved.[106]

The agent's efforts to distance the colonel from the abuses of the municipal police and to reduce opposition to mere inter-elite horse-trading are unconvincing. All accounts of the conflict agree that the head of the municipal police, another army officer from Jalisco, arrived in the town along with Martínez Cairo as a dual appointment by the governor; indeed, the two men also eventually left the town together. None were sure of the chief of police's proper rank and name, and he was in no hurry to reveal them; in their absence he was referred to colloquially as "The Great Hand."[107] While the agent's identification of local elites working to stoke opposition is probably true, the Avilacamachista affiliation of Martínez Cairo's local opponents is somewhat debatable. After Maximino Ávila Camacho's death, many local factions claimed the Avilacamachista mantle. However, the inner circle of Avilacamachista officers and politicians did not consider the colonel a major political obstacle. Colonel Nava Castillo found little fault with Martínez Cairo in June 1949. In early 1950, agents reported that the colonel had started to promote Rafael Ávila Camacho's bid for the governorship.[108]

Martínez Cairo's methods alienated many people in the town. Don Graciano López, one of those leading opposition to the colonel after 1949, had originally been Governor Betancourt's candidate for local deputy, whose defeat by Adalberto García prompted the governor's imposition of the colonel in the first place. López's about-face was probably due to widespread discontent with Martínez Cairo. The army received complaints from townspeople who were evidently no fans of López, sent before López got involved in opposition to the colonel.[109] Some of the self-consciously "respectable" sectors of Matamoros wrote to the SDN to express their disappointment at the colonel's behavior, arguing that they had expected far better from someone sent to protect the "*gente de orden*" of the town from candidates pushed by the *ejidatarios* of Atencingo.[110] However, letters were signed by groups including the chamber of commerce, the union of market venders, truck drivers, parents associations, merchants, fruit sellers, and groups of Zapatista veterans.[111] *Matamorenses* also accused the colonel of making a fortune from rice plots at Atencingo and of having the backing of the mill administration and William Jenkins, an infamous former U.S. consul, previous owner of the Atencingo mill, and a business tycoon who had allied with the Avilacamachistas in the 1930s.[112] After the colonel started to intercept mail, he reportedly discovered that the seventy-six-year-old Don Arnulfo G. Pérez had been writing to various journalists in Mexico City, including Martín Luis Guzmán. Pérez was promptly beaten up by the police, prompting more open letters to the president to be published in the press on May 10, 1949.[113]

That Martínez Cairo found the town difficult to mollify is not surprising; Matamoros had 10,597 inhabitants, and in the late 1930s and 1940s it had already seen lively Sinarquista rallies and bitter, cross-class antidraft protests; in 1947, a small independent "Morelos Party" had been formed to contest local elections.[114] Some of the language used by the protest had echoes of political Catholicism, as one might expect given that the colonel was accused of killing the local priest. In a 1949 pamphlet, a "Song of Hate and Liberty" protests against the "tyrant": "Do not fear anything; strike because God is your friend, and by your arm, sometimes, his punishment is delivered."[115] Most tellingly, townspeople continued to complain about Martínez Cairo long after he had left the municipality and returned to Mexico City. They urged the army to refuse him a promotion and demanded that criminal charges be brought against him for murders carried out by his driver and bodyguard.[116]

The protests against Martínez Cairo balanced outrage with tactful obfuscation. Over time, public complaints drew attention to the colonel's misdeeds while concealing his connections to the army. The colonel was a decorated, trusted member of the army; in 1944, he had served on a military tribunal that tried a mutinous officer; while he was in Matamoros, he remained a member of the army, but his service file noted that he was "attached" to the state government of Puebla; when he took over the town's administration, Puebla's zone commander even complained to the SDN that the colonel "constantly goes about wearing his uniform."[117] While letters to the government did mention Martínez Cairo's membership in the army, complaining about his wearing his uniform and his boasts about being a member of the Presidential Guard, public complaints were more circumspect. The first pamphlets produced in Matamoros mention that Martínez Cairo wore an army uniform and that he was dishonoring it with his behavior.[118] A few press articles did connect Martínez Cairo to contemporary army misdeeds. *El Universal* reported that he had been present at the army's massacre of protesters at León in 1946, but also reported, inaccurately, that he had been purged from the army.[119]

Public complaints connected Martínez Cairo to an anachronistic military tradition rather than the existing federal army. By 1950, the case received an unusual amount of press attention. This was partly because *matamorenses* forwarded complaints to the relatively independent *La Prensa*, but also because Colonel José García Valseca, who owned the *Sol de Puebla*, had fallen out with Governor Betancourt in 1945 after being denied a senatorial nomination. In May 1949, the *Sol de Puebla* published an open letter to the president from a group called the Frente Revolucionario de Matamorenses. The authors were cautious about mentioning the colonel's military status. He appeared less as a serving, uniformed soldier and more as an archetype: "He is the capricious and brutal *soldadón* who throws everyone in jail."[120] Although Martínez Cairo attended to municipal affairs in his army uniform, he was never in fact accused of colluding with the local cavalry regiment and instead relied heavily on the municipal police forces. Nevertheless, in open letters to the press locals happily stretched the military metaphor and dubbed these police forces Martínez Cairo's fellow "praetorians."[121]

Protest against Martínez Cairo also reveals how people still drew on the old liberal tradition that associated military repression with officers' dubious personal morals and mental equilibrium.[122] Complaints published in the press did not dwell on Martínez Cairo's membership in the army but described him as an old-fashioned, disorderly "*coronelazo*" whose nature was to carouse, brawl, and generally affront respectable people: "Martínez Cairo constantly gets drunk and causes scandals, shoots off bullets, and is extremely dangerous when drunk; he is always in the cantina 'El Tampico,' or he orders them to bring bottles to his hotel that he drinks alone or with some women."[123] Martínez Cairo's drinking and womanizing became a steady theme in complaints. He was even likened to the archetypal counterrevolutionary, inebriated officer; one pamphlet noted that on his arrival "all the inhabitants saw him bent over, decrepit, with a riding crop in his hand and we thought that Victoriano Huerta the dipsomaniac had been resuscitated."[124] In early 1949, the army issued an order for Martínez Cairo's transfer, but secretary of defense General Gilberto Limón quickly reversed it.[125]

The colonel finally left Matamoros as a result of some astute political maneuvering by Rafael Ávila Camacho shortly before he became governor. In October 1950, Rafael Ávila Camacho paid the town a visit and, after hearing dozens of complaints, brokered a deal that allowed for a civilian municipal council to take over the town and prepare for new elections once he became governor. Press accounts in most of the major national newspapers describe Martínez Cairo narrowly escaping a lynching as he and his chief of police were chased from the town by an angry mob.[126]

By the time the colonel left town, the press completely obscured his connection to the military. In the various accounts of his downfall, Martínez Cairo was transformed into a hidebound, "small-town," "regional" cacique, something he evidently was not (although perhaps something he had fancied becoming).[127] An editorial in La Prensa argued that the case was an example of the "caciquismo that is still alive in some villages."[128] The press only mentioned the army in relation to the benevolent cavalry regiment commanded by Colonel Nava Castillo that occupied the town to keep order after the "cacique" had happily been vanquished.[129] In this way the press obscured the troubling aspects of the story, particularly the questionable institutional and legal position Martínez Cairo had occupied as a serving, uniformed officer in municipal office, and his clear ties to the central government. Indeed, some of the inhabitants of the town remained fully aware of the colonel's position in the army; in late 1950, Vicente Sánchez wrote to the SDN complaining that, despite Martínez Cairo's removal from Matamoros, press reports had not reported the "full color" of the story, particularly the colonel's military background and methods. Sánchez sarcastically asked that the army place his letter in the colonel's military file as a "brilliant note on his military duties."[130]

In Matamoros, pressure from below to remove Martínez Cairo was helped by Rafael Ávila Camacho and the leadership of some well-connected townspeople. The Sol de Puebla, which was owned by another influential Avilacamachista disgruntled with Betancourt's governorship, contributed greatly to the publicity the case enjoyed. In nearby Chietla, peasant groups who protested the imposition of another military officer at the head of their municipality enjoyed no such publicity.[131] Rafael Ávila Camacho improvised and tried to take as much credit as possible for removing Martínez Cairo and show himself capable of taming disorder, but he did not conjure popular protest from nothing. Atlixco's cavalry forces descended on the town to oversee Martínez Cairo's departure for good reason.

The lasting effects of the Matamoros affair were ultimately meager. The affair hardly sparked a radical change in rule or accountability. One judge pursued charges against Martínez Cairo, urged on by the town, but the colonel refused to come back to the state to answer charges and promptly received a promotion to brigadier general. The new civilian municipal president of Matamoros in 1951, Manuel Sánchez Espinosa, was a close ally of Atencingo's wealthy former owner William Jenkins and hardly a political outsider.[132] In many ways, the case illustrates the limits rather than the scope of public debate about the army. Without some local discontent there would have been little need to remove Martínez Cairo at all and return to some semblance of civilian municipal rule. In the future, Rafael Ávila Camacho still relied on soldiers to rule the conflictive south of the state, but in the 1950s they would at least operate from formal military commands or, when placed in state administration, become more attentive to civilian appearances.[133]

Protests at the University of Puebla provide the clearest example of a reversal in the government's use of the army. In the summer of 1952, Governor Rafael Ávila Camacho appointed nine military officers to the university's administrative hierarchy. He also reintroduced the Military Pentathlon, a student sports club with stern disciplinary and patriotic aims, and made basic military training and marching exercises compulsory for the students.[134] Students and faculty believed that the governor had "militarized the University, if not legally, then de facto."[135] In the late 1940s, university students had engaged in rowdy street protests against an increase in bus fares and the cost of living, and they were becoming a political nuisance. Rafael Ávila Camacho's move was a response to recurring calls for greater university autonomy and the spread of left-wing groups among the students prior to the presidential election. It also reflected his long-held belief that military training could spread discipline and patriotism.[136]

Students and faculty responded to the governor's move by organizing campus meetings and street protests. After Rafael Ávila Camacho visited the campus to mediate the conflict, a crowd of students erupted in jeers and forced the furious governor to leave the podium.[137] Students attacked the governor's use of soldiers as retrograde and unsuitable for a modern university and as symptomatic of a lack of autonomy in the university and a dearth of democracy in the state as a whole.[138] After meetings with dissident railwaymen, another group subject to military repression in the recent past, student groups tied their protests to struggles for union democracy elsewhere in the country.[139] This was a controversial move; students engaged in fierce internal debates about the tone they should take in their protests. Faculty who urged "moderation" lost out, and some were denounced as CIA agents for their trouble.[140] The range and tenor of criticism were beyond what the press would report; students complained that the press either ignored them or portrayed them as Communist agitators. In response, they communicated with the public through street protests, circulated pamphlets, and installed loudspeakers in the streets outside of the campus.[141]

The protests succeeded in persuading Rafael Ávila Camacho to abandon the militarization of the university administration. After being shouted down by students at a campus meeting, the governor told the students that "they can keep their university." Before storming out, he promised to deny the university state funding. There followed a tense couple of days during which it was rumored that the governor would accede to demands, remove the officers, and appoint a new civilian rector; another rumor rapidly spread insisting that the governor was going to use troops to stage a "*cuartelazo*" on the campus. Eventually the first rumor proved more accurate, and the university rector removed the army officers before promptly resigning.[142] While protest fell short of achieving university autonomy, it forced the state government to adopt somewhat subtler tactics. According to Héctor Silva Andraca, a teacher in Puebla at the time, although Rafael Ávila Camacho was furious after being jeered by students, calmer voices in the governor's political circle convinced him of the need to appoint a prestigious civilian rector "who could govern with the discipline of an army officer, without necessarily being one."[143] The governor managed to regain some ground in the institution by other means; he restricted the university budget and promoted an anticommunist witch hunt overseen by the new rector that allowed him to split student groups and remove more radical student leaders.[144] However, the governor never again tried to impose military officers or training directly on the university. The removal of the officers led to a new phase in university politics; thereafter the state government sought to control the politics and curriculum of the university through anticommunist student gangs and by involving conservative business leaders in the university government.[145]

Conclusion

As we saw in the previous chapter, the role of Mexico's military officers in national politics changed in important ways in the 1940s and 1950s. In contrast, the story of military policing is ultimately one of profound, if contested and controversial, continuities. The Avilacamachistas wrought many changes in Puebla's politics and society, but the demilitarization of policing was not one of them. Not all of this police work was viewed as political and illegitimate, but a good deal of it was. In the 1940s and 1950s, the army carried out many of the tasks of policing and collective repression familiar elsewhere (disarmament drives, crowd control, mediating agrarian disputes, raiding recalcitrant *ejidos*, strikebreaking, harassing and intimidating unionizers, low-level assassinations), along with some particularly brazen Avilacamachista innovations such as the imposition of uniformed officers at the head of town councils and the state university.

It would be easy to exaggerate the effects of protest, which did not curtail military impunity or force the government to stop military policing. Direct public criticism of the army remained risky. However, criticism of army policing was not entirely futile. Protests were more successful when they occasionally exposed divisions within the Avilacamachista group, or when they focused on the most flagrant and legally questionable appointments of officers to civilian posts. Paul Gillingham has recently argued that popular protests under the PRI, while they rarely led to dramatic shifts in policy, could still function subtly and cumulatively "as bank deposits of resistance, reminding politicians and elites of the high operating costs of unpopularity."[146] Protest at Matamoros and the university perhaps fall into this category—a modest function, but one that made sense to the people who engaged in it. Throughout the 1960s, left-wing student groups once more demanded university autonomy from the state government and would look back to their earlier successes as a source of inspiration.[147]

Given the state of contemporary research, it is difficult to assess how typical Puebla's experience of army policing was. Puebla probably suffered an unusually high level of militarization, given the Avilacamachistas' penchant for putting army officers in charge of civilian institutions in a quasi-formal capacity. There is ample evidence that military violence in Veracruz and Guerrero in the 1940s helped to increase the PRI's control of local politics. However, other state governments were not quite so cavalier in disregarding the institutional boundaries between civilians and the army. In Oaxaca, according to Benjamin Smith, the army was absent from great swathes of the state, hamstrung by daunting terrain and a feeble budget and rendered unnecessary due to powerful local caciques.[148] On the other hand, evidence from Michoacán shows that outright militarization of conflictive provincial municipalities occurred elsewhere. In the Huasteca, the government tried to impose order in conflictive municipalities by sending a military officer to take over the police force. However, the frequency and meaning of such episodes are difficult to probe due to the army's own secrecy and, not least, local people's apparent reluctance to talk about them.[149]

The story of military policing in Puebla has larger implications that are important for our understanding of Mexican political development. By understanding the ways the government relied on violence—channeled through the army—to rule, and contrasting these practices with the attitudes of various groups in civil society, we can correct overly consensual views of state-society relations that have emphasized smooth bureaucratic co-optation, institutional mediation, and the hegemonic nature of postrevolutionary political culture. Unlike much of Latin America, Mexico did not suffer a military coup during the Cold War. The regime liked to portray this as a symptom of deep-rooted consensus and stability. However, the PRI had already woven the thread of military force subtly into the fabric of the regime, rendering such overt militarization unnecessary.

CHAPTER SIX

The Army, Veterans, and the Historical Memory of the Revolution

In Mexico City's Museo del Ejército, a curious pair of military documents sits mounted inside a glass case, sandwiched between showcases of military uniforms and racks of antiquated rifles. The first is a report from General Pablo González, military commander in Morelos in 1919, neatly typed under the letterhead of the Department of War. In it, González describes the Constitutionalist army's assassination of Emiliano Zapata and its strenuous efforts to spread the news among Morelos's incredulous villagers. Alongside sits an official certificate issued by the SDN in 1939 formally recognizing Zapata as a "Veteran of the Revolution" and confirming his military rank of division general. The museum certainly emphasizes the Mexican army's origins in the revolution's popular uprising. However, it also implicitly contrasts the revolution's factionalism and violence with the army's subsequent evolution into a professional, apolitical institution respectful of all revolutionary factions. Faced with this image, one cannot help but wonder at how the details of Zapata's death were eventually subsumed into this image of bland inclusiveness.

After the 1940s, Mexican officers liked to describe the army as a "mute" institution that remained silent on matters of politics and policy.[1] This chapter argues that the army spoke in various ways, and frequently told stories about its origins in the Mexican Revolution. While previous chapters have explored conflicts about how to reform and modernize the army, this chapter explores how the army tried to maintain a rhetorical connection to the past and promote a particular historical memory of the revolution. The army had various ways to disseminate its version of history, including public ceremonies, military magazines and manuals, and rare public dismissals of officers. Conversely, the military hierarchy could also apply backstage pressure on filmmakers and journalists to suppress other competing versions of history. This chapter focuses particularly on the army's policy toward revolutionary veterans and their families.

Many scholars have used the history of military veterans to explore the politics of historical memory in the wake of civil war, revolution, and colonialism.[2] In postrevolutionary Mexico, veteran policy is a particularly useful way to understand how and why the army's version of history changed over time. The government saw veteran policy as playing an indispensable role in linking the army to the revolution. However, it was very controversial for a number of reasons. First, the government suffered from a dramatic lack of bureaucratic records, and the military ranks and trajectories of many revolutionaries were downright opaque to the victors. In the mid-1920s, the army's records of some of its most prominent cavalry commanders remained incomplete.[3] Many officers tried to edit or embellish their military credentials; the *coronelazo* of Matamoros, Colonel Salvador Martínez Cairo, spent years trying (and failing) to convince military authorities that he had not served in the federal army under Victoriano Huerta.[4]

Veteran policy also required the government to clearly define the meaning and boundaries of revolutionary military service. The government tended to refer to the revolution as a "clearly defined, consistent entity, as a kind of club, with approved paid-up members inside, and black-balled cads outside."[5] However, the forces that emerged under Madero were crosscut by factionalism, and, after the fall of Huerta in 1914, Mexico experienced several years of full-blown civil war between the major revolutionary leaders. Revolutionary factions themselves could be very blurry around their edges; countless men and women moved from one to another according to shifting allegiances, political context, material inducements, or outright coercion. Women participated in the revolution alongside men in a variety of ways— as camp followers, spies, political dissidents, and sometimes as soldiers and officers. Veteran policy also had to define the nature of men's and women's involvement in the revolution. Finally, postrevolutionary veteran policies also demanded that the army conceptualize its relationship with the old, prerevolutionary army and its surviving veterans and define how the new revolutionary army fit into the larger sweep of patriotic military history. Veteran policies, then, helped to create revolutionary history as much as they simply represented it.

The government tried to use veteran policy to impose its version of history and restore a conservative gender order. However, the challenges faced by the government were political as well as conceptual. In this chapter, I use the history of veteran policy to identify three distinct periods in the army's version of revolutionary history. I argue that these changes occurred, in part, because revolutionary veterans and their families organized in different ways and tried to obtain political influence and material benefits from the government. In response, the army gradually adopted a broader, more inclusive policy toward revolutionary veterans. However, enduring factionalism among veterans and meager material benefits ensured that the government struggled to convert its expansive rhetoric into top-down bureaucratic control. The conclusion discusses some of the implications of this story for our understanding of the politics of history after the revolution.

A Revolutionary Army for Constitutionalist Men, 1920–1931

In the early 1920s, the army bequeathed by the revolution was a decentralized, fractious, and factionalized entity. In 1920, Obregón's rebellion brought the Sonorans to national power and marked the end of the major armed phase of the revolution. However, it also further swelled the ranks of the revolutionary army with soldiers from previously antagonistic factions. Obregón's defeat of part of the old Constitutionalist military elite loyal to Carranza, and his alliance with other Constitutionalist officers, ex-Zapatistas, Villistas, Felicistas, and various regional caudillos such as Manuel Peláez and Saturnino Cedillo, ensured that some observers felt that it was "no longer possible to know who was a revolutionary and who was an enemy of the revolution."[6]

Initially, Obregón was forced to be quite pragmatic and flexible in deciding who deserved recognition and reward for their participation in the revolution. He skillfully demobilized numerous armed groups, distributed land grants, and even paid homage to the revolutionary legacy of Zapata, as did Calles during his presidential campaign.[7] The government also distributed some pensions to the families of various revolutionaries. In 1917, the Constitutional Congress began to grant pensions to the relatives of the few revolutionary heroes on whom all its participants could agree, such as Madero and his vice president, José María Pino Suárez; in 1919, Congress awarded President Carranza extraordinary faculties to grant pensions to civilian and military revolutionaries and their relatives.[8] Obregón continued to use these powers with a degree of flexibility. While he tactfully urged military veterans and their families to request pensions through the proper legal channels, the new state also recognized the reality of a social revolution in which people's "revolutionary service" did not equate to formal membership in the army.[9] For example, the mother of Guerrero's famed Escudero brothers, Juan and Francisco, received a pension after the army decided that it would "consider them, only for the sake of a pension, as equal to majors in the army."[10] Distributing pensions to veterans in this fashion removed the need for official documents, but it frequently put the presidency at odds with the Department of the Treasury, as Obregón sought to balance budgetary constraints with the need to placate the military.[11]

As the government began to rebuild some basic military institutions, the army began to equate revolutionary military service with Constitutionalism. In 1922, the army's commission for revising soldiers' service records favored those who had served continually under the Constitutionalists for the purposes of recognizing ranks and benefits, although this apparently earned the head of the commission, General Jacinto Treviño, the enmity of many other officers. The *coahuilense* Treviño was no great friend of the Sonoran faction; in 1929, he joined the Escobar rebellion and went into exile until 1941. However, in 1924, he founded the Centre for Veterans of the Revolution, a political club in Mexico City that pushed for the exclusion of non-Constitutionalist officers from the army through the 1920s.[12] Although the Sonorans at times presented themselves as inheriting Zapatismo's legacy quite early in the context of agrarian reform, the Sonoran army certainly did not incorporate Zapatismo institutionally or symbolically. Ex-Zapatista officers complained that the army was less willing to recognize their ranks than those of Constitutionalist officers, and that some Sonoran officers saw them as unreliable and dangerous.[13] In Chihuahua, when the army amnestied and demobilized Villistas they were briefly equated with legitimate soldiers, as they received military pay and privileges according to their military ranks. After demobilization they simply became civilians, and their agricultural colonies were overseen by the Department of Agriculture.[14] Secretary of War Amaro (1925–31) codified new laws that granted military pensions to ex-Constitutionalists. The law included an explicit clause excluding those who had ever "fought against the constitutional government or against the regime of Francisco I. Madero"—that is, Zapatisas, Villistas, and Felicistas.[15]

Veteran policy was one of the new regime's first efforts to dictate history and political legitimacy. After all, in the 1920s the school system still relied on Porfirian textbooks, what historiography existed tended to be written by old Porfirian intellectuals, and Mexico City's celebrated muralist movement was only taking shape (and contained divergent interpretations of the revolution anyway).[16] The law's system for awarding bonuses divided the revolution into major national stages, awarding extra years' service for certain periods. The law provided a basic narrative of the revolution, albeit one seen

The Historical Memory of the Revolution 147

through a strictly military lens in terms of length of service, valor displayed, and battles fought. Bonuses of fifteen years were awarded to those enlisted during the initial Maderista uprising (November 20, 1910, to April 30, 1911). This fell to a bonus of eight years for those enlisted during the less taxing years of Madero's presidency. Those who had signed on to defeat Huerta from February 20 to December 31, 1913, enjoyed a bonus of thirteen years; the bonus fell to ten years thereafter for those who had enlisted up until August 15, 1914 (the date of the final fall of Huerta's regime and the Treaty of Teoloyucan). Troops who had enlisted after this date until "the end of the revolution," a terminus that the law did not specify, could expect a bonus of a mere two years.[17]

Amaro's reform of army benefits proved unpopular with many people: some reservists were not convinced that their military service was less deserving than that of regular soldiers; others protested the overly strenuous and unrealistic bureaucratic requirements, the graft in the pensions department, and the different standard the army applied to soldiers killed by disease instead of warfare. Rumors of political favoritism abounded; in the mid-1920s, the commission revising service records was part of the Department of War but functioned "under the direct supervision of the president."[18] Some people also thought that legitimate military service extended beyond Constitutionalism and wrote to the government to make their case. As early as 1921, some Zapatista widows tried to press their claims for military pensions. Doubtless such claims were encouraged by the alliance of many ex-Zapatista generals with Obregón around 1920 and by Obregón's initial cautious embrace of Zapata's agrarian legacy as he sought to broaden his base of political support. While widows sought out old ex-Zapatista generals such as Genovevo de la O to write recommendations for them, de la O in turn removed any controversial notions about the Zapatistas' contributions to the revolution from his recommendations and simply stressed how such appeals were made by "abnegated" and honorable mothers and might be fulfilled as a personal favor to him.[19]

Under Amaro, the Department of War was evasive and euphemistic but nonetheless firm when rejecting claims that fell outside the boundaries of Constitutionalism. When faced with difficult cases the army tended to respond with a dry technicality rather than enter into an explicit discussion of the boundaries of revolutionary service. For example, in 1925, Amaro received a report from his general staff explaining that the wife of General Encarnación Díaz was ineligible for a pension because Díaz had fought "in the ranks of the Zapatistas." Amaro's secretary then composed a tactful note to Díaz's family explaining that a pension was not possible because, as the general had died more than nine years ago, the five years allowed for making pension claims had expired.[20] Such exchanges reveal a certain sensitivity to these obvious ruptures in the fabric of revolutionary military history, perhaps heightened in this case by Díaz's widely known and admired role in routing the federal forces at Chilpancingo in 1914.[21]

Other cases that threatened to uncover discontinuities and murky episodes in Constitutionalism's own military history (in which Amaro himself was sometimes involved) were similarly rejected, somewhat disingenuously, on the basis of technicalities. Eulalia García's sons Elías and Eliseo had died after doing "a great deal of revolutionary work." In 1913–14, they had fought under the orders of General Gertrudis Sánchez in Michoacán. After Huerta's defeat, Gertrudis Sánchez eventually sided with Carranza, but not before ordering Amaro, then serving under him, to attack Constitutionalist forces in Michoacán in 1914. At least one of the García brothers chose differently and defected to Villismo.[22] Amaro's office again replied that the period for making pension requests had unfortunately elapsed, thus implying that García might have been eligible if she had applied earlier. In the case of the son who had joined the Villistas, at least, this was clearly untrue.[23]

The government also defined revolutionary military service as strictly masculine, while women were cast in a purely dependent, supportive role. Amaro's pension law assumed that all military veterans were male heads of household. Women who requested pensions as mothers, wives, or daughters thus did so as dependents who had been robbed of patriarchal protection, for which a pension could offer a substitute. Logically then, if a widow or daughter married, she entered into a new patriarchal relationship, and the state's responsibility ended. Women also lost their pensions if they entered into a consensual union or engaged in prostitution "in public." Thus, common-law marriage to a soldier was insufficient to claim pension rights, but subsequent common-law marriage was sufficient to strip a woman of a pension she had received. Men lost their military pensions only for treason or open rebellion, or if they changed their citizenship.[24] The army did recognize the military status of Amelio Robles, a transgendered Zapatista colonel. Amelio's performance of revolutionary machismo was thorough and convincing, and he enjoyed the friendship of two powerful ex-Zapatista officers, Adrián Castrejón and Rodolfo López de Nava.[25] However, the army downgraded Amelio's rank from colonel to sergeant.[26] In the 1920s, as far as we know, the army ignored women who fell outside the notion of dependency set out in the law and claimed to have fought in the revolution.[27] In her correspondence with Obregón, Josefina Arce chose to downplay her later participation in the "revolutionary army of the South" and instead stressed her earlier "revolutionary work since 1910 at the side of the martyr Aquiles Serdán and in the Liberal Club of Puebla"; in 1921 she received a brief audience with Obregón during which she showed him documents and photographs attesting to her revolutionary work, but little else.[28]

Responding to Amaro's campaign of moralization, dozens of women wrote to the army in the 1920s and used the government's rhetoric of female dependency to hold the army up to the standards of an institutional patriarch that it implicitly set for itself. These petitions find women caught somewhere between demanding a right and requesting a favor by appealing to sentiment and Amaro's "humanitarian and philanthropic instincts."[29] Alongside complaints about the morals, promiscuity, and abusiveness of officers, some women used these arguments to try to broaden the definition of military service. For example, Matilde Durán emphasized the army's paternal responsibilities while requesting a pension for her husband who had been killed while fighting as a federal soldier under Huerta. The governor of Guanajuato had promised Durán that she would receive an army pension, and she entered into an exchange with Amaro that lasted several weeks.[30] Durán wrote in a frank, unapologetically passionate style: "I do not value disguised words, I write to you as if I were speaking to you . . . with my tears I beg of you to concede what I wish . . . I speak to you with my heart in hand." In her argument ideas of rational justice and patriarchal benevolence jostle together: "I do not want a defender; the defender? That will be me. You will be the Judge; but be my kind and benevolent judge that considers the tears of a widow, and assuages the hunger of an orphan."[31] Amaro's office took an extremely solicitous tone and even absolved Durán's husband from association with Huertismo on the basis of her own feminine and maternal virtues: "It makes sense that you argue that your husband was not affiliated with an unconstitutional regime, since your love as a wife and a mother would never permit such a thing."[32] This was purely a rhetorical flourish—Durán had argued that her husband was not actually affiliated with Huerta because he had only been obeying military orders. However, it served to remind her of a woman's proper role and tone. In her final letter Durán had put all legal arguments to one side and appealed to Amaro "not as a severe and implacable judge but as a protector that . . . will favor me."[33]

Well into the 1920s, officers were divided about how much the army should build on the prerevolutionary institutions and ideology, and how much it ought to break with them. These divisions were particularly clear in matters of military education. In 1915, some radical revolutionaries connected to anarcho-syndicalism advocated the complete destruction of the old Military College at Chapultepec as a symbol of old regime militarism. Although Obregón intervened to prevent this, arguments continued in the 1920s.[34] The Sonorans initially staffed the new military schools with many officers who had served in the Porfirian army. These officers argued that the new army should see itself as a continuation of the best traditions of the old Military College, whose cadets had famously remained loyal to Madero in 1913. They faced opponents who considered the Porfirian army "a nest of reactionaries," thought that the Military College's cadets had been "pure aristocrats," and wanted military education to renounce the past.[35]

Ultimately, the Sonorans encouraged the new army to see itself as a continuation of certain aspects of the past and not others. The army's policy toward prerevolutionary veterans was indicative. In the early 1920s, the Department of War was careful to include prerevolutionary veterans in military ceremonies and provide benefits for them.[36] The new military college quickly revived its cult to the cadet heroes who died fighting the U.S. invasion of 1847–48.[37] Obregón granted military pensions to prerevolutionary officers based on whether they had fought against the French or not.[38] The 1926 military pension law conceded pensions "equivalent to full pay" to all veterans who had fought against the United States and France in the nineteenth century and had been recognized as having done so by earlier governments.[39] Such solicitude is not so surprising. Mexican revolutionaries looked toward the past for ideological inspiration in many respects, and these policies offered a way of knitting revolutionary warfare into a longer fabric of patriotic struggle.[40] It was also relatively easy and inexpensive to identify these men compared to managing the amorphous and opaque mass of revolutionary veterans. Of course, those who had been certified as veterans prior to 1910 were themselves the product of earlier policies that were selective and sometimes bitterly contested, but these controversies had long since faded away to leave an indisputable group of heroic survivors. In 1941, the army invited a ninety-seven-year-old veteran of the French Intervention to don military uniform and attend military exercises in Puebla as the guest of honor.[41] However, army regulations did not allow for the granting of new pensions to these men or their families; those who requested pensions for prerevolutionary services, or asked that such rights be passed on to new generations, were directed to the Congress. In 1931, the Congress granted the nieces of General Mariano Monterde a pension because of their uncle's service in the U.S.-Mexican War.[42]

Nevertheless, it was difficult for the new regime to construct such continuity in historical memory. Celebrating earlier patriotic struggle against foreign invaders was easy enough but raised the question of when this heroic body of men had mutated into Porfirio Díaz's militarist institution responsible for the press-gang, strikebreaking, and *matalos en caliente*.[43] The new regime's solicitude for old soldiers could have unpredictable results, and prerevolutionary veterans did not always judge the new regime favorably. The homage for General Juan J. Navarro, held in December 1927 in Culiacán, Sinaloa, illustrates these problems. Navarro was unquestionably a bona fide military veteran and hero, having fought for the liberals against conservatives and the French, most notably at San Pedro in Sinaloa under the orders of General Antonio Rosales. In 1927, Navarro was the sole surviving veteran of a battle remembered by many as "one of our greatest victories."[44] General Juan Manuel Torrea, an army historian and graduate of the prerevolutionary military college, edited an homage to Navarro and celebrated the veteran's long and distinguished service record. While this confirmed Navarro's deeds against the French, it also described how Navarro had subsequently risen through the Porfirian military, reaching the grade of brigadier general in 1910. He had also fought the Maderista forces at Ciudad Juárez in May 1911, retired, and then rejoined the military under Huerta before retiring a second and final time as Huerta's regime disintegrated.[45] In the homage, retired General Joaquín Beltrán commented on Navarro's counterrevolutionary conduct. Far from demonstrating Navarro's dubious political judgment, Beltrán insisted, the veteran's conduct had only demonstrated his "indisputable military bravery," given that he had defended the city for fifty-six hours without water or reinforcements and outnumbered ten to one. Navarro did not even surrender once the inhabitants of the town had defected to the insurgents and started to attack the federal troops from their own homes. Beltrán also sought to downplay revolutionary conflicts by invoking U.S. malevolence. While defending Ciudad Juárez, Navarro could not effectively return fire to the north "in order to avoid complications with the Yankees, who have been and always will be the eternal threat, who signify to us the abuse of strength, and the exploitation and provocation of our internal divisions [*divisions intestinas*]."[46] According to Beltrán, it was in recognition of

Navarro's bravery that Madero and other "honorable elements of the Revolution" had decided to save his life. Beltrán finally added with a flourish that Navarro had "always sustained the legally constituted government," an odd assertion given his service to Huerta.[47]

The homage, which included about thirty telegrams from diverse admirers, allowed for a variety of interpretations of the revolution. Some contributors praised how the new revolutionary army had begun to respect earlier heroes, and how Navarro's services against the French might serve as an example for the new "soldiers of the Revolution" and for Mexico's youth.[48] Some simply pointed out that Navarro was more heroic than most revolutionaries because he had fought against foreigners rather than in "*guerras intestinas.*"[49] Others, many of them old companions of Navarro, went further and drew unfavorable comparisons between "our old and beloved federal army" and the current crop of revolutionary soldiers and *políticos*.[50] Angel García Conde saw the homage as an illustration that "in this country there are still patriots who understand what a civic education means, something that has unfortunately been abandoned by our leaders, and is practised very little by the majority of the citizens of the republic, who have only been concerned with other *radicalismos*."[51] Journalist Manuel Haro suggested that since Navarro was now being honored, Porfirio Díaz's remains might also be returned to the country to be buried, since he also knew "how to make the land fruitful with his blood, in defense of the Fatherland."[52]

Broadening the Meaning of the Revolutionary Army, 1931–1940

In the early 1930s, as Thomas Benjamin has shown, the government began to present itself as the product of a single, abstract revolution that transcended factionalism. Calles's founding of the PNR in 1928 gave this idea a new impetus; themes of reconciliation and unity came to dominate official rhetoric. In 1931, the government inscribed Zapata's and Carranza's names in gold in the Congress. Using the foundation of an earlier Porfirian structure, the government also built Mexico City's Monument of the Revolution, a striking attempt to present an image of revolutionary unity.[53] The first efforts to create a national organization of veterans began during the Maximato, and the groups that emerged in the early 1930s were tied to the PNR. By 1933 the Legion of Revolutionary Veterans, made up of ex-Constitutionalists, was parading on November 20 each year.[54] However, the party's new rhetoric opened up an uncomfortable gap between the idea of a revolution that transcended factionalism and the army's continuing, more restrictive definition of military service. In 1932, the National Union of Veterans pledged support to Calles and the PNR. The group never became politically prominent, but it illustrates the growing disjuncture between official rhetoric and army policy. Article 5 of the group's regulations demanded that members show that they had joined "the Constitutionalist movement" after Huerta's coup but did not address subsequent divisions in the movement. The group only explicitly excluded ex-Huertistas and Felicistas. This vagueness encouraged some ex-Zapatistas from Puebla to ally with them, along with the ex-Zapatista General Gildardo Magaña.[55]

After 1935, Cardenismo mobilized and polarized the country, brought the question of veterans' rights to the fore, and eventually led to some changes in army policy. Opponents of Cardenismo seized on the identity of the revolutionary veteran. In part, this simply reflected a situation in which participation in the revolution remained the root of political legitimacy, even as possibilities for actual revolt and rebellion—the preferred option for many veterans in the 1920s—were rapidly disappearing. Veterans' claims also had a certain elective affinity with opposition to radical class-based politics. While Cardenistas promoted the idea of the revolution as an anonymous (often bitter and tragic) mass social struggle, revolutionary veterans tended, almost by definition, to represent the revolution as a matter of individual men's virtuous, virile (and violent) exploits. For the right-wing veterans groups that proliferated after 1934, the vertical bonds tying individual veterans to the government superseded any horizontal ties of class solidarity. Joaquín Rodríguez, the brother of the leader of Mexico's fascist Gold Shirts, offered an extreme but nonetheless telling version of this narrow understanding of the revolution that proved useful to many right-wing groups opposing Cardenismo. In February 1935, he argued that it was necessary to form a "truly revolutionary party; that is, of men who have fought with arms and are recognized as such."[56]

Veterans groups were a crucial part of the conservative opposition to Cardenismo that grew steadily through the *sexenio*. The most important and vocal group was the National Union of Veterans of the Revolution (Unión Nacional de Veteranos de la Revolución, or UNVR), founded in 1935 and headed by generals Cesáreo Castro and Daniel Ríos Zertuche. However, Mexican intelligence agents insisted that the main organizing force within the UNVR was Colonel Gabino Vizcarra, a shady figure alleged to have stolen thousands of pesos from both Carranza and Villa and sometimes rumored to have been married to a U.S. intelligence agent.[57] The UNVR was based in Mexico City and was part of a dense web of secular right-wing groups that sprang up after 1935. These groups often cooperated and had overlapping memberships and similar sources of funding (Cedillo, conservative businesses and governors).[58] On July 14, 1937, the UNVR took out a paid advertisement in *El Universal* and condemned Cárdenas's violation of the constitution, communistic education, the collective *ejido*, labor's growing power, and the mounting public debt. The U.S. military attaché estimated that the advertisement was "the sharpest rebuke received by the government of President Cárdenas since his break with Calles two years ago."[59]

Throughout 1936 and 1937, the provinces were littered with veterans' organizations that may or may not have had any functional relationship to the UNVR. It is true that the UNVR, like the Gold Shirts, never enjoyed anything like the mass membership of which it boasted. In 1936, Vizcarra claimed the UNVR had 100,000 members. In 1940, according to lists obtained by Mexican intelligence, the group had 980 paid-up members in the Federal District.[60] However, veterans' claims to be the true representatives of a revolution that had been hijacked by "mystifiers" and Communists became standard rhetoric for provincial opposition. In Sonora, the local UNVR became one of Governor Román Yocupicio's "main pillars of support" in his efforts to subvert Cardenismo and was financed by the state and municipal governments. In 1939, the UNVR had roughly a thousand members in chapters spread across Sonora. Veterans demanded the creation of privately owned military colonies for themselves and formed part of various yellow-dog unions. The Cardenista zone commander, General Henríquez, even marched into Governor Yocupicio's office brandishing his pistol and demanded that the group be disbanded, to no avail.[61] In Coahuila, the Madero family "hired" UNVR veterans to help defend their properties against local *agraristas*.[62] In the late 1930s, another shadowy veterans group had reportedly received 80,000 pesos from various conservative governors.[63]

Cárdenas's response to this cacophony of right-wing veterans varied. Initially, the government tried to discredit these groups by arguing that groups of military veterans represented an anachronism since they had, according to the "new norms of the life of Mexico," been superseded by class identity. An editorial in the government's *El Nacional* argued that, while veterans should be respected for their service and might gather to reminisce or form mutual-aid associations, they could not expect to form a defined political group or a "collective opinion," since they did not in themselves possess a "common class interest." Rather, veterans ought to demonstrate their commitment to the true meaning of the revolution by joining a sector of the peasantry or working class and identifying with their interests. Days before the editorial was published, Cárdenas had argued along the same lines in a radio broadcast from Torreón.[64]

This strategy of discounting veterans' claims altogether was not viable, however. While emphasizing the importance of class, Cárdenas simultaneously allied with other veterans groups. Just as Cárdenas relied on ex-Carrancista, ex-Villista, and ex-Zapatista military officers to displace Calles, he cultivated ties to veterans who might provide some kind of loyal counterweight to right-wing groups such as the UNVR. In 1935, a group of Zapatista veterans and freemasons from Cuautla contacted Cárdenas and asked that their children be admitted into Cárdenas's new schools for soldiers' children. Cárdenas replied to their petitions warmly, urging that they send a list of children and orphans of ex-Zapatistas, who would then be admitted to the school in Coyoacán pending the completion of a school in Morelos.[65] Under Cárdenas, the army started to catch up with the party's symbolic embrace of Zapata. In 1937, new military ceremonial regulations declared that the army would honor the date of Zapata's death each year.[66]

In the 1930s, army widows and soldaderas became more organized and assertive, formed unions, and adopted the rhetoric of revolutionary citizenship to claim rights and benefits. The recognition of consensual unions for the purpose of pensions was a major demand, and one to which the government ceded in 1940.[67] The groups that emerged to claim benefits as relatives of Zapatista veterans or as veteranas in their own right were part of this general growth in women's organizing. In 1935, Guadalupe Narváez founded the Bloc of Precursors of the Revolution in the Federal District to press for women's pension rights and for recognition of herself and some other women as veteranas. In 1935, Ana María Zapata, a daughter of Emiliano Zapata, organized the Union of Revolutionary Women to demand pension rights for widows and children of ex-Zapatistas as an act of "social justice." The group expanded its activities from Morelos into Guerrero, Puebla, Hidalgo, and Oaxaca and claimed some 8,000 members by the late 1930s. At points, Cárdenas encouraged such efforts. In September 1938, Cárdenas personally authorized annual payments of one hundred pesos each to widows and orphans of Zapatistas. By 1941, these payments totaled one hundred thousand pesos, at which point the Ávila Camacho administration stopped them.[68] However, these groups were not simply tools of the ruling party. The main organization of Zapatisa widows and *veteranas* in Morelos allied with Almazán in the 1940 election.[69]

The Cárdenas administration also began a first tentative reconciliation with organized groups of Villista veterans. Friedrich Katz suggests that Cárdenas sought a reconciliation with Villismo to secure support among agrarian radicals in the Laguna region for whom Villa was an enduring popular hero. In the middle of 1936, groups of Villista veterans led by Nicolás Fernández were formed in the Laguna region in support of Cárdenas and the agrarian reform.[70] In 1936, the Cardenista colonel Enrique Calderón became governor of Durango and emphasized the government's new relationship with Villismo. At government functions, he handed out copies of Baltasar Dromundo's *Pancho Villa y la "Adelita,"* recently published by the state government. Dromundo sought to recover the memory of Villa as a popular revolutionary "whose memory has not been respected as it should by some Villistas" and professed his respect for those "authentic revolutionaries of the Division of the North, linked today to the government and the interests of the Mexican proletariat." Dromundo particularly attacked "those who name themselves Villistas, perhaps because today the chief is dead and cannot come and contradict them nor teach them the difficult road of manliness."[71] In the 1970s, several Villista veterans dated the change of the government's attitude toward them to Cárdenas's presidency.[72] More conservative Villista groups such as the Legion of Veterans of the Revolution, which enjoyed pockets of support across the states of Chihuahua, Coahuila, and northern Durango, kept their distance from Cardenista radicalism. However, Cárdenas did authorize them to build a statue of Villa in Lerdo and to name a market after Villa in Torreón as a "friendly gesture."[73] In 1939, Cárdenas even authorized the Villista Legion to negotiate with the remaining Cristero rebels in the south of Durango, part of a strategy of making peace with powerful regional groups that would soon bring a new conservative group to power in the state. In 1940, the leader of Durango's Legion of Veterans of the Revolution, Villista general Máximo García, obtained one of two posts for state senator.[74]

Cárdenas also tried to distance the army from the more obvious episodes of factional violence and strife. While Cárdenas mended fences with members of the old Carrancista military elite such as Francisco Urquizo and Juan Barragán, he also sought to render their reinclusion in the army less symbolically jarring. On May 11, 1937, the officer responsible for killing Carranza in 1920, General Rodolfo Herrero, was publicly purged from the military, although he was not formally tried. In one sense, this was clearly a modernizing measure that emphasized the distance the army had come from the violence of the revolution. However, it also fostered the idea that the revolution's inter-elite violence stemmed merely from the caprices of a few rogue generals.[75] For a time the problem of dealing with the officers directly responsible for Zapata's death had been solved by their subsequent military revolt and exile shortly afterward. However, Pablo González's return from exile in 1937 triggered a storm of protest by ex-Zapatistas, which eventually persuaded the government not to allow him to reenter the army.[76]

However, the Cárdenas administration struggled to control veterans. While government-backed groups such as the Confederation of Veterans of the Revolution or the Laguna region's Villista unions provided some sort of counterweight to right-wing groups, the proliferating claims of veterans in the public sphere, most of them still hostile or at least ambivalent to the regime, frustrated attempts at basic political control, let alone the fostering of a hegemonic interpretation of the Mexican Revolution. Naming oneself a veteran, wearing a military uniform, and insinuating ties to high military figures were useful ways to extort and intimidate opponents in local politics.[77] In 1938, the UNVR's right-wing veterans in Coahuila wielded sufficient local influence to get their families admitted to the government's schools for soldiers' children, although the government later succeeded in removing most of them. The powerful dissident candidate for the 1940 presidential election, General Almazán, promised to give justice to the veterans of the revolution regardless of factions, and the UNVR sided with Almazán's presidential bid.[78] In February 1939, thousands of veterans reportedly attended rallies in Mexico City organized by Amaro's Revolutionary Anticommunist Party.[79]

Eventually the government attempted a compromise; it recognized the wider utility of this political language but tried to exert some control over its use. Any revolutionary regime could hardly cede such potent rhetorical terrain to opponents. In 1939, the government created the Pro-Veterans of the Revolution Commission within the SDN to certify the true status of revolutionary veterans. The commission considered all factions eligible for recognition, although it conveniently only concerned itself with the "heroic" phase of the revolution prior to 1915. Anyone who had served in the "liberating movements of 1910–11 and 1913–14" was eligible for recognition, provided they sent in relevant documents or, lacking these, certificates issued by "revolutionary *jefes*" attesting to their involvement in specific battles and campaigns. The commission only excluded those who had backed Orozquismo or Felicismo or participated in Huerta's coup against Madero. Those who had served in Madero's government could be recognized as veterans provided they had joined the revolution before a seemingly arbitrary deadline of ninety days after Huerta's coup.[80] The commission also allowed the army to bestow official veteran status on civilians who had never joined one of the revolutionary armies, provided that they could obtain certificates from military authorities confirming their contribution to the revolution. The admission of civilians as veterans ensured that women were also in theory able to claim recognition as *veteranas*, without the government having to formally recognize their military ranks. The several hundred *veteranas* who obtained army recognition in subsequent decades tended to be women who had either fought in the ranks or served as important political agents, spies, or messengers.[81]

In 1940, the government passed a new law on military retirements that also adopted a broader definition of revolutionary military service for those revolutionary veterans still serving in the army. Episodes such as the defense of Veracruz in April 1914 and the clash with U.S. forces at Carrizal in July 1916 were now covered by the law and entitled those who had fought to a full army pension. Although the law kept the basic structure of military bonuses from 1926, it did not explicitly rule out military pensions for those who had fought against Madero (such as the Zapatistas).[82]

The new policies were announced with great fanfare, and military authorities throughout the country were instructed to hand out application forms and urge people to send the army their credentials. The ultimate goal of the commission was to gather all revolutionary veterans in an "honorific legion" recognized and organized by the SDN. To this end, the SDN formally recognized the National Unification of Revolutionary Veterans as the only official veteran organization, in which it was hoped one day could be gathered all the authentic veterans.[83] Along with these laws the government passed decrees that suggested that where symbolic recognition went, material benefits might follow. The commission promised somewhat vaguely to promote the employment of certified veterans in state, municipal, and federal government posts "where it was possible that such posts could be filled, according to personal circumstances."[84] In 1939, Congress approved the "Pro-Patrimony of the Veteran" decree and promised 1.5 million pesos to construct "Pro-Veteran Colonies."[85]

The Struggle to Institutionalize Veteran Unity, 1940–1960

After 1940, the regime's shift rightward allowed for a rapprochement with right-wing anticommunist organizations that had dominated headlines in the 1930s. The UNVR changed its name to the Mexican Legion of Revolutionaries in 1941. Although in the early 1940s the group was still connected to fractious regional conservative movements such as Berberismo in Guerrero, later in the decade it supported the Alemán administration's curtailment of land reform.[86] After the Gold Shirts had jettisoned their more rebellious members in 1940, they also enjoyed some closer relations with Alemán, basking in the glow of renascent official anticommunism.[87]

However, it remained difficult for the government to gather revolutionary veterans in one supportive and neatly choreographed organization. Veterans groups continued to be an important political resource for as long as army officers resisted party discipline. In the 1940s, successive heads of official veteran organizations tried to use these groups as springboards for their own political ambitions. General Agustín Castro had tried to use his position as head of the National Unification of Veterans of the Revolution to bolster his political fortunes in the 1946 presidential election; when these efforts faltered he neglected the group and retired to his properties in Chihuahua, while splinter groups of veterans promptly appeared condemning him.[88] In 1948, the groups of dissident generals discussed in chapter 4 courted veterans' support. Old Carrancistas such as Juan Barragán and Cándido Aguilar and the group led by General Ríos Zertuche demanded solicitude for revolutionary veterans. However, generals Alamillo and Amaro could count on little support from veterans, many of whom resented Amaro for having removed them from the army in the 1920s.[89]

By the end of September 1948, Alemán had survived this resurgence of military pressure, although he thought it wise to try to placate veterans. In November 1948, the National Unification of Veterans of the Revolution held a conference in Mexico City. Generals Agustín Castro and Cándido Aguilar announced that they had hammered out a deal with Alemán that would finally give justice to all the revolutionary veterans. However, an atmosphere of mistrust and tension pervaded the conference. After Alemán's delegation had left on the first day, the conference became distinctly rowdy, with low-ranking veterans openly attacking their "betrayal" by previous regimes; scuffles broke out when intelligence agents, disguised as journalists, tried to obtain the personal details of some of the more outspoken veterans.[90]

In January 1949, Alemán created the Mexican Legion of Honor to address veterans' concerns and exert some control over their politics. The legion represented a last major effort to reconcile factions, extinguish forever revolutionary "passions," and organize army and revolutionary veterans together in a single institution. It also promised more material benefits to revolutionary veterans, particularly their possible readmittance into the national army so that they could receive a full military pension, although such promises were carefully made "subject to economic capacity."[91] The legion also sought to integrate various groups of "precursors" of the revolution that had sprung up during the 1940s. A group in Sinaloa dated the activities of precursors from 1902.[92] The first director of the legion, General Cándido Aguilar, tried to turn the organization into a personal political machine, although he was replaced by the far more reliable General Urquizo in 1951.[93] However, General Henríquez's presidential campaign kept the question of veterans' rights politically charged. Henriquistas issued their own certificates and credentials to revolutionary veterans who worked for them.[94] In 1950, a group of Zapatista veterans allied with Henríquez took out a one-page advertisement in La Prensa demanding that the government remove General Rodolfo Sánchez Taboada (then head of the PRI) from the army for his role in the "assassination of Zapata": "We have never understood by what merit—since laurels are won for acts of infamous treachery—Sánchez Taboada has reached the very highest rank in the army."[95]

By the mid-1950s, the government's defeat of these dissident officers allowed it to disseminate a more coherent image of unity. In 1949, General Aguilar had interpreted the code of the Mexican Legion of Honor to exclude Zapatistas on the basis that they had fought against Madero, and he generally ignored petitions from Villistas. Under Urquizo, the legion operated as a more reliable vehicle of reconciliation, although the wording of the law was only eventually altered to explicitly admit Zapatistas in 1954, after protests from the Zapatista Front of the Republic.[96] Under General Urquizo, the Legion of Honor produced a particularly bland and frictionless version of military history through its monthly publication, El Veterano. The magazine celebrated what had become a predictable pantheon of revolutionary heroes, rarely commented on the contemporary army except in effusive praise of its technical progress, and called on veterans to put an end to infighting, political "passions," "partisanship," and "thoughts of revenge and grudges."[97] The army carefully instructed regional heads of the legion in each state to "exalt the figures of all the *caudillos* of the Revolution with a sense of consideration and equality."[98] In the 1950s, the magazine invited veterans to write in with their own memories of the revolution, and many did; the stories that were printed stuck to the technical and narrative details of particular battles and encounters, generally hewing to the "battle piece" genre of military history that presented revolutionary warfare as orderly, officer-coordinated, and concerned mainly with tactical and technical considerations.[99] Similarly, the magazine rarely discussed veterans' revolutionary citizenship in social terms but focused on the military virtues of honor, sacrifice, patriotism, and individual self-improvement and discipline.[100] It also published critiques of contemporary Mexicans' lack of honor and "self-respect" and attacks on leftist public school teachers who "poison young minds with exotic and unreal theories."[101]

Despite these efforts, the idea of gathering all the veterans together in a single, neatly choreographed organization proved a chimera. Veterans from the different factions continued to gather in an array of groups and subgroups defined by faction, region, or a combination of both.[102] General Ramón Iturbe's offhand comments recorded at a dinner held after the 1948 veteran conference were prophetic: "the day they gather all the veterans into one organization will be the day they 'move mountains.'"[103]

Veterans continued to prefer their own groups partly because at the local level they could still adopt different political stances. Official organizations such as the National Unification of Veterans of the Revolution, dominated by Carrancistas, increasingly tended to focus on the veterans as neglected, poverty-stricken men whom the regime had thoughtlessly, even cruelly, abandoned.[104] Groups that were connected to agrarian politics employed an altogether more assertive rhetoric that tied their demands as veterans to broader social rights.[105] The Villista groups in Durango who collaborated with Jacinto López's UGOCM, and blended their claims as veterans with familiar *agrarista* tactics, are indicative. At times, at the local level, these diverging tactics rendered the facade of revolutionary unity extremely fragile. A group of Villista veterans in Durango started to petition for lands in the Agricultural Colony "El Centenario" in 1953, which President Alemán had promised them in 1949. A group of influential Constitutionalist veterans led by Domingo Arrieta and Dámaso Carrasco also had designs on the property, however, and a bitter conflict ensued after they allegedly paid off the Department of Agriculture. In November 1956, the leader of the Villista veterans, Major Esteban Mendiola Palacios, wrote to the president describing an assassination attempt made on him by Carrasco's henchmen. Eventually, in July 1957, the Constitutionalist group took over the property with the aid of the military zone commander, denounced the Villistas to the press as "traitors to the Revolution," and renamed the property the "Colonia V. Carranza."[106]

Some regional veterans groups were also successful in obtaining material benefits in the wake of symbolic recognition. Since 1939, the regime had promised far more material support to revolutionary veterans than it was ever likely to deliver. Unfortunately, it is very difficult to quantify the material benefits veteran policy actually delivered after 1939. Between 1939 and 1975, the army received 60,000 applications from people eager to be recognized as revolutionary veterans, but it remains reluctant to release any figures indicating how many veterans from each faction were recognized, or how many were readmitted into the army to receive a pension.[107] Still, there is plenty of anecdotal evidence that veterans' requests for jobs, pensions, and lands percolated down from the state in a discretionary fashion, subject to local politics and personal connections. Many veterans complained that the promises of military pensions and government jobs that accompanied the Legion of Honor proved to be a "dead letter" for most of them.[108] In Puebla, even José Martínez Castro, one of the state's most influential local bosses and a certified veteran Constitutionalist, fruitlessly spent twenty years asking the government to readmit him to the army so he could receive a pension.[109] In the 1950s and 1960s, Villistas and Zapatistas regularly complained that it was only ever well-connected ex-Constitutionalists who received army pensions. However, through the 1950s some northern veterans groups in Nuevo León, Chihuahua, and Coahuila succeeded in pushing their state governments to institute special benefits for revolutionary veterans who had been authorized by the army.[110] By the 1960s, officially recognized veterans received, if not admission to the army, then free treatment in military hospitals.[111]

The state could not organize veterans into a single group, but it did nevertheless increase its control in some ways. In the 1950s, the army was still frustrated by the existence of unofficial Villista veterans groups, who regularly invited political generals to act as honorary presidents and whose members, according to one military lawyer, "frequently commit violations of laws by awarding recognition and military rank to Veterans of the Revolution in a way that contravenes official dispositions." However, the army did start to prevent commanders from sponsoring these groups.[112] In the face of Henriquismo, the army increasingly clamped down on veterans who sought to use military uniforms and insignia.[113] In September 1953, five veterans were locked up by military police for wearing uniforms in public.[114] Veterans increasingly turned to groups that had at least obtained recognition from the SDN; a veterans group in San Luis Potosí that had no such recognition had increasingly little to show for the quotas demanded of members.[115] Factional differences endured in veteran organizations, but the army was capable of gathering enough veterans together for annual veteran banquets in Mexico City, and plenty showed up to ceremonies to receive medals from members of the army's general staff. By the late 1950s, large veterans organizations offered few open criticisms of the PRI. For example, the leaders of the Zapatista Front of the Republic, which lobbied for veterans, understood that what influence they enjoyed largely depended on their members learning to "discipline themselves to our PRI."[116]

Revolutionary veterans' tendency to gather in their own groups at a distance from the official party may not, in the end, have been unduly damaging to the PRI's public image. The regime, for which the politics of unity was normally "an irrepressible compulsion," eventually gave up trying to group veterans in one national organization.[117] It also permitted a loyal opposition in the form of the Authentic Party of the Mexican Revolution (Partido Auténtico de la Revolución Mexicana, or PARM), led by officers who justified their stock liberal-democratic criticisms of the PRI largely on the basis of their status as revolutionary veterans.[118] Veterans were increasingly old and few, which probably made schemes to control them less urgent for the government. However, veterans' authority and public image had always been somewhat dubious; even at a moment of great historical recognition in 1939, the secretary of defense's statement to the press was hardly a ringing endorsement, simultaneously acknowledging and casting doubt on veterans' claims: "some who are aren't and some who aren't are."[119] Some civilians worried about the undue costs of veterans' claims.[120] Expressions of popular culture that lightly mock the proliferation of military ranks during the revolution, and the subsequent enrichment of revolutionary veterans, are probably as old as the revolution itself.[121] Alongside the bland coverage of veterans' poverty and neglect in the press, it is not difficult to find representations of veterans as proud, squabbling, slightly ridiculous figures.[122] While the national press was normally respectful of General Jacinto B. Treviño's PARM, provincial journalists were sometimes blunter—in Guerrero journalists likened the group's members to arthritics.[123] The original meeting of the PARM in Mexico City descended into a rowdy farce, and the press considered it a ridiculous spectacle. If veterans at times continued to argue among themselves, form their own fractious organizations, or follow leaders such as General Jacinto B. Treviño, who were seen by "proletarian groups" as men "from another time, with an exaggerated military spirit," in a sense this could reflect well on the benefits of a civilian PRI that was rational, modern, and free of the passions of the revolution.[124]

Conclusion

The Mexican army contributed in different ways to the formation of the postrevolutionary state; it helped blunt Cardenista radicalism and policed much of the countryside, while its officers traded national political submission for continuing informal powers. The army was also necessarily involved in disseminating a particular version of revolutionary history. It did this not only through parades and official publications but more prosaically through its policy toward revolutionary veterans. However, the army's version of revolutionary history—its definition of what constituted legitimate military service during (and prior to) the revolution—was not static. It changed, in part, because in the early 1930s the official party began to present itself as the heir of an abstract revolution that transcended factionalism. However, it also changed because of the ways veterans and their families tried to claim benefits and justify their criticisms of the regime. During the 1920s, the army's definition of revolutionary military service was limited to Constitutionalism and was strictly masculine. Veteran policies also served to tie the new army into a larger narrative of patriotic military history. During the 1930s, Cárdenas sought to counter right-wing veterans groups by arguing for the precedence of class identity and by cultivating other loyal veteran organizations from those factions who had previously been denied recognition. The Cárdenas *sexenio* ended with the state broadening the definition of revolutionary military service in factional and gender terms, while giving the army the authority to certify who could use this potent political language. Rather than deal with an array of disparate, irreconcilable factions, the regime wanted to gather veterans in a well-defined, orderly group whose unity and support for the government could prove that it was the heir to a coherent, national revolution. Tense military politics in the late 1940s and early 1950s, continuing divisions among veterans themselves, and limited material incentives offered by the government ensured that this remained difficult to achieve.

This story has several implications for our understanding of the development of the myth of the Mexican Revolution. The turn toward cultural analysis since the 1980s has ensured that we now know a lot more about how the postrevolutionary state tried to shape history through official historiography, commemorations, radio programs, and school textbooks. This chapter shows how the military contributed to this project. It confirms the arguments of scholars such as Thomas Benjamin and Mary Kay Vaughan that it took considerable time for the myth of a reified, unified revolution to emerge, and that the struggles of the 1930s were particularly important in producing a broader and more inclusive understanding of the revolution, whether in social, factional, or gender terms. The hardest question to answer is whether this policy actually helped to enhance the legitimacy of the regime. Few historians would now echo Ilene V. O'Malley's argument about wholesale popular credulity in the face of official mythmaking.[125] By the 1950s, the sight of revolutionary veterans lining up to receive medals from military officers, gathering at commemorative banquets, or using their official recognition to gain access to care at military hospitals probably helped, over time, to lend some credibility to the idea that the army remained the direct descendent of the revolution. However, veteran policy, and the development of the myth of the Mexican Revolution as a whole, should be understood as the result of a dynamic political process; veterans helped reshape government policy and the historical assumptions that underpinned it. Revolutionary veterans were often querulous, sometimes well-connected people in possession of a rhetorical authority that any revolutionary administration could never entirely ignore. While the development of veteran policy certainly involved conflict, frustration, and disappointment for many veterans, the government was also frustrated in its plans to convert its broader rhetorical embrace of veterans into tight bureaucratic control.

CONCLUSION

In the 1970s and 1980s, it seemed to most observers that the single most important story that could be told about Mexico's army was the country's emancipation from the praetorian militarism that had dominated its nineteenth-century history and remained so obviously potent in much of Latin America. A common metaphor likens the transformation of the army to the progressive "taming" of a wild and irrational militarist tradition.[1] If the revolution achieved anything, surely it was the postrevolutionary army's subjection to state control and its extrication from rebellions and praetorianism. Even those scholars who take a generally negative view of the achievements of the PRI find much to admire in the postrevolutionary regime's subordination of the military.[2] Certainly, there is some truth to this familiar narrative of government-led centralization, institutionalization, and stabilization. Praetorianism fell away, and the army acquired a formal institutional framework, more specialized roles, and education requirements. These were important changes, familiar to most students of the period, but they can only take us so far in understanding the nature and limits of postrevolutionary demilitarization. Moreover, as Alan Knight has argued, the terms and evidence used in this national-level story "are misleadingly narrow and elitist: it takes in one dramatic form of political violence (national praetorianism) but ignores the more mundane but pervasive political violence of daily local life."[3]

Historians now have ample materials with which to move away from the perspective of Los Pinos and tell a broader range of stories that can reveal how protracted Mexico's process of demilitarization was, how it was shaped by many forces in state and society, and how it remained incomplete. First, it took some time for the postrevolutionary regime to actually settle on a political and ideological project for the army, as official policy shifted from the Sonorans' emphasis on military neutrality to Cardenas's vision of a class-conscious and politically engaged army, before sharply veering back to the Sonoran blueprint again under Manuel Ávila Camacho. These changes in official policy were driven by factional conflicts within the revolutionary elite but, I have tried to show, also reflected competing understanding of the revolution's broad and multifaceted ideology.

When it came to officers' political powers, it took most of the 1940s and early 1950s for the PRI regime to appreciably narrow the gap between official rhetoric and reality. Having helped secure Manuel Ávila Camacho's ascent to the presidency, the officer corps remained factionalized, ambitious, and independent. A series of tense political conflicts among officers themselves, and between officers and the Alemán administration, eventually produced a new set of unspoken political rules for the army. In exchange for national acquiescence, officers could still expect to wield political influence in the provinces, to graft, to resist central policies of rotation and retirement, and to enjoy autonomy in operational matters, provided that these powers were never acknowledged in public and that they restricted their own speech to the anodyne platitudes of presidentialism or the varieties of loyal opposition proposed by the PARM. While the changes of the 1940s hemmed in officers' political options, their remaining autonomy had a solid institutional basis: the army's continuing importance in providing the hard edge of coercion the PRI required to rule.

Ironically, the official rhetoric emphasizing the army's top-down, technical reform overlooked those fleeting moments when popular attitudes and protest really did affect military policy. Beyond the ambivalence and weary skepticism that often met officers' claims of political disinterest and administrative competence, popular resistance stymied conscription in many places. By 1950, public antipathy helped persuade the state to abandon conscription and replace it with a less onerous and less ambitious system of military training. After 1939, the government responded to the proliferation of groups pushing for veteran benefits by broadening the army's definition of revolutionary veterans to include men and women from all the revolutionary factions. This reshaped the army's version of history and opened some meager but meaningful channels for material benefits. By the late 1940s, the state had even reduced the military's role in the campaign against foot-and-mouth disease, judging that it was usually counterproductive and that military participation ensured that "bullets are more apt to fly."[4]

However, when it came to the army's most important role as an agent of social and political control, the evidence of the military's impunity and insulation from popular pressure is far more imposing than its responsiveness. After the scandal over army violence at León in 1946, the government tried to make the army avoid bloody repression in Mexico's main towns and cities, at least until the early 1960s. However, the army remained central to police work in the countryside; like other political actors, officers continued to enjoy a much freer hand in bloodshed in rural areas.[5] In Puebla, people complained about officers' corruption and meddling, as well as the state government's use of soldiers to enforce unpopular policies and get PRIístas elected. Although complaints did not lead to a transformation in the substance of Avilacamachista rule, they could elicit some kind of government response when they exploited divisions within the regional political elite or when they protested the gratuitous imposition of officers in civilian posts.

The history of modern Latin America often seems to move in circles rather than straight lines and requires historians to think about change within an overall context of continuity.[6] Postrevolutionary Mexican demilitarization confirms this pattern in some ways and bears a number of similarities to Porfirian demilitarization in the late nineteenth century. Both periods saw the reestablishment of new professional schools for officers, a gradual reduction in the army's size and budget and the number of officers in civilian posts, and the gradual replacement of battle-hardened veterans of civil war with new officers. However, the Porfirian continuities that revisionist scholars such as Jean Meyer have emphasized conceal some important differences.[7] Twenty-five years after his ascent to power, Díaz had largely removed the veterans of the French Intervention from the military hierarchy and replaced them with the new products of professional education. In contrast, revolutionary veterans dominated the hierarchy of the postrevolutionary army—the SDN, the zone commands—into the 1960s. Whereas Díaz disbanded the National Guard in the 1880s, the postrevolutionary government maintained the army's institutional connection with the rural militia. Finally, while the postrevolutionary army was certainly flawed—it was never technologically advanced or immune from desertions—it was a more effective instrument than its Porfirian predecessor. In part this was because the army's air power, machine guns, and infrastructure ensured that it was farther along "the learning curve of state repression."[8] Its recruits were also predominantly volunteers; when the postrevolutionary government did attempt an ambitious project of conscription, it had the flexibility and sensitivity not to push the matter in the face of popular hostility and changing political circumstances.

In 2001, Arthur Schmidt argued that historical research into the foundational years of the PRI would point to "indeterminate, ambiguous outcomes" long obscured by dominant models of centralization, presidentialism, and corporatism and would clarify how Mexico's period of revolutionary reform came to an end.[9] This story of demilitarization confirms this prediction. Even the military, that apparently most centralized and monolithic institution, was shaped by profound ideological conflicts, divisions within the government, and public opinion, and it reflected a multilayered political system that worked differently in the provinces than in the national capital. This work thus contributes to a growing number of studies seeking to understand the difficulty the central government had imposing its authority across the country, even after 1940, let alone having it accepted as legitimate. Regardless of the chosen metaphor—"Swiss cheese" instead of solid cheddar, jalopies instead of juggernauts—conflicts over military policy and repression afford a crucial perspective on weakness of the state.[10]

By revealing the state's enduring reliance on military force, this story corrects overly consensual interpretations of postrevolutionary politics. There is a long tradition of seeing Mexico's postrevolutionary regime as isolated and exceptional in Latin America. Guillermo O'Donnel's model of military-led bureaucratic authoritarianism, so influential in the 1970s, encouraged this perspective by grouping southern cone military regimes in contrast to those in Mexico and elsewhere.[11] Of course, the PRI were often happy to encourage this sense of a fundamental contrast between Mexico's political system and repressive militarism elsewhere in the hemisphere. However, this way of contrasting Mexico's experience with military authoritarianism elsewhere in Latin America is less than satisfactory. In part, this is because we now know a lot more about the many political, ideological, and institutional variations among the Cold War military dictatorships of Brazil, Argentina, Chile, and elsewhere.[12] New studies of PRIísmo, particularly during the post-Cárdenas and Cold War periods, also reveal the ways that Mexico's postrevolutionary regime, for all its peculiarities, relied on violence. Of course, Mexico's army never seized national power, and Mexico always had fewer soldiers per citizen than other countries of comparable size in South America.[13] However, like armies elsewhere, Mexico's remained a deeply factionalized institution in the middle of the twentieth century, and one that played an important role in limiting and containing the challenge of mass politics and radicalism.[14] Moreover, in terms of militarized policing, Mexico's experience was not as different from elsewhere as often assumed. South America's larger armed forces developed in a context of international competition and "militarized bargaining" that was absent in Mexico, and substantial portions of these armies were deployed and trained with external roles in mind.[15] Mexico's armed forces were smaller but domestic in their focus, and they developed their own close institutional relationship with the police. The army was only one of a panoply of "violence workers" on whom the PRI relied to consolidate itself, but it remained central.[16]

For all its complexities, by the end of the 1950s Mexico's demilitarization had left a clear legacy. The dominance of civilians in national politics is usually seen as a basically progressive legacy that, for all of PRIísmo's numerous faults, represented a fundamental first step on the way to democracy. Aside from the teleology implicit in this perspective, on closer inspection other legacies affecting the quality of Mexican democracy emerge. To be sure, subsequent decades would see changes in the army's organization and relationship to society. In the 1960s and 1970s, the government used the army in much more visible repression of urban student movements and in bloody rural counterinsurgencies that, at least in Guerrero, involved more troops than any of the small campaigns that pockmarked the terrain of provincial politics in the 1940s and 1950s. In the 1960s, the presidential general staff emerged once more as a powerful group within the PRIísta system; its officers were deeply anticommunist, well paid, and closely tied to the president. They controlled their own system of intelligence, and they opened fire on student protesters and other soldiers at Tlatelolco in 1968.[17]

However, in many ways the political, institutional, and ideological foundations for this repression had already been laid by around 1960. Efforts to reduce the scope of military education in the 1940s endured, although some of the army's counterinsurgency techniques of the 1960s may have been influenced by exposure to U.S. training and Cold War ideology.[18] But the Mexican army's basic internal orientation had been decisively confirmed by the early 1950s. The Mexican army, as exemplified by officers such as Puebla's Ochoa Moreno, had little need to import wholesale a new doctrine of domestic repression, because it had already—quietly, discreetly—developed its own repertoires of repression, hitherto deployed largely in rural areas, that included both brutal and exemplary violence, or the more subtle cultivation of pistoleros and paramilitaries. The rules governing these practices were rarely written down or theorized. However, they can be seen in military practice, or sporadically illuminated in the remarks muttered by officers in private meetings or scribbled down in complaints. Greg Grandin has discussed how, in much of Latin America, right-wing political violence gradually became more public and ideologically explicit through the Cold War. For better or worse, the PRI's political repression, particularly that which involved the army, never made this transition and remained stuck for much longer in the coy and discreet style developed in the 1940s and 1950s, a public secret more than a fully articulated ideology.[19]

Finally, this story also allows us to place contemporary militarization in historical perspective. There is little doubt that since the early 1980s, increases in the Mexican army's size, budget, policing roles, and political leverage indicate a remilitarization of the Mexican state.[20] Even as Mexico's political system gradually opened in the 1990s, the growth in crime, peasant insurgency, and drug trafficking provoked calls for an increased military role in domestic policing and fed concerns about human rights abuses, impunity, and the army's local political influence.[21] However, arguably much of what came to define the PRIísta state's relationship with the army in the 1950s— an alliance between military and civilian elites based on a murky blend of professional, political, and economic incentives; a balance of national obedience with regional and operational autonomy; an underlying commitment to militarized social control; and an agreement by soldiers and civilian politicians alike to insulate the army from public scrutiny—has continued to shape this more recent process of militarization. One particular legacy is public discussion of the army's history. After the 1950s, the government put considerable effort into presenting the history of the postrevolutionary army as one of institutional unity, neutrality, and unquestioned obedience to presidential authority. It censored representations of military repression, factionalism, and corruption and encouraged officers to repeat this version of history in public. Although public debate about the army is far more lively and open today than fifteen years ago, the army has generally "stonewalled" efforts to investigate past crimes and has argued, in any case, that the army bears no responsibility for any past abuses because soldiers were following orders from civilian presidents.[22] Politicians and journalists have justified the militarization of policing by pointing to polls suggesting that the army enjoys greater public trust than the police, but also by evoking this simplistic, sanitized version of the army's history.[23] It provides a poor guide for either historical understanding or public policy.

NOTES

Abbreviations

AGN	Archivo General de la Nacíon, Mexico City
AHSDN	Archivo Histórico de la Secretaría de la Defensa Nacional, Mexico City
ALM	Ramo Presidentes, Adolfo López Mateos
ALR	Ramo Presidentes, Abelardo L. Rodríguez
APECFT	Fideicomiso Archivos Plutarco Elías Calles y Fernando Torreblanca, Mexico City
ARC	Ramo Presidentes, Adolfo Ruiz Cortines
ASEP	Archivo de la Secretaría de Educación Pública, Mexico City
CESU	Centro de Estudios Sobre la Universidad, Universidad Nacional Autónoma de México, Mexico City
CNC	Confederación Nacional Campesina
CTM	Confederación de Trabajadores de México
DESTIC	Departamento de Enseñanza Superior Técnica Industrial y Comercial
DF	Distrito Federal
DFS	Dirección Federal de Seguridad
DGG	Dirección General de Gobierno
DGIPS	Dirección General de Investigaciones Políticas y Sociales
EHE	Escuela Hijos del Ejército
exp.	expediente (file)
FEMOSPP	Fiscalía Especial para Movimientos Sociales y Políticos del Pasado
FFU	Fondo Francisco Urquizo
FHJ	Fondo Heriberto Jara
FJA	Fondo Joaquín Amaro
FO	Foreign Office Reports
FSTE	Federación de Sindicatos de Trabajadores del Estado
FTP-CTM	Federación de Trabajadores de Puebla–Confederación de Trabajadores de México
G-2	U.S. Military Intelligence Division
IAMSD	Internal Affairs of Mexico, U.S. State Department, 1944–54 (Microfilm)
LC	Ramo Presidentes, Lázaro Cárdenas
leg.	legajo (bundle)
MA	Military Attaché

MAC	Ramo Presidentes, Manuel Ávila Camacho
MAV	Ramo Presidentes, Miguel Alemán Valdés
MIDRF	Record Group 165, Military Intelligence Division Regional Files (Mexico)
NA	National Archives, London
NARA	National Archives and Records Administration, Washington, D.C.
OC	Ramo Presidentes, Obregón-Calles
PHO	Archivo de la Palabra, Instituto Mora, Mexico City
POR	Ramo Presidentes, Pascual Ortiz Rubio
RG 84	Record Group 84, Consular Reports
RG 319	Record Group 319, Records of Army Staff
SD	U.S. State Department
SDN	Secretaría de la Defensa Nacional Collection
UGOCM	Union General de Obreros y Campesinos de México
UNS	Unión Nacional Sinarquista
UNVR	Unión Nacional de Veteranos de la Revolución
USMIR	United States Military Intelligence Reports, 1920–41 (Microfilm)

Introduction

1. See complaints by Vicente Lombardo Toledano about the "*cacicazgo avilacama-chista*" in Taracena, *La vida en México*, 1:21–24.

2. Women of Cuauxocota, Puebla, to Ruiz Cortines, March 14, 1957, AGN, ARC, 404.1/4035.

3. Various correspondence, 1957, AGN, ARC, 404.1/4035; Report on Teziutlán, 1965, AGN, DGIPS, caja 431, exp. 14.

4. For a discussion of sociological and institutional definitions of militarization, see Skjelsbaek, "Militarism."

5. Lutz, "Militarization," 320.

6. For a very useful recent overview that bucks this trend, see Plasencia de la Parra, *Historia y organización*. For a discussion of the limitations of officer-centered and national-level analysis of the military in contemporary Latin America, see Davis and Pereira, "New Patterns of Militarized Violence."

7. For a useful survey of debates about militarism, see Berghahn, *Militarism*.

8. Lorenzo Meyer, "Historical Roots." For a concise critique of scholars' emphasis on Cardenista corporatism, see Rubin, "Decentering the Regime."

9. Lieuwen, *Mexican Militarism*, 121.

10. Preface in Joseph and Nugent, *Everyday Forms of State Formation*, xvi.

11. Roseberry, "Hegemony and the Language of Contention." See also Vaughan, *Cultural Politics in Revolution*; Dawson, *Indian and Nation*; Rubenstein, *Bad Language, Naked Ladies*; Vaughan and Lewis, *The Eagle and the Virgin*. For a detailed discussion of state cultural policy, transnational intellectuals, and indigenous artisans, see López, *Crafting Mexico*. For a postrevisionist approach applied to the 1920s, see Boyer, *Becoming Campesinos*.

12. For a useful historiographical survey, see Schmidt, "Making It Real Compared to What?" For a collection of newer studies that explore the post-1940 period, see Gillingham and Smith, *Soft Authoritarianism in Mexico*.

13. Lieuwen, *Mexican Militarism*. See also Lieuwen, "Depoliticization of the Mexican Revolutionary Army"; Lozoya, *El ejército mexicano*; Casanova, *Democracy in Mexico*, 36–39; Wager, "The Mexican Army"; Ackroyd, "Military Professionalism"; Loyo Camacho, *Joaquín Amaro*.

14. Tobler, "Las paradojas"; Hernández Chávez, "Militares y negocios."

15. Cited in McAlister, "Mexico," 236.

16. Camp, *Generals in the Palacio*, 24.

17. Alamillo, *Memorias*, 612–14.

18. Brandenburg, *The Making of Modern Mexico*, 158–59; McAlister, "Mexico"; Ronfeldt, "Mexican Army and Political Order"; Margiotta, "Civilian Control of the Military."

19. Camp, *Generals in the Palacio*; Servín, *Ruptura y oposición*; Navarro, *Political Intelligence*. For a discussion of the military in the last two decades, see Camp, *Mexico's Military on the Democratic Stage*.

20. Jean Meyer, *La Cristiada*, 1:146–68, 3:249–56.

21. Boils, *Los militares y la política*; Córdova, *La ideología de la Revolución Mexicana*, 368–79.

22. Pansters, "Zones of State-Making"; Fallaw and Rugeley, *Forced Marches*; Tanalís Padilla, *Rural Resistance*; Sierra Guzmán, *El enemigo interno*; Veledíaz, *El general sin memoria*.

23. FEMOSPP, *Informe histórico*; Markarian "Los debates públicos."

24. Sierra Guzmán, *El enemigo interno*; Reyes Peláez, "El largo brazo del estado."

25. James McKinley, "Mexican Report Cites Leaders for 'Dirty War,'" *New York Times*, November 23, 2006.

26. Skurski and Coronil, "States of Violence," 2.

27. For a concise overview of this process, see the introduction in Gillingham and Smith, *Soft Authoritarianism in Mexico*.

28. Grandin, "Coming to Terms," 6.

29. Taussig, *The Magic of the State*, 95. On the problems of applying Foucauldian theories of diffuse disciplinary power in Latin America, see Centeno, "Disciplinary Society in Latin America."

30. Adelman, "Spanish-American Leviathan?"

31. For a selection, see Knight, "Political Violence in Post-revolutionary Mexico," 110; Bellingeri, *Del agrarismo armado a la guerra de los pobres*, 112; Serdán, *Memorias de un Guerrillero*, 81–84.

32. Some recent studies are helping to clarify the relationship among violent actors under the PRI: Pensado, "Political Violence and Student Culture"; McCormick, "The Political Economy of Desire"; Davis, "The Political and Economic Origins."

33. Shawn Smallman describes a similar process in his *Fear and Memory*.

34. Tobler, "Las paradojas."

35. Guardino, *The Time of Liberty*, 7–14.

Chapter 1

1. Monsiváis, "Foreword"; Piccato, *City of Suspects*, 179.

2. Blasco Ibáñez, *Mexico in Revolution*, 96–97.

3. Lockhart and Schwartz, *Early Latin America*, 358.

4. Vinson, *Bearing Arms for His Majesty*; Vinson and Restall, "Black Soldiers, Native Soldiers." In the central areas, the colonial government considered indigenous militia service a "last recourse," and it became less common over time, especially after the 1770s. Ibid., 40.

5. Irigoin and Grafe, "A Stakeholder Empire."

6. Santoni, "A Fear of the People," 269.

7. Vázquez, "Iglesia, ejército y centralismo"; Fowler, *Forceful Negotiations*.

8. For a useful historiographical discussion, see Fowler, *Military Political Identity*.

9. Vázquez, "Political Plans."

10. Fowler, *Military Political Identity*, 54.

11. Ibid.; Archer, "The Politicization of the Army."

12. Hernández Chávez, "Origen y ocaso."

13. Hale, "José María Luis Mora"; Johnson, *The Military and Society*, 59; Santoni, "A Fear of the People."

14. Thompson, "Los indios y el servicio militar"; Mallon, *Peasant and Nation*; McNamara, *Sons of the Sierra*; Forment, *Civic Selfhood and Public Life*.

15. Hernández Chávez, "Origen y ocaso."

16. Nugent, *Spent Cartridges of Revolution*; Alonso, *Thread of Blood*.

17. Fowler, *Military Political Identity*.

18. Whitehead, "State Organization," 402.

19. Knight, *The Mexican Revolution*, 1:1–36; Craib, *Cartographic Mexico*, 127–92; Vanderwood, *Disorder and Progress*.

20. Hernández Chávez, "Origen y ocaso," 285. On Latin American trends, see Rouquié, *The Military and the State*, 72–97.

21. Hernández Chávez, "Origen y ocaso."

22. Ibid., 258–59, 261; Jean Meyer, "Grandes compañias," 1027–28; "Report: The Mexican Army," 1927, USMIR, reel 7, 951–90.

23. Neufeld, "Servants of the Nation," 245–59; Santoni, "'Where Did the Other Heroes Go?'"

24. Macías-González, "Presidential Ritual in Porfirian Mexico."

25. Neufeld, "Servants of the Nation," 43–98.

26. McKee Irwin, McCaughan, and Rocío Nasser, "Introduction."

27. Hernández Chávez, "Origen y ocaso," 284–95.

28. Ibid.

29. Knight, *The Mexican Revolution*, 1:463–64.

30. Ibid., 1:388–490.

31. Aguilar Camín, "The Relevant Tradition"; Jean Meyer, "Grandes compañias"; Warman, "The Political Project of Zapatismo"; Brunk, *Emiliano Zapata!*, 106–7.

32. Katz, *Life and Times of Pancho Villa*, 801.

33. Ibid.; Knight, *The Mexican Revolution*, 2:141.

34. For debates about the strategic, political, and ideological causes of Villa's defeat, see Salmerón Sanginés, "Los historiadores y la guerra civil."

35. Knight, *The Mexican Revolution*, 1:57–58; Almada, *Con mi cobija*, 208.

36. Knight, *The Mexican Revolution*, 2:240.

37. Haber, Razo, and Maurer, *The Politics of Property Rights*; Knight, *The Mexican Revolution*, 2:240–51, 456–65; Hernández Chávez, "Militares y negocios."

38. Katz, *Life and Times of Pancho Villa*, 339, 397–403.

39. Lieuwen, *Mexican Millitarism*, 40–44.

40. Knight, *The Mexican Revolution*, 2:255, 450–53, 477.

41. Hernández Chávez, "Origen y ocaso," 270.

42. Lear, *Workers, Neighbors and Citizens*, 282.

43. MA to G-2, August 22, 1930, USMIR, reel 6, 454–55.

44. Knight, *The Mexican Revolution*, 1:457.

45. Ibid., 2:317; "El Soldado," *Regeneración* 92, June 1, 1912.

46. Buchenau, *Plutarco Elías Calles*.

47. General Joaquín Amaro, DF, to Escuela Superior de Guerra, January 1932, APECFT, FJA, 04/01, exp. 8.

48. Loyo Camacho, *Joaquín Amaro*, 121–33, 137–46.

49. Lieuwen, *Mexican Militarism*, 111.

50. General José Álvarez quoted in *El Universal*, May 7, 1925; Dillon, *President Obregón*, 69–96.

51. Cravioto Leyzaola, *Historia documental*, 3:304; *Génesis de la Escuela Superior de Guerra*; *Los estudios de la Escuela Superior de Guerra*.

52. Translation of 1933 speech by President Rodríguez, in MA to G-2, May 12, 1933, USMIR, reel 8, 56.

53. Fallaw, "Varieties of Mexican Revolutionary Anticlericalism," 489.

54. Loyo Camacho, *Joaquín Amaro*, 29.

55. Colonel Rubén García, Santiago de Chile, to Amaro, January 22, 1926, APECFT, FJA, 03/04, leg. 1, exp. 22.

56. Bliss, *Compromised Positions*, 64, 74–75, 128–29.

57. Gruening, *Mexico and Its Heritage*, 289–334; Rath, "Gender and Military Reform."

58. Gustavo Salas, *El servicio militar obligatorio*, 50.

59. Osten, "Peace by Institutions," 173–74.

60. Lieuwen, "Depoliticization of the Mexican Revolutionary Army," 55.

61. Pani, *El cambio de regímenes*, 9.

62. Dulles, *Yesterday in Mexico*, 194–96.

63. Osten, "Peace by Institutions," 373–443.

64. Ibid., 444–54.

65. Jean Meyer, *Estado y sociedad con Calles*, 60–76.

66. "Report: The Mexican Army," 1927, USMIR, reel 7, 951–90, 987.

67. Almada and Díaz Babio, "La estrategia nacional"; Jean Meyer, "Grandes compañias," 1028.

68. Jean Meyer, *Estado y sociedad con Calles*, 69–70; Gruening, *Mexico and Its Heritage*, 289–334.

69. Some studies that illuminate these variations include Benjamin and Wasserman, *Provinces of Revolution*; Saragoza, *The Monterrey Elite*; Ankerson, *Agrarian Warlord*; Brewster, *Militarism, Ethnicity and Politics*; Fallaw and Rugeley, *Forced Marches*.

70. Jean Meyer, *Estado y sociedad con Calles*, 69–70.

71. Lieuwen, *Mexican Militarism*, 164.

72. López de Nava, *Mis hechos de campaña*, 127.

73. Jean Meyer, *Estado y sociedad con Calles*, 60.

74. Cravioto Leyzaola, *Historia documental*, 3:226; Ackroyd, "Military Professionalism."

75. Camp, *Generals in the Palacio*, 67.

76. Lieuwen, *Mexican Militarism*, 106–9; Jean Meyer, *Estado y sociedad con Calles*, 60.

77. On citizenship and notions of "revolutionary time," see Olcott, *Revolutionary Women*, 10.

78. Pani, *El cambio de regímenes*; Lieuwen, *Mexican Militarism*, 71.

79. On Amaro, see Loyo Camacho, *Joaquín Amaro*, 146–49; MA to G-2, December 16, 1935, USMIR, reel 4, 553.

80. For examples, see Quezada, *El sistema*, 24; Ravelo Lecuona, *Los jaramillistas*, 144.

81. Centro Revolucionario de Estudios Políticos, DF, to Rodríguez, November 1933, AGN, ALR, 580/121; Lieuwen, *Mexican Militarism*, 106–9.

82. MA to G-2, January 1934, USMIR, reel 7, 6–20.

83. MA to G-2, January 20, 1930, USMIR, reel 8, 34.

84. Meyer, "Grandes compañias," 1020; Meyer, *Estado y sociedad con Calles*, 60–76; "Report: The Mexican Army," 1927, USMIR, reel 7, 951–990. For further discussion of ethnic stratification in the army, see Brewster, *Militarism, Ethnicity and Politics*; Smith, "Heliodoro Charis Castro."

85. MA to G-2, January 1934, USMIR, reel 7, 6–20; "Report: The Mexican Army," 1927, USMIR, reel 7, 951–90.

86. Meyer, *Estado y sociedad con Calles*, 64–70; MA to G-2, June 14, 1932, USMIR, reel 8, 151.

87. Krauze, *General Misionero*.

88. Santos, *Memorias*, 349.

Chapter 2

1. "¿Libertad . . . para asesinar al pueblo? El Ejército de la Revolución desprecia a los 'periodistas' amigos de Victoriano Huerta, que hoy hipócriticamente lo adulan," reproduced in Méndez, *Leopoldo Méndez y su tiempo*, 85.

2. Monsiváis, "Leopoldo Méndez," 23. See also Diego Rivera's illustrations in Beals, *Mexican Maze*.

3. "¿Pos pa'que luchamos? (La familia del general y el 'Juan')," reproduced in Méndez, *Leopoldo Méndez y su tiempo*, 63.

4. On the Popular Graphic Workshop and Cardenismo, see Caplow, *Leopoldo Méndez*, 123–58.

5. McAlister, "Mexico," 205; Krauze, *La presidencia imperial*, 66.

6. Camp, *Generals in the Palacio*, 20.

7. Lieuwen, *Mexican Militarism*, 113–38.

8. Knight, "Cardenismo," 104.

9. *Reglamento de las comandancias de las zonas militares*; *Reglamento del ceremonial militar*.

10. Camp, *Mexico's Military on the Democratic Stage*, 21.

11. Hernández Chávez, *La mecánica cardenista*, 77–81.

12. Azcárate, *Escencia de la Revolución*, 180. See also Hernández Chávez, *La mecánica cardenista*, 91–95; Navarro Valdez, *El cardenismo en Durango*, 94–101. Command circulation is discussed in more detail in chapter 4.

13. Gilly, *El cardenismo*, 166n40; Hernández Chávez, *La mecánica cardenista*, 77–81.

14. Speech by Margarita Díaz de Téllez, director of EHE No.2, August 22, 1937, in CESU, FHJ, caja 32, exp. 1216.

15. Carrasco Cuéllar, *Hacia la república socialista*, 24, 26, 47.

16. Ibid., 39.

17. Vaughan, *Cultural Politics in Revolution*, 39; Teja Zabre, *Breve historia de México*.

18. Carrasco Cuéllar, *Hacia la república socialista*, 24.

19. Corona del Rosal, *Moral militar y civismo*, 212–18, 252, 280.

20. Captain Luis Macedo, "Desarrollo histórico e ideológico de la Revolución," *El Soldado*, November 1936, 702–3.

21. MA to G-2, April 25, 1933, and MA Report "Soldiers' Day," April 28, 1936, USMIR, reel 8, 581, 585–91.

22. See photoessay "Día del Soldado," *El Nacional*, April 28, 1938.

23. Ibid.

24. Speech by President Cárdenas on April 27, 1935, *El Maestro Rural*, May 15, 1935, 3–5; *Los pinceles de la historia*, 150.

25. MA Report "Soldiers' Day," April 28, 1936, USMIR, reel 8, 585–91.

26. Gabino Palma, "El militarismo mexicano y las 'Escuelas Hijos del Ejército,'" *El Nacional*, April 28, 1938. The featured poem is "No sé por qué piensas tú . . .," by Nicolás Guillén, a Cuban communist.

27. MA to G-2, April 25, 1933; and G-2 Report "Soldiers' Day," April 28, 1936, USMIR, reel 8, 581, 585–91.

28. *El Nacional*, April 28, 1938.

29. *Excélsior*, April 30, 1938.

30. Joaquín Jara Díaz, Circ. No. ll-32-97, April 9, 1936, ASEP, caja 2136, exp. ll/356(015)/.

31. On the difficulty of gathering information on the militia, see Plasencia de la Parra, *Historia y organización*, 276; MA to G-2, June 4, 1926; and MA to G-2, August 22, 1930, USMIR, reel 6, 36, 454–55. On the social background and political tendencies of the militia, see Fallaw, "Militaries and Paramilitaries."

32. Arellano Cruz, "Las defensas rurales," 55–57. See also Calderón, *El ejército y sus tribunales*, 190–92.

33. Boyer, *Becoming Campesinos*, 213.

34. September 1, 1936, *Diario de los Debates*, Diario 2. See also MA to G-2, September 4, 1936, USMIR, reel 4, 656.

35. Vaughan, *Cultural Politics in Revolution*, 39–40.

36. *Memorias de la Secretaría de la Defensa Nacional*, August 1938–September 1939, 38–46; *Anales gráficos de la historia militar*, 550.

37. See speeches by deputies Arnulfo Pérez and F. Altamirano, December 17, 1935, *Diario de los Debates*, Diario 21.

38. Suárez Suárez, *Breve historia*, 65.

39. Ibid., 67, 66, 73.

40. Ibid., 62.

41. Lieuwen, *Mexican Militarism*, 119.

42. MA to G-2, December 16, 1935, USMIR, reel 4, 553.

43. *El Soldado*, January 1936, 1–3.

44. General Heriberto Jara, Project for Reform of Military Justice, 1933, CESU, FHJ, caja 29, exp. 1057.

45. MA to G-2, January 8, 1937, USMIR, reel 7, 879. On the large salary and bonuses that Amaro paid himself as secretary of war, see Plasencia de la Parra, *Historia y organización*, 28.

46. MA to G-2, February 11, 1936, USMIR, reel 4, 602–10.

47. General Heriberto Jara quoted in *El Nacional*, September 18, 1937.

48. Colonel Ignacio Beteta, radio address, April 27, 1937, reproduced in Bosques, *The National Revolutionary Party*, 357.

49. Lázaro Cárdenas quoted in *Informe del Secretario de la Defensa Nacional*, 24.

50. *El Universal Gráfico*, February 17, 1938.

51. *Excélsior*, December 3, 1935; MA to G-2, February 3, 1938, USMIR, reel 2, 624.

52. Meacham, "Mexican Federalism," 34.

53. *Informe del Secretario de la Defensa Nacional*, 10, 27, 63.

54. "Reglamento Interior del Bloque Militar" and "Normas de Conducta Aprobados por los Representantes del Sector Militar," March 28, 1938, in *Informe del Secretario de la Defensa Nacional*, 73–80.

55. MA to G-2, September 11 and 16, 1936, USMIR, reel 4, 653–56.

56. Ankerson, *Agrarian Warlord*.

57. Various reports, March–April 1938, AGN, DGIPS, caja 80, exp. 7.

58. Lieuwen, *Mexican Militarism*, 91; Camp, *Generals in the Palacio*, 251; Saragoza, *The Monterrey Elite*, 124–25.

59. MA to G-2, September 11 and 16, 1936, USMIR, reel 4, 653–56; Hernández Chávez, *La mecánica cardenista*, 113.

60. Santos, *Memorias*, 711. For useful overviews of the 1940 election, see Navarro, *Political Intelligence*, 13–79; Michaels "Las elecciones de 1940."

61. I discuss the army's institutional roles from the 1930s to the 1950s in more detail in chapter 5.

62. Bantjes, *As If Jesus Walked on Earth*, 189.

63. Estrada Correa, *Sin reconocimiento oficial*, 29–45.

64. Anguiano Equihua, *Lázaro Cárdenas*, 148–56. Ireta was sector commander in Uruapan in 1935, Michoacán's zone commander in 1938–40, and state governor in 1940–44. "Extracto de Antecedentes," AHSDN, XI/III/1–574 (Ireta Viveros).

65. General Brigadier Carlos Martín del Campo, Mixcoac, DF, to Manuel Ávila Camacho, November 7, 1941, AGN, MAC, 534/92; Vega González, *Cadetes mexicanos*, 20–21; Report by S19, DF, May 12, 1938, AGN, DGIPS, caja 80, exp. 7. On tensions between the military sector and the CTM at the party assembly, see also reports by S19 from March 29 and April 1, 1938, AGN, DGIPS, caja 80, exp. 7.

66. MA to SD, 1 June 1937, USMIR, reel 4, 124–26.

67. Fallaw, *Cárdenas Compromised*, 59, 69–74. On the incompetence or the mutable loyalties of the apparently Cardenista generals sent to Baja California, see Vanderwood, *Juan Soldado*, 162–63. On the government's problems managing the politically useful but independent General Agustín Castro, see Navarro Valdez, *El cardenismo en Durango*, 91–104, 242–52.

68. De la Peña, "Populism, Regional Power, and Political Mediation," 204–5.

69. Confidential report dated September 11, 1936, reproduced in Gojman de Backal, *Camisas, escudos y desfiles*, 345–48.

70. *Excélsior*, March 20, 1939, 10; Colonel Ignacio Beteta, radio address, April 27, 1937, reproduced in Bosques, *The National Revolutionary Party*, 357–67.

71. *El Soldado*, February 1936, 65.

72. *Memorias de la Secretaría de la Defensa Nacional*, August 1938–September 1939, 15.

73. MA to G-2, October 6, 1936, USMIR, reel 2, 747; MA to G-2, April 23, 1937, USMIR, reel 2, 72.

74. General Alejo González, Mazatlán to Cárdenas, March 1939, AGN, LC, 559.1/69; various correspondence, Secretaría de la Defensa Nacional to Cárdenas, October 1937–November 1938, AGN, LC, 556.7/6; Francisco Padilla, *Lo que el tiempo no se llevó*, 35–72.

75. Army circular, May 14, 1937, reproduced in MA to G-2, May 18, 1937; and MA to G-2, July 27, 1937, USMIR, reel 7, 465–67, 481.

76. Santos, *Memorias*, 583–88.

77. Ibid., 647–48, 665–66; Hernández Chávez, *La mecánica cardenista*, 118.

78. Various correspondence, MA to G-2, October–November 1938, USMIR, reel 2, 136–47.

79. Valencia Castrejón, *Poder regional y política nacional*, 125–51; Bantjes, *As If Jesus Walked on Earth*, 182–86, 223.

80. Dawson, *Indian and Nation*, 3–33; Photomontage "Los niños españoles," *El Nacional*, June 13, 1937. The orphans were briefly housed in the Escuela Hijos del Ejército in Colonia Del Valle and posed for a round of press photographs with army children. Photographs of the orphans' visit are available in the Archivo Fotográfico Enrique Díaz Delgado y García at the AGN.

81. Bosques, *The National Revolutionary Party*, 264–65.

82. Suárez Suárez, *Breve historia*, 71. See also Juan de Dios Bátiz, DESTIC, to General Brig. Salvador Sánchez, Secretaría de Guerra, September 7, 1936, ASEP, caja 2146, exp. V/356(8-5)/-1; "Informe gráfico de la Escuela Industrial Superior 'Hijos del Ejército, No. 2,'" 1938, reproduced in *Los pinceles de la historia*, 19, 55.

83. Gregorio Lara, "Mi visión de las Escuelas Hijos del Ejército," July 1936, in AGN, LC 534.4/47, 2; Juan de Dios Bátiz to Cárdenas, October 1, 1935, AGN, LC, 534.4/47, caja 721.

84. Gregorio Lara, "Mi visión de las Escuelas Hijos del Ejército," July 1936, in AGN, LC 534.4/47, 2. See also speech by Margarita Díaz de Téllez, director of EHE No. 2, August 22, 1937, in CESU, FHJ, caja 32, exp. 1216. On the radicalization of teachers in the 1930s, see Vaughan, *Cultural Politics in Revolution*, 25–46.

85. Gregorio Lara, "Mi visión de las Escuelas Hijos del Ejército," July 1936, in AGN, LC 534.4/47, 19. See also Carlos M. Peralta, "Dictamen sobre el proyecto que para la educación de los hijos del ejército presenta a la consideración del c. Presidente de la República el C. Profesor Marcelino M. Murrieta," March 20, 1935, AGN, LC, 534/64, caja 687, 3, 6.

86. *El Soldado*, February 1936, 85–88.

87. Margarita Díaz de Téllez, director of EHE No. 2, to Jara, August 22, 1937, in CESU, FHJ, caja 32, exp. 1216.

88. 1935 budget for "Centro Escolar Hijos del Ejército, de obreros, y campesinos," AGN, LC, 534/64, caja 687.

89. *El Nacional*, August 16, 1935. The postcards are available in AGN, LC, 534/64, caja 687.

90. Gregorio Lara, "Mi visión de las Escuelas Hijos del Ejército," July 1936, in AGN, LC 534.4/47, 9.

91. Copy of speech by Colonel Tomás Martínez Catache at the opening of EHE No. 1, DF, AGN, LC, 534/64, caja 687.

92. *El Maestro Rural*, November 15, 1935, 21–23. See also Gabino A. Palma, "El militarismo mexicano y las 'Escuelas Hijos del Ejército,'" *El Nacional*, April 28, 1935.

93. Margarita Díaz de Téllez, director of EHE No. 2, to Jara, August 22, 1937, in CESU, FHJ, caja 32, exp. 1216.

94. Margarita Díaz de Téllez, director of EHE No. 2, to Jara, August 24, 1937, CESU, FHJ, caja 32, exp. 1216.

95. Castillo Ramírez, Dorantes González, and Tuñon Pablos, *La noble tarea*, 130; Cravioto Leyzaola, *Historia documental*, 3:350.

96. On widespread support for developmentalism among elites, see Knight, "Popular Culture and the Revolutionary State."

97. Cárdenas, *Apuntes*, 261–62; *El Soldado*, February 1936, 85; *Memorias de la Secretaría de Educación Pública*, 1936–37, 136–37.

98. Gregorio Lara, "Mi visión de las Escuelas Hijos del Ejército," July 1936, in AGN, LC 534.4/47, 19.

99. Lieuwen, *Mexican Militarism*, 93; *Memorias de la Secretaría de Guerra y Marina*, August 1930–July 1931, 28–29; MA to G-2, June 19, 1934, USMIR, reel 7, 83; Draft of "Ley de Retiros y Pensiones Del Ejército Y Armada Nacionales," 1940, in CESU, FFU, caja 8.

100. General José Riverón, Zone Command, Guadalajara, Jalisco, to Cárdenas, January 8, 1937, and Cárdenas, DF, to General José Riverón, January 13, 1937, AGN, LC, 534.4/47, caja 721.

101. Humberto Cerdio y Conde, Inspector General de Policía, Toluca, Mexico, to Cárdenas, September 22, 1936, AGN, LC 534/64.

102. Capitán Lauro J. Flores, Ayudante del 51 Batallón, Veracruz, Veracruz, to Cárdenas, July 9, 1937, AGN, LC 534/64, caja 687.

103. Candelaria S. Vda. de Arcovedo, Salamanca, Guanajuato, to Cárdenas, July 25, 1937, AGN, LC 534/64, caja 687.

104. *New York Times*, June 29, 1938. For parent and student discontent at teaching in EHE No. 2, see also *El Nacional*, October 5, 1938.

105. "Memo: War Department General Staff," October 11, 1934, USMIR, reel 8, 751; MA to G-2, December 26, 1934, USMIR, reel 4, 32.

106. General Brigadier Carlos Martín del Campo, Mixcoac, DF, to Manuel Ávila Camacho, November 7, 1941, AGN, MAC, 534/92.

107. MA to G-2, October 31, 1933, USMIR, reel 8, 658–59.

108. General Brigadier Carlos Martín del Campo, Mixcoac, DF, to Manuel Ávila Camacho, November 7, 1941, AGN, MAC, 534/92.

109. Cárdenas, *Apuntes*, 329.

110. FSTE to Cárdenas, May 22, 1940, AGN, LC, 534.4/47, caja 721.

111. Niblo, *Mexico in the 1940s*, 106–8.

112. Castillo Ramírez, Dorantes González, and Tuñon Pablos, *La noble tarea*, 133.

113. Margarita Díaz de Téllez, DF, to Doña Amalia Solórzano de Cárdenas, 7 August 1939, AGN, LC, 534/64, caja 687. See also report by Miguel Chavez, to Cárdenas, n.d., AGN, LC, 534/64, caja 687.

114. C. Calderón Rabanales, Tapachula, Chiapas, to Cárdenas, March 27, 1940, AGN, LC, 534/64, caja 687; Castillo Ramírez, Dorantes González, and Tuñon Pablos, *La noble tarea*, 130; Rafael Teja, Sec. Gen. Grupo Acción Revolucionaria del Sindicato de la EHE No. 4, Guadalajara, Jalisco, to Cárdenas, September 29, 1938, AGN, LC, 534.4/47, caja 721; *Excélsior*, March 12, 1939.

115. Transcription of report by General José Inocente Lugo, in Subjefe EM, Gen. Brigadier Luis Rueda Flores, to Rómulo Meza Miralles, June 7, 1941, AGN, MAC 534.6/121, caja 651. See also Estado Mayor del Secretario de la Defensa to Rómulo Meza Miralles, Sec. Gen. Union General de Trabajadores Materiales de Guerra, DF, June 23, 1941; Rómulo Meza Miralles, DF, to Manuel Ávila Camacho, May 7 and July 29, 1941; Prof. Roberto Abrego, DF, to Manuel Ávila Camacho, May 15, 1941; FSTE, DF, to Manuel Ávila Camacho, January 21, 1942, in AGN, MAC 534.6/121, caja 651.

116. *La Prensa*, February 28, 1941; Correa, *El balance*, 26–27.

117. *La Prensa*, March 3–4, 1941; Transcription of report by General José Inocente Lugo, in Subjefe EM, Gen. Brigadier Luis Rueda Flores to Rómulo Meza Miralles, June 7, 1941, AGN, MAC, 534.6/121, caja 651.

118. Prof. Roberto Salinas, DF, to Manuel Ávila Camacho, February 20, 1943, AGN, MAC, 534/92, caja 623; Calderón, *El ejército y sus tribunales*, 51.

119. Muñoz Cota, cited in Estrada Correa, *Sin reconocimiento oficial*, 203.

120. Bermúdez and Véjar Vázquez, *No dejes crecer la hierba*, 55–57; Cárdenas, *Apuntes*, 636–37.

121. *Historia documental de la CNOP*, 1:45–46.

122. *Memorias de la Secretaría de la Defensa Nacional*, August 1937–September 1938, 17, 55. See also "Colegio Militar: Convocatoria para el concurso de admisión a los cursos del año escolar 1943-4," *El Nacional*, January 21, 1943. Camp dates the formal end of enlisted men's entry to the Military College to 1944, although he notes that examples of such officers in his database stop "several years" before this. A more modest program admitting enlisted men started again in 1955. Camp, *Mexico's Military on the Democratic Stage*, 54.

123. Chancery to Foreign Office, September 26, 1955, NA, FO 371/114260, 137; *Anales gráficos de la historia militar*, 590.

124. "El Dia del Ejército y de la Unificación," *Novedades*, February 17, 1965.

125. *Excélsior*, March 3, 1941.

126. García de León, *Fronteras interiores*, 81; Vera Salvo, *Historia de la cuestión agraria mexicana*, 3:38–39.

127. Calderón, *El ejército y sus tribunales*, 194.

128. Arellano Cruz, "Las defensas rurales," 72.

129. MA to G-2, October 4, 1940, NARA, MIDRF, box 2516, file 6750–66.

130. Sosa Elízaga, *Los códigos ocultos del cardenismo*, 455.

131. Memorandum on Henriquista propaganda, July 1951, AGN, DGIPS, caja 24, exp. 15, 75–76. See also various complaints about military education and corruption sent to President Adolfo López Mateos by General Heriberto Jara, 1961-2, CESU, FHJ, caja 6, exp. 475.

Chapter 3

1. The chapter title is from Mexico's national anthem, itself the focus of government wartime propaganda efforts. *Un soldado en cada hijo te dió.*

2. Serrano, *El contingente de sangre*; De Palo, *The Mexican National Army*, 90; Reina, *Las rebeliones campesinas*, 162–63, 354–56.

3. Thompson, "Los indios y el servicio militar"; Brewster, *Militarism, Ethnicity and Politics*; Mallon, *Peasant and Nation*.

4. Paz, *El servicio militar obligatorio*.

5. Womack, *Zapata*, 168–69.

6. Deas, "The Man on Foot," 79.

7. Madero cited in Knight, *Mexican Revolution*, 1:457.

8. Jean Meyer, *La Cristiada*, 149.

9. MA to G-2, September 20, 1927, NARA, MIDRF, box 2512, file "recruitment."

10. Nunn, *Yesterday's Soldiers*.

11. Moran and Waldron, *The People in Arms*.

12. Gustavo Salas, *El servicio militar obligatorio*, 6.

13. Reports from Colonel Rubén García, Santiago de Chile, to Amaro, 22 January 1926, APECFT, FJA, 03/04, leg. 1, exp. 22, 1924–6; García, *El servicio militar obligatorio*; *El Universal*, 7 May 1925.

14. Gustavo Salas, *El servicio militar obligatorio*, 50.

15. Cárdenas, *Apuntes*, 196.

16. Loyo Camacho, *Joaquín Amaro*, 133.

17. Álvaro Obregón, Cajeme, Sonora, to General Gabriel Gavira, DF, August 9, 1925, AGN, ALR, 580/121.

18. Abelardo Rodríguez, copy of speech at Asociación de Ciclos de Información de Generales, 1943, NARA, MIDRF, box 2511, file 6000–6500; Pansters, *Power and Politics in Puebla*, 106.

19. Anonymous Report on Conscription Conference, November 1, 1933, AGN, ALR, 580/121; Centro Revolucionario de Estudios Políticos, DF, to Rodríguez, November 1933, AGN, ALR, 580/121.

20. Schuler, *Secret Wars*, 56–82.

21. Almada and Díaz Babio, "La estrategia nacional"; MA to G-2, October 5, 1934, NARA, MIDRF, box 2511, file 6000–6500.

22. Schuler, *Mexico Between Hitler and Roosevelt*, 153–71; Torres Ramírez, *México en la Segunda Guerra Munidal*, 144; Colonel Juan Beristain, DF, to Manuel Ávila Camacho, May 26, 1942, AGN, MAC, 545.2/14-8.

23. Prewett, *Reportage on Mexico*, 291.

24. Manuel Ávila Camacho, "Mensaje a los jóvenes conscriptos clase 1926, Grupo B, al separarse de las filas del Servicio Militar Nacional," June 15, 1946, AGN, MAC, 708.1/42.

25. MA to G-2, October 5, 1934, NARA, MIDRF, box 2511, file 6000–6500; García, *El servicio militar obligatorio*; Cárdenas, *Apuntes*, 196.

26. García, *¿Qué y cómo es el servicio militar obligatorio?* 7.

27. Rubén García, DF, to Manuel Ávila Camacho, February 8, 1941, with attached essay "El servicio militar obligatorio," AGN, MAC 545.2/14-8, 20.

28. Federación de Ligas del Sector Popular del Estado de Morelos, Cuernavaca, to Cárdenas, June 20, 1940, AGN, LC, 545.3/46.

29. Pedro Rocha, DF, to Cárdenas, August 7, 1936, AGN, LC, 545.3/46.

30. Alejandro Macías, DF, to Cárdenas, September 12, 1940, AGN, LC, 545.3/46.

31. Mondragón, "El servicio militar," 354. On the founding of the Military Pentathlon, see MA to G-2, August 19, 1939, USMIR, reel 8, 526. On the group's wholehearted support for conscription, see Dr. Manlio Hernández Hernández to Ruiz Cortines, January 1954, AGN, ARC, 111/398, caja 11.

32. General Rubén García, DF, to Manuel Ávila Camacho, February 8, 1941, AGN, MAC, 545.2/14-8.

33. Mondragón, "El servicio militar," 227, 229.

34. Carlos Marín Foucher, "Iniciativa para crear el servico militar obligatorio del indio" (June 1938), cited in Knight, "Racism, Revolution and *Indigenismo*," 92–93.

35. *Excélsior*, December 12, 1939.

36. Amezcua, *Estudio de los sistemas de reclutamiento*, 70.

37. Minutes of cabinet meeting, August 1940, AGN, LC, 545.3/46, 3. See also, Cárdenas, *Apuntes*, 196.

38. Gen. Rubén García, DF, to Manuel Ávila Camacho, February 8, 1941, AGN, MAC, 545.2/14-8.

39. MA to G-2, January 21, 1941, and "General System: Pre-military training," April 15, 1942, NARA, MIDRF, box 2512, file "recruitment"; minutes of cabinet meeting, August 1940, AGN, LC, 545.3/46.

40. "Reglamento de la Ley del Servicio Militar," *Diario Oficial*, November 1, 1942.

41. 1942 press reports from *El Porvenir*, reproduced in Garza Guajardo, *Los conscriptos*, 33–38.

42. Ibid.; Naval attaché to G-2, March 30, 1943, NARA, MIDRF, box 2515, file 6600–6650.

43. General de Brigada Vicente Escobedo Mercadillo, Jefe del Estado Mayor, Defensa Nacional, to Manuel Ávila Camacho, September 18, 1942, AGN, MAC, 545.2/14-8.

44. See note from Colonel Alberto Violante Pérez, Jefe del Estado Mayor, Guanajuato, to Manuel Ávila Camacho, January 7, 1943, AGN, MAC, 545.2/14-12.

45. Naval attaché, Tampico to G-2, January 7, 1943, NARA, MIDRF, box 2512, file "recruitment."

46. Beattie, *The Tribute of Blood*, 267.

47. María Verdusco de Quiñones, Cubiri de Portela, Sinaloa, to Manuel Ávila Camacho, March 18, 1943, AGN, MAC, 545.2/14-24; Rogelio G. and Rafael Molina, Municipios Nacajuca and Jalpa de Méndez, Villahermosa, Tabasco, to Manuel Ávila Camacho, November 25, 1942, AGN, MAC, 545.2/14-26; Petition from Tlaxiaco, Oaxaca, to Manuel Ávila Camacho, October 3, 1944, AGN, MAC, 545.2/14-19.

48. Pedro Aquino, San José Tetla, Municipio de Piaxtla, Puebla, to Manuel Ávila Camacho, December 21, 1942, AGN, MAC, 545.2/14-20.

49. Redfield, *A Village That Chose Progress*, 131.

50. Xatepuztla, Municipio de Tlaola, Puebla, to Manuel Ávila Camacho, December 25, 1942, AGN, MAC, 545.2/14-20.

51. A. Juárez y demás, Ziritzicuaro, Michoacán, to Manuel Ávila Camacho, August 17, 1942, AGN, MAC, 555.2/46.

52. Juan José Ahumada, Mazatlán, Veracruz, to Manuel Ávila Camacho, April 6, 1945, AGN, MAC, 545.2/14-29; Confederación Regional Obrera, Puerto Angel, Oaxaca, to Manuel Ávila Camacho, December 1942, AGN, MAC, 545.2/14-16; Erasmo Hernández, Presidente Municipal, Ixtapan de la Sal, México, to Manuel Ávila Camacho, August 6, 1942, AGN, MAC, 545.2/14-14.

53. Petition from Comalco, Tabasco, to Manuel Ávila Camacho, May 22, 1943, AGN, MAC, 545.2/14-26. See also Juan Silveti, XETM, Naco, Sonora, to Manuel Ávila Camacho, September 21, 1942, and Rafael Gutiérrez, Naco, Sonora, to Manuel Ávila Camacho, November 4, 1942, AGN, MAC, 545.2/14-25; Report on Defensa Civil of Córdoba, Veracruz, by Ríos Thivol, Córdoba, Veracruz, November 24, 1942, AGN, DGIPS, caja 84, exp. 1.

54. MA to G-2, July 15, 1943, NARA, MIDRF, box 2555, file "June–July."

55. José Lugo Guerrero, Gobernador del Estado, Pachuca, Hidalgo, to Manuel Ávila Camacho, November 9, 1942, AGN, MAC, 432/454.

56. General Matías Ramos, Comm. del 18/a Zona Militar, Venta Prieta, Hidalgo, to Manuel Ávila Camacho, November 13, 1942, AGN, MAC, 432/454.

57. Tepejillo, Puebla, to Manuel Ávila Camacho, December 24, 1942, AGN, DGG, 2/382.2(18)16.

58. Report for CNC by Narciso Livas, Secretario General del Comité Regional, Riogrande, Zacatecas, January 23, 1943, AGN, MAC, 545.2/14-31.

59. Bravo Izquierdo, *Soldado del pueblo*, 320–21.

60. See various reports by Francisco Quezada, "P.S. 13," and Francisco Vega Canseco, "P.S. 28," January–February 1943, AGN, DGIPS, caja 89, exp. 2-1/131/714; Ma. Refugio S. Vda de Adame, Nieves, Zacatecas, to Manuel Ávila Camacho, July 22, 1943, AGN, MAC, 545.2/14-31; *Time*, January 11, 1943.

61. Whetten, *Rural Mexico*, 484.

62. See various reports by Francisco Quezada, "P.S. 13," and Francisco Vega Canseco, "P.S. 28," January–February 1943, AGN, DGIPS, caja 89, exp. 2-1/131/714.

63. Jaramillo, *Autobiografía*, 54–58; Ravelo Lecuona, *Los jaramillistas*, 55n7, 56n8.

64. Report by Gen. Brig. Ramón Cortés González, Secretaría de Comunicaciones y Obras Públicas, May 8, 1943, AGN, MAC, 559.1/51.

65. MA to G-2, September 17, 1943, NARA, MIDRF, box 2553, file "Sept.–Oct."; Taracena, *La vida en México*, 2:114.

66. Rubén Jaramillo, Tlaquiltenango, to Manuel Ávila Camacho, June 22, 1942, and poster produced by "the guiding committee of the *ejidatarios* of Zacatepec," September 1942, both in AGN, MAC, 523.1/13; Rubén Jaramillo, DF, to Manuel Ávila Camacho, November 22, 1944, AGN, MAC, 559.1/5; Jaramillo, *Autobiografía*, 50–91.

67. Cited in Tanalís Padilla, *Rural Resistance*, 94.

68. Ramírez Melgarejo, "La bola chiquita." My reading of the story is somewhat more skeptical of the role of "Don Cecilio" than Ramírez's interpretation.

69. Taracena, *La vida en México*, 2:109, 110, 115.

70. Ibid., 2:108.

71. Ibid., 2:117.

72. General Brigadier Comandante del 11/a Regimiento de Caballería to Defensa Nacional, March 22, 1943, AGN, DGG, 2/385.(14)1, caja 1 (Morelos).

73. Lic. J. Lelo de Larrea, Jefe del Departamento, DGIPS, to Manuel Hernández, Inspector de Departamento, Secretaría de Gobernación, transcribing report on Morelos and Puebla, March 1, 1943, AGN, DGIPS, caja 775, exp. 2; Lic. Jorge Mena Baca, Cuernavaca, Morelos, to DGIPS, October 4, 1943, AGN, DGIPS, caja 775, exp. 2.

74. Lewis, *Life in a Mexican Village*, 37.

75. Torres Ramírez, *México en la Segunda Guerra Mundial*, 136; G. Ray, Embassy to SD, January 13, 1943, NARA, MIDRF, box 2512, file "recruitment."

76. Francisco Quezada and Francisco Vega Canseco, Zacatecas, Zacatecas, 16 January 1943, AGN, DGIPS, caja 89, exp. 2-1/131/714.

77. Memo on June 19, 1944, report on UNS by Raleigh Gibson, U.S. Embassy Secretary, NA, FO 371/44478, AN20/20/26.

78. CROM to Manuel Ávila Camacho, January 5, 1943, AGN, MAC, 545.2/14-29.

79. Sindicato de Trabajadores Ferrocarrileros de la República Mexicana to Manuel Ávila Camacho, July 23, 1942, AGN, MAC, 545.2/14-8; José Hernández, DF, to Manuel Ávila Camacho, December 7, 1942, AGN, MAC, 545.2/14-8.

80. Daniel and Matías Astudillo, Tixtla, to Manuel Ávila Camacho, October 26, 1943, Alfonso Salmerón, Tixtla, to Manuel Ávila Camacho, October 11, 1942, and Desiderio Fuentes, Chilapa, Guerrero, to Manuel Ávila Camacho, December 11, 1942, AGN, MAC, 545.2/14-11.

81. Juan Macías, Hotel Regis, DF, to Manuel Ávila Camacho, July 2, 1942, AGN, MAC, 545.2/14-24.

82. Niblo, *Mexico in the 1940s*, 121–24.

83. Joseph, "Rethinking Mexican Revolutionary Mobilization," 149–50.

84. Letter from Ma. Refugio S. Vda de Adame, Nieves, Zacatecas, to Manuel Ávila Camacho, July 22, 1943, AGN, MAC, 545.2/14-31.

85. Telegram from Ezequiel Navarro, Comité Regional Campesino, Tuxtepec, Oaxaca, to Gobernador del Estado (Oaxaca), copied to Manuel Ávila Camacho, December 22, 1942, AGN, MAC 545.2/14-19. *El Popular* also reported rebellions against conscription in Colima and Teloloapan, Guerrero, along with serious demonstrations in Tlaxcala. Cited in Torres Ramírez, *México en la Segunda Guerra Mundial*, 136.

86. "Memo: Anti Axis Measures," November 3, 1943, NA, FO 371/33993, F10041.

87. General Lázaro Cárdenas transcribing message from Comandante de la 14/a Zona Militar, Aguascalientes, to Manuel Ávila Camacho, December 1, 1942, AGN, MAC, 545.2/14.

88. Nicolasa Hurtado Raya, Morelia, to Manuel Ávila Camacho, September 20, 1942, 545.2/14-15; and various correspondence, September 1942, AGN, MAC, 545.2/14-33.

89. Mayor Candelario Castillo Romero, "Las corporaciones sin mujeres y el servicio militar obligatorio," *La Prensa*, June 18, 1936. I discuss changing gender roles in military reform in more detail in "Gender and Military Reform."

90. MA to G-2, July 15, 1943, NARA, MIDRF, box 2551, file "June–July"; *Memorias de la Secretaría de la Defensa Nacional*, September 1942–August 1943, 38. In an earlier published version of this research I underestimated how many conscripts the government obtained in 1943 because the published figures did not include the second group. Rath, "'Que el cielo un soldado en cada hijo te dio. . . .'"

91. Confidential memo from General Francisco Urquizo, Defensa Nacional, to Manuel Ávila Camacho, August 9, 1943, AGN, MAC, 545.2/14-33; MA to G-2, July 29, 1943, NARA, MIDRF, box 2551, file "June–July."

92. General Francisco Urquizo quoted in Garza Guajardo, *Los conscriptos*, 28; "Cuerpos Regionales: Summary of Information," Assistant Chief of Staff, G-2, April 17, 1943, NARA, MIDRF, box 2512, file 6240.

93. MA to G-2, November 30, 1943, NARA, MIDRF, box 2553, file "Nov.-Dec."

94. MA to G-2, July 15, 1943, NARA, MIDRF, box 2551, file "June–July"; MA to G-2, December 6, 1943, and May 18, 1944, NARA, MIDRF, box 2553, files "April–June," "Nov.–Dec. 43."

95. Scott, *Weapons of the Weak*.

96. Garza Guajardo, *Los conscriptos*, 198–210.

97. Confidential memo from General Francisco Urquizo, Defensa Nacional, to Manuel Ávila Camacho, August 9, 1943, AGN, MAC, 545.2/14-33; testimony of Mario Flores Serrano in Garza Guajardo, *Los conscriptos*, 160–75; various reports from naval attaché, Tampico, to G-2, 1943, NARA, MIDRF, box 2512, file "recruitment."

98. MA to G-2, September 1943, NARA, MIDRF, box 2553, file "Sept.–Oct."

99. MA to G-2, July 15, 1943, NARA, MIDRF, box 2555, "June–July." The attaché chose to protect the anonymity of his informant.

100. On military maneuvers in Jalisco, see *Memorias de la Secretaría de la Defensa Nacional*, August 1942–September 1943; Soto Oliver, *Entre soldados y cabos*, 67–75.

101. Rafael Pascacio Gamboa, Tuxtla Gutiérrez, Chiapas, to Manuel Ávila Camacho, December 14, 1942, AGN, MAC, 545.2/14-6.

102. Margarito Rosales, Nayarit, to Manuel Ávila Camacho, October 25, 1943, and Manuel Ávila Camacho, Tren Presidencial, Tepic, Nayarit, to Margarito Rosales, Jesús María, Nayarit, October 29, 1943, AGN, MAC, 545.2/14-33.

103. Ravelo Lecuona, *Los jaramillistas*, 17; copy of open letter from state governor Jesús Castillo López to villages of Yecapixtla, Ocuituco, Tetela del Volcán, Zacualpan, Jantetelco, Jonacatepec, Tepalcingo, Axochiapan, Tlaltizapan, Tlaquiltenango, and Jojutla, October 1943, AGN, DGIPS, caja 775, exp. 2; Frente Zapatista de la República, DF, to Manuel Ávila Camacho, January 30, 1946, AGN, MAC, 545.2/14-20.

104. U.S. Consulate, Durango, to SD, January 6, 1943, NARA, MIDRF, box 2512, file "recruitment."

105. "325 Madres de Familia," Senguio, Michoacán, to Manuel Ávila Camacho, December 14, 1942, AGN, MAC, 545.2/14-15.

106. Cabrera, *El servicio militar obligatorio*.

107. Fein, "Myths of Cultural Imperialism and Nationalism."

108. See poster by Crescenciano Brígido, San Andrés Tuxtla, Veracruz, July 1943, AGN, MAC, 545.2/14-29.

109. Petition from ninety-five *"agraristas"* of "Emiliano Zapata," Tabasco, to Manuel Ávila Camacho, August 24, 1942, AGN, MAC, 545.2/14-26.

110. Higinio Mazariegos, Presidente Comis. Ejidal, "Aldea la Libertad Calera," Municipio de Motozintla, Chiapas, to Manuel Ávila Camacho, August 7, 1942, AGN, MAC, 545.2/14-6.

111. Petition from Itzamatitlán, Morelos, to Manuel Ávila Camacho, December 14, 1942, AGN, MAC, 545.2/14-16.

112. Petition from Chauzumba, Rancheria del Municipio de Chiautla de Tapia, Puebla, to Manuel Ávila Camacho, January 15, 1943, AGN, MAC, 545.2/14-20.

113. El Oiganal, Municipio de Huaquechula, Ex-distrito de Atlixco, Puebla, to Manuel Ávila Camacho, December 1942 (exact date illegible), AGN, MAC, 545.2/14-20.

114. Petition from "Rancho La Enredadora," Municipio de Jerécuaro, Guanajuato, to Manuel Ávila Camacho, October 1, 1942, AGN, MAC, 545.2/14-12. On the use of the term "campesino" by Sinarquistas, see Gill, *El Sinarquismo*.

115. Petition from Cuauhtémoc, Municipio de Centla, Tabasco, to Manuel Ávila Camacho, November 17, 1942, AGN, MAC, 545.2/14-26.

116. Fein, "Myths of Cultural Imperialism and Nationalism," 172–82.

117. Jaramillo, *Autobiografía*, 52, 94–95; Ravelo Lecuona, *Los jaramillistas*, 61.

118. Petition from Ranchería San Luis, Municipio de Matías Romero, Oaxaca, to Manuel Ávila Camacho, November 21, 1942, AGN, MAC, 545.2/14-16.

119. Petition from Tlaquiltenango, Morelos, to Manuel Ávila Camacho, August 3, 1942, AGN, DGG, 404.1/2392.

120. Letter from Gerardo Ramírez, DF, to Manuel Ávila Camacho, August 20, 1942, AGN, MAC 545.2/14-16.

121. Saúl Peralta, Escuela Industrial, DF, to Manuel Ávila Camacho, January 11, 1943, AGN, MAC, 545.2/14-8.

122. Juan Nieto, Pres. del Comis. Ejidal de Emiliano Zapata, Municipio de Arriaga, Chiapas, to Manuel Ávila Camacho, June 10, 1941, AGN, MAC, 545.2/14-6.

123. Petition from Cuautempan, Puebla, to Manuel Ávila Camacho, August 20, 1942, AGN, MAC, 545.2/14-20. On Juan Francisco Lucas and nineteenth-century traditions of local mobilization, see Thompson with LaFrance, *Patriotism, Politics and Popular Liberalism*.

124. Juan Gómez, Guadalajara, to Manuel Ávila Camacho, April 4, 1941, AGN, MAC, 545.2/14-8.

125. Letter from Celerino Estrada, delegate for the Liga General de Communidades Agrarias de la Republica for Acatlán de Pérez Figueroa, Oaxaca, to Manuel Ávila Camacho, October 20, 1942, AGN, MAC, 545.2/14-19. Emphasis mine.

126. Centeno, *Blood and Debt*, 211.

127. Mariano Hernández Zarate y demás, Zinacantán, Chiapas, to Manuel Ávila Camacho, September 2, 1943, AGN, MAC, 545.2/14-6.

128. Naval attaché, Tampico, to G-2, April 27, 1943, NARA, MIDRF, 2512, "recruitment"; Ramírez Melgarejo, "La bola chiquita."

129. Vaughan, *Cultural Politics in Revolution*, 39.

130. Petition with fifteen signatories, Matamoros, Puebla, to Manuel Ávila Camacho, June 30, 1943, AGN, MAC, 545.2/14-20.

131. Beattie, *The Tribute of Blood*. For an example of Mexicans associating military service with punishment in the early nineteenth century, see Caplan, *Indigenous Citizens*, 87–88.

132. Angela Pérez, Sindicato Femenil de Trabajadores de Playa Vicente, Veracruz, to Manuel Ávila Camacho, December 8, 1942, AGN, MAC, 545.2/14-29.

133. Felipe Neri Roblero, Bejucal de Ocampo, Chiapas, to Manuel Ávila Camacho, March 31, 1945, AGN, MAC, 545.2/14-6.

134. Cabrera, *El servicio militar obligatorio*, 33.

135. Juvenal Aceves and Ing. Juan B. Rodríguez, La Piedad, Michoacán, to Manuel Ávila Camacho, March 9, 1943, AGN, MAC, 545.2/14-15.

136. Hermelindo Velázquez, Pijijiapan, Chiapas, to Manuel Ávila Camacho, December 1940 (exact date illegible), AGN, MAC, 545.2/14-6.

137. General Lázaro Cárdenas, "Ciudadanos oficiales de la antigüedad 1940," August 10, 1940, AGN, LC, 545.3/46, 3.

138. Luis Gurza, DF, to Manuel Ávila Camacho, July 8, 1943, AGN, MAC, 545.2/14-8.

139. *Memorias de la Secretaría de la Defensa Nacional*, September 1943–August 1944, 157–62.

140. MA to SD, February 8, 1943, NARA, MIDRF, box 2552, file "Jan.–July 1943," and various correspondence, November–December 1943, box 2553, file "November 2662."

141. For a detailed discussion of changes in service conditions, see Rath "Gender and Military Reform."

142. González Luna, *Servicio militar*; press clippings enclosed in the letter by Gregorio Delgado Ibarra, Mazatlán, Sinaloa, to Manuel Ávila Camacho, December 20, 1943, in AGN, MAC, 550/107.

143. See reports on "Casino del Conscripto," Inspectors P.S. 1, 2, and 19, August 24, 1944, AGN, DGIPS, caja 89, exp. 2–1/131/726.

144. *Diario Oficial*, November 26, 1943.

145. MA to G-2, April 14, 1944, NARA, MIDRF, box 2553, file "March–April"; Taracena, *La vida en México*, 2:232.

146. Harrison, "United States–Mexican Military Collaboration," 238–39.

147. Ranchería San Luis, Municipio de Matías Romero, Oaxaca, to Manuel Ávila Camacho, November 21, 1942, AGN, MAC, 545.2/14-16.

148. "Reglamento de la Ley del Servicio Militar," *Diario Oficial*, November 1942.

149. The files on military service in Alemán's presidential archive contain mainly these types of petitions. AGN, MAV, 545.2/1-1 to 1-31.

150. Suprema Corte de Justicia to Gobernación, February 2, 1949, AGN, MA, 545.2/1; *Memorias de la Secretaría de la Defensa Nacional*, September 1949–August 1950, 34; Lozoya, *El ejército mexicano*, 107.

151. McAlister, "Mexico," 231.

152. Urquizo, *Tres de Diana*, 109; Circular número 5 de la Secretaría de Gobernación, March 26, 1946. Copy provided by Paul Gillingham.

153. Junta de Reclutamiento, Amilcingo, Morelos, to Gobernador del Estado, September 2, 1946, AGN, MAC, 545.2/14-16. For continued complaints of corruption, see AGN, MAV, 545.2/1-20 (Puebla).

154. Report from Ing. Gerardo Rafael Catalán Calvo, Governor of Guerrero, to Manuel Ávila Camacho, October 21, 1943, AGN, MAC, 545.2/14-11. On the heavy military presence in Puebla and Morelos in 1943–44, see Bravo Izquierdo, *Soldado del pueblo*, 320–22; Ravelo Lecuona, *Los jaramillistas*, 57.

155. *Memorias de la Secretaría de la Defensa Nacional*, September 1943–August 1944, 76; Elodia Arévalo, Tuxtla Gutiérrez, Chiapas, to Manuel Ávila Camacho, August 20, 1943, AGN, MAC, 545.2/14-6; Gillingham, "Force and Consent," 129.

156. Díaz Escobar, *Alemán y la democracia mexicana*, 175–77; Cárdenas, *Apuntes*, 610; General Francisco L. Urquizo, "Plan de Re-organización del Ejército," July 1952, in CESU, FFU, caja 8, exp. 10.

157. Vaughan, *Cultural Politics in Revolution*, 195.

158. Guardino, *The Time of Liberty*, 7–14.

Chapter 4

1. Garza Guajardo, *Los conscriptos*, 29.
2. Open letter to Alemán, 1947, AGN, MAV, 577/7.
3. Camp, *Generals in the Palacio*, 69.
4. Servín, "Reclaiming Revolution," 551–52.
5. Alfredo Leal Cortés, "El gabinete de Alemán," *Mañana*, 1 August 1959; General Miguel Molinar Simondy, Comdte. 12/a zona militar, San Luis Potosí, to Alemán, September 20, 1949, AGN, MAV, 708.1/9, caja 841.
6. Servín, *Ruptura y oposición*; Navarro, *Political Intelligence*. For two useful earlier studies, see Sánchez Gutiérrez, "La política en el México rural" and "Los militares."
7. Navarro, *Political Intelligence*, 270.
8. "Report: The Mexican Army," 1927, USMIR, reel 7, 951–90, 984.
9. Military reports on Latin America, October 20, 1943, NA, FO 371/33939, 9514.
10. MA to G-2, February 28, 1941, USMIR, reel 4, 21.
11. *El Soldado*, March 31, 1944, 3. See also Urquizo, *Charlas cuarteleras*; Sánchez Lamego, ¿*Debe tener México militares profesionales?*
12. Corona del Rosal, *Moral militar y civismo*.
13. Cravioto Leyzaola, *Historia documental*, 3:419–22.
14. "Strength of Mexican Army," MA to G-2, October 1937, USMIR, reel 7, 493; MA to G-2, October 1, 1937, USMIR, reel 8, 937.
15. Camp, *Mexico's Military on the Democratic Stage*, 208.
16. McAlister, "Mexico," 218–22; Camp, *Generals in the Palacio*, 100–132.
17. "Presidential Guard," June 10, 1935, NARA, MIDRF, box 2555, file "6100: Combat Info. Digests"; Camp, *Generals in the Palacio*, 194; Lieuwen, *Mexican Militarism*, 147.
18. MA report on military organization, April 16, 1942, NARA, MIDRF, box 2551, file "April–June."
19. Almada and Díaz Babio, "La estrategia nacional," 156–65; Col. Juan M. Carrasco Cuéllar, 2 Infantry Battalion, Chilpancingo, Guerrero, to Alemán, May 10, 1950, AGN, MAV, 545.3/47, caja 585; General Franciso L. Urquizo, "Plan de Re-organización del Ejército," July 1952, in CESU, FFU, caja 8, exp. 10, 9–10.
20. N. P. Wright to Foreign Office, July 6, 1945, NA, FO, 371/44476, AN2267, 29.
21. General Heriberto Jara, Veracruz, to López Mateos, June 12, 1963, CESU, FHJ, caja 6, exp. 475.
22. Author's calculation based on bimonthly reports on military commands, 1934–41, USMIR, reel 7.
23. Niblo, *Mexico in the 1940s*, 116–17.
24. Cited in Harrison, "United States–Mexican Military Collaboration," 196.
25. Naval attaché to G-2, January 6, 1943, NARA, MIDRF, box 2555, file "Jan.-Feb."; Ríos Thivol, October 1, 1949, DGIPS, caja 84, exp. 2; "Leading Personalities," July 4, 1944, NA, FO 371/38354; Bateman to Foreign Office, May 8, 1944, NA, FO 371/38312, 83; Harrison, "United States–Mexican Military Collaboration," 196.
26. Bateman to Foreign Office, December 27, 1943, NA, FO 371/38312, AN138, 3.

27. Various correspondence, MA to G-2, October–November 1938, USMIR, reel 2, 136–47. On Arias Barraza, see: "Enclosure to FBI letter of 12/15/41," NARA, MIDRF, box 2555, file "6100 Mexico"; Extract from Captain Raúl Arias Barraza, Veracruz, to Miss Laila Lezli, Los Angeles, February 11, 1944, U.S. Office of Censorship, February 17, 1944, NARA, MIDRF, box 2547, file "Entry 77."

28. MA to G-2, December 15, 1943, NARA, MIDRF, box 2553, file "Nov.–Dec."

29. Alamillo Flores, *Memorias*, 543–611.

30. MA to G-2, July 27, 1937, USMIR, reel 7, 944.

31. Report on Captain Jerónimo Gomar Suástegui, April 1, 1943, MA, NARA, MIDRF, box 2552, file "March–April"; Political Report, MA, February 11, 1944, NARA, MIDRF, box 2553, file "Jan.–Feb."; Report on General Cristóbal Guzmán Cárdenas, September 30, 1949, AGN, DGIPS, caja 84, exp. 2; Bateman, "Leading Personalities in Mexico," May 2, 1947, NA, FO 371/60955.

32. Navarro Valdez, *El cardenismo en Durango*, 245, 250, 277–78.

33. Bateman to Foreign Office, February 14, 1944, NA, FO 371/38312, AN798, 37.

34. Gruening, *Mexico and Its Heritage*, 329; José Valadés quoted in Estrada Correa, *Sin reconocimiento oficial*, 49.

35. Gillingham, "Military Caciquismo."

36. Inspectors P.S. 1 and P.S. 2, DF, to DGIPS, August 7, 1945, AGN, DGIPS, caja 89, exp. 2-1/131/726.

37. Report on Blas Corral Martínez, June 18, 1942, NARA, MIDRF, box 2551, file "June–July."

38. Consul, Durango, to SD, February 26, 1944, NARA, MIDRF, box 2555, file "5990-Mexico."

39. Santos, *Memorias*, 587; Francisco F. Quezada, Inspector 13, Durango, to DGIPS, March 14, 1943, AGN, DGIPS, caja 89, exp. 2-1/131/726.

40. Consul, Durango, to SD, February 26, 1944, NARA, MIDRF, box 2555, file "5990-Mexico."

41. Consul, Monterrey, to SD, October 6, 1943, NARA, RG 84, Mexico Consular Reports, box 62, "Confidential Supplement," 820.02.

42. Inspector P.S. 2, Mazatlán, Sinaloa, to DGIPS, October 26, 1943, AGN, DGIPS, caja 89, exp. 2-1/131/726.

43. Geraldo, *Sobre las armas*, 149; Bateman to Foreign Office, April 9, 1945, NA, FO 371/44478, AN1380.

44. Bateman to Foreign Office, April 9, 1945, NA, FO 371/44478, AN1380.

45. "Acusación contra el General Macías Valenzuela, Gobernador de Sinaloa y Ex-Secretario de la Defensa Nacional, diligencias preparatorias del Consejo de Guerra próximo," AGN, MAC, 541/907, 1, 4–5.

46. Ibid., 7, 11; Jesús González Gallo, Secretario de la Presidencia, DF, to Cárdenas, Defensa Nacional, April 4, 1945, AGN, MAC, 541/907.

47. Hernández, *Amistades, compromisos y lealtades*, 37–52, 328.

48. Santos, *Memorias*, 767, 824–26, 842.

49. Consular Reports on Monterrey Municipal Elections, July–September 1945, NARA, RG 84, Classified General Records, box 5; Arthur Goodfriend, "Ejército Mexi-

cano," *Infantry Journal*, May 1947, 48–49; MA report on General Salvador Sánchez, 1944, NARA, MIDRF, box 2553, file 1; Report on General Alberto Salinas Carranza, March 1944, NARA, MIDRF, box 2553, file "MA Reports."

50. Anonymous Memo, October 1948, AGN, DGIPS, caja 24, exp. 3.

51. General Brig. Ignacio Alberto Martínez León, Justicia y Pensiones, Defensa Nacional, to Manuel Ávila Camacho, February 15, 1944, AGN, MAC, 418.2/47.

52. MA to G-2, March 27, 1944, NARA, MIDRF, box 2553, file "March–April."

53. Harrison, "United States–Mexican Military Collaboration," 155.

54. Inspector 42, Salvatierra, Guanajuato, to DGIPS, July 29, 1946, AGN, DGIPS, caja 87, exp. 1; Inspectors 31 and 34, Oaxaca, Oaxaca, to DGIPS, March 26, 1947, AGN, DGIPS, caja 84, exp. 1, 3–4; Liga Nacional Campesina "Ursulo Galván," report to Vocal Ejecutivo de Asuntos Campesinos de la Presidencia de la República, July 22, 1947, and Juan Caccia Bernal, Marcelo Fernández, to DGIPS, August 11, 1947, AGN, DGIPS, caja 16, exp. 31.

55. Francisco Quezada, "P.S. 13," and Francisco Vega Canseco, "P.S. 28," January 16, 1943, AGN, DGIPS, caja 89, exp. 2-1/131/714.

56. Geraldo, *Sobre las armas*, 57–60, 80, 129. For contemporary complaints about Olachea protecting and commissioning *pistoleros* in Nayarit, see various correspondence, July–August 1943, AGN, MAC, 444.1/433. For similar practices by General Mange in Veracruz, see Gillingham, "Military Caciquismo."

57. Astorga Almanza, *El siglo de las drogas*, 68–82, 86; Report on General Arias Sánchez, Delegado 36, Culiacán, Sinaloa, to DGIPS, May 27, 1950, AGN, DGIPS, caja 803, exp. 2.

58. González Gallo to Ciclo de Infomación de Generales, February 1944, AGN, MAC, 550/35.6.

59. *La Prensa*, January 25, 1950, AGN, DGIPS, caja 803, exp. 1; Liga Nacional Campesina "Ursulo Galván," report to Vocal Ejecutivo de Asuntos Campesinos de la Presidencia de la República, July 22, 1947, AGN, DGIPS, caja 16, exp. 31.

60. San Hipólito Soltepec, Puebla, to Alemán, April 15, 1950, AGN, MAV 404.1/275, caja 217.

61. Memo, Cuernavaca, to DGIPS, June 17, 1940, AGN, DGIPS, caja 140, exp. 5; MA to G-2, January 28, 1944, NARA, MIDRF, box 2553, file "Jan.–Feb."; Veterans, Morelos, to Alemán, May 29, 1948, AGN, MAV, 556.63/48.

62. Francisco F. Quezada, Inspector 13, Durango, to DGIPS, March 14, 1943, AGN, DGIPS, caja 89, exp. 2-1/131/726.

63. Santos, *Memorias*, 852–53.

64. *El Universal*, June 19 and July 4, 1946, CESU, FFU, caja 6, exp. 6.

65. Bethel and Roxborough, *Latin America*; Agustín, *Tragicomedia mexicana*, 1:75; Díaz Escobar, *Alemán y la democracia mexicana*.

66. Newcomer, *Reconciling Modernity*, 165–68; Niblo, *Mexico in the 1940s*, 153–58.

67. *Seis años de actividad nacional*, 37–38.

68. See commission report on General Marcelino García Barragán's governorship of Jalisco, *Diario de los Debates*, August 1, 1945.

69. Unsigned memo "Zacatecas," May 1950, AGN, DGIPS, caja 803, exp. 2.

70. *Excélsior*, February 7, 1950, AGN, DGIPS, caja 803, exp. 1.

71. *La Prensa*, October 22, 1948, AGN, DGIPS, caja 24, exp. 3.

72. Memo, August 23, 1948, AGN, DGIPS, caja 24, exp. 3; Alfonso Corona del Rosal and Gregorio Ortega, DF, to Alemán, August 12, 1948, AGN, MAV, 565.32/88.

73. Servín, *Ruptura y oposición*, 44–45; Lieuwen, *Mexican Militarism*, 144.

74. *El Nacional*, July 4, 1945; *New York Times*, July 5, 1945.

75. Author's calculations based on "Escalafón de la Plana Mayor del Ejército" of 1953, AGN, ARC, 556.1/105, and the British military attaché's estimates of total number of serving generals in July 1945 in Bateman to Foreign Office, July 6, 1945, NA, FO 371/44476 (1945), AN2267. Although Camp calculates that President Alemán promoted 379 officers to general, according to calculations based on the 1953 table some of these promotions must have been issued as a result of colonels being promoted a grade as they retired from active service. Camp, *Generals in the Palacio*, 179–80.

76. "Escalafón de la Plana Mayor del Ejército" of 1953, AGN, ARC, 556.1/105, 1–2.

77. Memo, August 23, 1948, AGN, DGIPS, caja 24, exp. 3.

78. Camp, *Mexican Political Biographies*, 592; "Escalafón de la Plana Mayor del Ejército," 1953, AGN, ARC, 556.1/105; Liga Nacional Campesina "Ursulo Galván," report to Vocal Ejecutivo de Asuntos Campesinos de la Presidencia de la Republica, July 22, 1947, and Juan Caccia Bernal, Marcelo Fernández, to DGIPS, August 11, 1947, AGN, DGIPS, caja 16, exp. 31.

79. Memo, August 31, 1948, AGN, DGIPS, caja 24, exp. 3.

80. *La Prensa*, September 6, 1948, AGN, DGIPS, caja 24, exp. 3.

81. *La Prensa*, August 21, 1948, AGN, DGIPS, caja 24, exp. 3; Embassy to SD, August 5, 1948, IAMSD, 812.00/8-548; Ramírez Faz to DFS, August 26, 1948, AGN, DFS, exp. 29-18-48.

82. Memo on Henriquismo, June 1951, AGN, DGIPS, caja 24, exp. 15. See also Inspector "JCB," April 21, 1950, AGN, DGIPS, caja 803, exp. 1; Inspector "FVC," April 21, 1950, AGN, DGIPS, caja 803, exp. 1; Memorandum "Futurismo Presidencial," May 10, 1950, AGN, DGIPS, caja 803, exp. 2, 3; Servín, *Ruptura y oposición*, 189–92; Quiles Ponce, *Henríquez y Cárdenas*, 25.

83. *La Prensa*, January 25, 1950, AGN, DGIPS, caja 803, exp. 1.

84. Ibid.

85. Inspector P.S., August 3, 1945, AGN, DGIPS, caja 788, exp. 8; *El Universal Gráfico*, June 8, 1950, AGN, DGIPS, caja 803, exp. 2.

86. Memo on Henriquismo, June 1951, AGN, DGIPS, caja 24, exp. 15.

87. *Excélsior*, August 17, 1951, AGN, DGIPS, caja 24, exp. 3; Quiles Ponce, *Henríquez y Cárdenas*, 25.

88. Memo, July 1951, AGN, DGIPS, caja 24, exp. 15, 75–76. See also Octavio Véjar Vázquez, various clippings, October 1951, in AGN, DGIPS, caja 24, exp. 3.

89. Jalisco rally report by "JNM," December 26, 1950, AGN, DGIPS, caja 805, exp. 1.

90. Press release by Agustín Leñero, transcribed in Memo on Henriquismo, July 1951, AGN, DGIPS, caja 24, exp. 15, 75–76.

91. Servín, *Ruptura y oposición*.

92. Estrada Correa, *Sin reconocimiento oficial*, 8–9, 69, 153, 218.

93. Gillingham, "Force and Consent," 81; Servín, *Ruptura y oposición*; Tanalís Padilla, *Rural Resistance*.

94. "Futurismo Presidencial," May 29, 1950, AGN, DGIPS, caja 803, exp. 2.

95. Biweekly reports, Rapp to Foreign Office, October 1948, NA, FO 371/67994 (1948), 86; Report, July 23, 1948, AGN, DGIPS, caja 111, exp. 2; Report, August 17, 1948, AGN, DGIPS, caja 111, exp. 2.

96. *Alemán y el ejército.*

97. Cravioto Leyzaola, *Historia documental*, 3:408; General Miguel Molinar Simondy, Comdte. 12/a zona militar, San Luis Potosí, to Alemán, September 20, 1949, AGN, MAV, 708.1/9, caja 841.

98. Navarro, *Political Intelligence*, 117.

99. Aguayo, *La charola*, 63–66.

100. Ibid., 79

101. Ibid., 78

102. Ibid., 79

103. Ibid., 74; Ronfeldt, "Mexican Army and Political Order."

104. G-2 memo on General Limón, 1948, NARA, RG 319, Army Intelligence Decimal Files, box 247, file 335.11; Bateman, "Leading Personalities in Mexico," May 2, 1947, NA, FO 371/60955.

105. General Manuel Solís, Military Archive, Defensa Nacional, to Alemán, April 9, 1950, attached to AGN, DGIPS, caja 803, exp. 1.

106. Comments of Colonel Raúl Alarcón, recorded in "Memorandum Confidencial," Inspector "X," April 19, 1950, AGN, DGIPS, caja 803, exp. 1; Servín, *Ruptura y oposición*, 197n53; Santos, *Memorias*, 870–71; Memorandum, December 5, 1950, AGN, DGIPS, caja 805, exp. 1; Camp, *Generals in the Palacio*, 60–61; Cárdenas, *Apuntes*, 652; Navarro, *Political Intelligence*, 110.

107. González, *Portesgilismo y alemanismo en Tamaulipas*, 157–59.

108. "Mexico: Leading Personalities," 1956, NA, FO 371/120161.

109. Anonymous note, 1953, AGN, ARC, 703.2/252, caja 1241.

110. Estrada Correa, *Sin reconocimiento oficial*, 77–78; *Últimas Noticias de Excélsior*, July 28, 1952.

111. Ramírez Faz to DFS, August 26, 1948, AGN, DFS, exp. 29-18-48.

112. Rapp to Foreign Office, August 29, 1950, NA, FO 371/81503, 27–28; *La Prensa*, November 10, 1948.

113. Turkel to Embassy, August 12, 1948, IAMSD, 812.00/8-1248; Niblo, *Mexico in the 1940s*, 169n29.

114. Various correspondence, President Alemán to López, 1952, AHSDN, X/III/1-16 (López Morales), 1955.

115. Santos, *Memorias*, 863.

116. Flores Arellano and Wences Román, *María de la O*, 68–70; personnel tables in AGN, MAV, 550/19 and 298/22349.

117. Memo, February 1949, AGN, DGIPS, caja 24, exp. 3. On earlier tensions between the Department of National Defense, the presidency, and commanders over the creation of a general staff, see Memo "War Dept. General Staff," MA to G-2,

October 11, 1934, USMIR, reel 8, 751; MA to G-2, January 17, 1939, USMIR, reel 7, 587.

118. Memo, December 1946, RG 319, Army Intelligence Decimal Files, box 173, "General Limón."

119. "Mexican Army," 1955, NA, FO 371/120173; Wager, "The Mexican Army," 32–33; lists of military commander appointments, 1959, AGN, ALM, 135.21/131.

120. McAlister, "Mexico," 214.

121. Margiotta, "Civilian Control of the Military"; Camp, *Generals in the Palacio*, 66, 68.

122. Medin, *El sexenio alemanista*, 164–66.

123. Gunther, *Inside Latin America*, 34–52.

124. General Heriberto Jara, Veracruz, to López Mateos, June 12, 1963, CESU, FHJ, caja 6, exp. 475.

125. AHSDN, XI/III/1-574 (Ireta Viveros); Veledíaz, *El general sin memoria*, 143–62; AHSDN, X/III/1-16 (López Morales); Ben Fallaw, personal communication, July 1, 2012.

126. Various correspondence, General Salinas, Guadalajara, to Defensa Nacional, 1954–56, AHSDN, XI/III/1-574 (Ireta Viveros); Monterrey Consulate to State, April 1, 1953, IAMSD, 712.00/4-153; Report of May 22, 1969, AGN, DFS, 100-17-3-69, H.105, L.18. Salinas Leal is the subject of an ongoing research project by this author.

127. Camp, *Generals in the Palacio*, 181–82; DFS report, January 14, 1953, AGN, DFS, 44-3-953, H.24, L.1.

128. Memorandum from president's office, "Observaciones sobre la naturaleza de las prestaciones sociales que el ejército ha dado a otras dependencias oficiales y a elementos civiles del país durante el año 1952," 1953, AGN, ARC, 550/24.

129. Embassy to SD, February 14, 1952, IAMSD, 712.5-MSP/2-1452; various correspondence, July–August 1950, NARA, RG 319, Army Intelligence Decimal Files, 000.7, box 174. On right-wing support for a military alliance with the U.S. government and left-wing hostility to the same, see Embassy to SD, February 6, 1952, IAMSD, 712.5/MSP-2-1252.

130. Sullivan to Foreign Office, March 23, 1954, NA, FO 371/114260, 46.

131. Sullivan to Foreign Office, January 12, 1955, NA, FO 371/114260, 2.

132. XA-1, Report, August 26, 1955, AHSDN, X/III/1-435 (Ochoa Moreno), leg. 13, 161.

133. McAlister, "Mexico," 233; Sullivan to Foreign Office, March 23, 1954, NA, FO 371/114260, 46; Lieutenant Colonel Veraza de los Ríos, Campo Mil. No. 1, DF, to Ruiz Cortines, August 27, 1957, AGN, ARC, 556.63/168.

134. Various correspondence, April–October 1956, Colonos de Reforma Social, DF, to Ruiz Cortines, AGN, ARC, 509/761; Primer Congreso Indígena, Guadalajara, to ARC, January 14, 1956, and Padilla, Ayotitlán, Jalisco, to Ruiz Cortines, March 25, 1956, AGN, ARC, 541/401, caja 786; Manuel Santos, Atlacomulco, México to Ruiz Cortines, July 1, 1958, AGN, ARC, 501.1/414; Mecapalapa, Puebla, to Ruiz Cortines, June 10, 1957, AGN, ARC, 710.1/1152; Gillingham, "Military Caciquismo"; Gordillo Jiménez, Tapachula, to Ruiz Cortines, May 18, 1958, MAC, ARC, 550/114.

135. Davis, "The Political and Economic Origins," 61n15.

136. Report of January 1964, AGN, DFS, 100-16-1-964, H.287, L.4.

137. 1973 reports, AGN, DFS, 100-12-1-73, H.208, L.21, and H.156, L.27. For further background on the context in which Amaya operated, see Aguayo, *La charola*, 216–23. For some anonymous but revealing reflections by government officials on systemic military corruption stretching back to the 1960s at least, see Pimentel, "The Nexus of Organized Crime and Politics."

138. López de Nava, *Mis hechos de campaña*, 162–69; Garduño Valero, "El ejército mexicano," 100, 106n11. On García Barragán's remarkable political rehabilitation, see Navarro, *Political Intelligence*, 252.

139. Bateman to Foreign Office, February 14, 1944, NA, FO 371/38312, AN798, 37; Mraz, *Looking for Mexico*, 201–50.

140. Memo, Presidential Secretary, March 14, 1953, AGN, ARC, 555/1.

141. LaFrance, *Revolution in Mexico's Heartland*, 59–114.

142. Pansters, *Power and Politics in Puebla*, 39–47; Tobler, "Las paradojas," 65–66; Almada, *Con mi cobija al hombro*, 201–3. For a detailed discussion of Puebla's autonomous and entrepreneurial commanders in the 1920s and early 1930s, see LaFrance, "The Military as Political Actor."

143. Various correspondence, AHSDN, X/111/1-8 (Maximino Ávila Camacho) September–October 1929, 514–40. For more detail on Maximino Ávila Camacho's career, see Alejandro Quintana, *Maximino Ávila Camacho and the One-party State*.

144. MA to G-2, March 19, 1935, USMIR, reel 6, 188.

145. Cummings to G-2, December 8, 1931, USMIR, reel 2, 812; various correspondence, September 1935, AHSDN, X/111/1-330 (Sánchez Cano), 945–50; Pansters, *Power and Politics in Puebla*, 47–77.

146. "Gran Centro Político, formado por miembros del PNR," Puebla, to H. Congreso de la Unión, DF, May 1935, AHSDN, X/111/1-8 (Maximino Ávila Camacho), 1218.

147. Pansters, *Power and Politics in Puebla*, 47–77; Vaughan, *Cultural Politics in Revolution*, 72–76; Inspector PS-2 to Gobernación, July 8, 1938, and unsigned report from Teziutlán, AGN, DGIPS, caja 140, exp. 3, 18–21.

148. Inspector PS-2 to DGIPS, July 11, 1938, AGN, DGIPS, caja 140, exp. 3.

149. "Group of peasants, organized workers, agraristas from Patlanalan, Quimixtlán, Puebla," Coatepec, Veracruz, to Manuel Ávila Camacho, January 19, 1941, AGN, MAC, 551.1/3; Gregorio Flores, Comité de Frente Único de Lucha por la Tierra, San Pablo Xochimihuacán, San Pablo del Monte, Puebla, to President Cárdenas, March 18, 1935, AHSDN, X/111/1-8 (Maximino Ávila Camacho) 1211; Crider, "Material Struggles," 228–37; Pansters, *Power and Politics in Puebla*, 50; unsigned report on visit to Xiutetelco, Teziutlán, to Gobernación, 1938, AGN, DGIPS, caja 140, exp. 3, 18–21.

150. Manjarrez, *Puebla*, 135.

151. Bravo Izquierdo, *Soldado del pueblo*, 318.

152. Sergeant Andrés Ros, Teziutlán, Puebla, to President Cárdenas, May 1, 1936, AHSDN, X/111/1-330 (Sánchez Cano), 1081.

153. Márquez Carillo, *Tiempo y su sombra*, 83–84.

154. *Puebla en marcha*, August 1939; Romano Moreno, *Anecdotario estudiantil*, 1:180–81, 197–98.

155. *Puebla en marcha*, May 1940. For images of the club marching through Puebla's streets in uniforms very similar to those used by army officers, see *Puebla en marcha*, March 1940.

156. Author's calculation, based on Camp, *Mexican Political Biographies*; *Diario de los Debates*.

157. Report on Nava Castillo, October 6, 1943, NARA, MIDRF, box 2553, file "Sept.–Oct."

158. Report of Ernesto Colín Enríquez, January 25, 1956, AGN, DFS, "Versiones Públicas: Antonio Nava Castillo," 1; "Extracto de Antecedentes" and Leyva Mancilla to Director General de Personal, January 17, 1957, AHSDN, XI/111/2-1249. I discuss officers' activities in municipal and university posts in chapter 5.

159. First Cavalry Captain José Nuñez Valdez, Atencingo, Puebla, to Manuel Ávila Camacho, June 14, 1942, Fidencio Morales and thirty other signatures, Calmeca, Puebla, to Captain José Nuñez Valdez, Atencingo, June 10, 1942, and Governor Gonzalo Bautista, Gustavo Díaz Ordaz, Puebla, to Manuel Ávila Camacho, July 6, 1942, all in AGN, MAC, 542.1/137, caja 684.

160. General Anacleto López Morales, 11 Jefatura de Operaciones Militares, "Certificado de servicio y hechos de armas del General de Brigada Maximino Ávila Camacho," November 16, 1931, AHSDN X/111/1-8 (Maximino Ávila Camacho), 744–49.

161. *Excélsior*, October 14, 1936; "Press Bulletin," October 15, 1936, in AHSDN, X/111/1-16 (López Morales), 954.

162. Roberto Barrios, CNC, to Defensa Nacional, October 3, 1947, AHSDN, XI/111/2-4444 (Álvarez Villaseñor); various correspondence, Tochtepec, Puebla, to Defensa Nacional, in AHSDN, X/111/1-435 (Ochoa Moreno) 1944–45; Francisco Escobedo, Juan F. Martínez, Macedonio M. Reyes, José Arroya, Mecapalapa, Puebla, to Ruiz Cortines, June 10, 1957, AGN, ARC, 710.1/1152; *Excélsior*, April 27, 1949.

163. Mottier, "Drug Gangs and Politics in Ciudad Juárez"; Wasserman, *Persistent Oligarchs*, 56–67.

164. Santos, *Memorias*, 583, 663; "Extracto de Antecedentes," March 20, 1967, and General Arnulfo González Medina, Justicia y Pensiones, Defensa Nacional, to Secretaria del Ramo, AHSDN, XI/111/1-403 (Quevedo Moreno), 104–6.

165. Romano Moreno, *Anecdotario estudiantil*, 1:197–98.

166. "Extracto de Antecedentes," AHSDN, 1-444 (Tapia Freyding); various correspondence, José María Tapia to Gobernación, 1943-4, AGN, DGIPS, caja 74, exp. 7; MA to G-2, January 11, 1944, NARA, MIDRF, box 2555, file "Jan.–Feb."

167. MA to G-2, July 12, 1927, USMIR, reel 6, 119.

168. Henderson, *The Worm in the Wheat*, 215–16; MA to G-2, November 13, 1931, USMIR, reel 8, 118.

169. Bravo to Defensa Nacional, March 22, 1940, Bravo to President Cárdenas, November 21, 1938, and Bravo to Defensa Nacional, February 13, 1939, AHSDN, XI/111/1-555 (Bravo Izquierdo) 1104–34.

170. "Extracto de Antecedentes," AHSDN, X/111/1-330 (Sánchez Cano); Gillingham, "Maximino's Bulls," 183.

171. Delegado RVS, Puebla, November 4, 1949, AGN, DGIPS, caja 801, exp. 8.

172. "Extracto de Antecedentes" and report by General Bravo, Puebla, to Defensa Nacional, June 14, 1947, AHSDN, X-2/III/456 (Demetrio Barrios Cabrera), 696. I discuss the career of Colonel Maximiliano Ochoa in chapter 5.

173. Cavalry Colonel Ricardo Jiménez Nava, 8 Cuerpo Guardia Regional, Villa Cuauhtémoc, Veracruz, to Manuel Ávila Camacho, June 29, 1944, AGN, MAC, 556.2/120, caja 866; various correspondence, 1944–46, AGN, MAC, 556.2/120, caja 866.

174. Embassy to SD, August 4, 1947, IAMSD, 812.00/8-147; Romano Moreno, *Anecdotario estudiantil*, 1:100–102; J.S.T., Puebla, to DGIPS, January 17, 1946, AGN, DGIPS, caja 87, exp. 1. Betancourt had been Maximino Ávila Camacho's undersecretary in the Department of Communications and Public Works. Peral, *El pelelismo en México*, 110–11.

175. Peral, *El pelelismo en México*, 83–84; José Martínez Castro, Puebla, Puebla, to Alemán, October 13, 1949, MAV, AGN, 544.4/20, caja 559; J.N.M. report, December 18, 1950, AGN, DGIPS, caja 805, exp. 1.

176. Gen. Div. Bravo Izquierdo, Puebla, to Alemán, March 16, 1948, MAV, AGN, 556.2/75.

177. Various correspondence, April 1950, AGN, MAV, 404.1/275, caja 217; report by M.A.O., DF, September 23, 1950, AGN, DGIPS, caja 801, exp. 8; Servín, *Ruptura y oposición*, 197n53.

178. Pansters, *Power and Politics in Puebla*, 51; "Mexico: The President's Other Brother," *Time*, April 14, 1941; Niblo, *Mexico in the 1940s*, 288.

179. José Narvaez Cano, Secretario General de Gobierno, Puebla, to Alemán, December 21, 1946, transcribing reports from Municipal President of Tlalchichuca, October 25 and December 18, 1946, AGN, MAV, 542.1/43; Report on Teziutlán, 1965, AGN, DGIPS, caja 431, exp. 14.

180. Embassy to SD, November 10, 1949, IAMSD, 812.00/11-1049. On cadets' responses to Rafael Ávila Camacho, see Beltrán González, *Mejores anecdotas del H. Colegio Militar*, 104–6.

181. Delegado RVS, Puebla, November 4, 1949, AGN, DGIPS, caja 801, exp. 8; Ronfeldt, *Atencingo*, 105–44; Pansters, *Power and Politics in Puebla*, 101.

182. Florencio Vega Aburto, Sec. Gen. Coalición de Obreros y Campesinos del Puebla, Puebla, to Ruiz Cortines, May 9, 1954; Octaviano Luján y otros, Teziutlán, Puebla, to ARC, October 29, 1957, AGN, ARC, 542.1/436, caja 800; Francisco Escobedo, Juan F. Martínez, Macedonio M. Reyes, José Arroya, Mecapalapa, Puebla, to Ruiz Cortines, June 10, 1957, AGN, ARC, 710.1/1152.

183. Ramos to Ruiz Cortines, 1953, AGN, ARC, 550/2.

Chapter 5

1. MA to G-2, September 19, 1941, extract copy, NARA, MIDRF, box 2516, file 6760; MA to G-2, March 13, 1943, NARA, MIDRF, box 2552, file "March–April"; Assistant MA to G-2, January 15, 1944, NARA, MIDRF, box 2554, file "Jan.–Feb."

2. MA to G-2, December 18, 1942, NARA, MIDRF, box 2552, file "Nov.–Dec."

3. Bravo Izquierdo, *Soldado del pueblo*, 312.

4. MA to G-2, May 22, 1944, NARA, MIDRF, box 2553, file "May–June."

5. "The Mexican Army," 1954, NA, FO 371/109037; General Franciso L. Urquizo, "Plan de Re-organización del Ejército," July 1952, in CESU, FFU, caja 8, exp. 10; Geraldo, *Sobre las armas*.

6. "The Mexican Army," 1954, NA, FO 371/109037; "The Mexican Army," 1955, NA, FO 371/97547.

7. Geraldo, *Sobre las armas*, iv.

8. Taylor to Foreign Office, April 10, 1952, NA, FO 371/97540, 12; "The Mexican Army," 1954, NA, FO 371/109037.

9. Author's calculation based on Estado Mayor, Defensa Nacional, "Estadística de prestaciones sociales que el ejército ha dado a otras dependencias oficiales y a elementos civiles del país, durante el año 1952," AGN, ARC, 550/24, caja 920, 11–12; Memo to Defensa Nacional, 1953, AGN, ARC, 550/24, caja 920. This report also noted that the army posted 730 troops in smaller "detachments" but did not provide a total number of units. AGN, ARC, 550/24.

10. Personnel tables in AGN, MAV, 550/19 and 298/22349.

11. Del Villar, *Where the Strange Roads Go Down*, 61–62; Army general staff, "Informe relativo a la impartición de garantias," January 9, 1954, AGN, SDN, caja 3, exp. 0010.

12. Tanalís Padilla, *Rural Resistance*; Greenberg, *Blood Ties*.

13. Army general staff, "Informe relativo a la impartición de garantias," January 9, 1954, AGN, SDN, caja 3, exp. 0010, 8.

14. Parra Mora, Javier, and Hernández Díaz, *Violencia y cambio social*, 139–54; introduction in Gillingham and Smith, *Soft Authoritarianism in Mexico*.

15. Army general staff, "Informe relativo a la impartición de garantias," January 9, 1954, AGN, SDN, caja 3, exp. 0010, 8.

16. Report by "I.P.S. 4," August 24, 1955, AGN, DGIPS, caja 2014-B, exp. 31; Robertson Sierra, "La casa de nuestra cultura."

17. Servín, "Reclaiming Revolution."

18. "I.P.S. 4" and "I.P.S. 9," DF, August 24, 1955, AGN, DGIPS, caja 2014-B, exp. 31.

19. Smith, *Pistoleros and Popular Movements*, 412.

20. MA to G-2, March 1, 1943, NARA, MIDRF, box 2552, file "March–April"; Gillingham, "Force and Consent"; Smith, *Pistoleros and Popular Movements*, 405.

21. *Memorias de la Secretaría de la Defensa Nacional*, September 1941–August 1942, 170. For examples of the mediation of agrarian conflict, see "Estudio relacionado con el funcionamiento de las defensas rurales," Colonel Toribio Beltrán Pulido, Tlaxcala, 1944, to Manuel Ávila Camacho, AGN, MAC, 550/24; Ricardo Trujillo Quirós, Inspector P.S. 12, DF, February 16, 1945, AGN, DGIPS, caja 788, exp. 5; Open Letter to the President of the Republic (175 Signatures), San Hipólito Soltepec, Puebla, April 15, 1950, AGN, MAV 404.1/275, caja 217, MAV.

22. Gillingham, "Force and Consent," xiii. See also Aguayo *La charola*, 8–80.

23. State governors' expansion of state police and judicial systems is a crucial but underresearched topic. Gillingham finds a clear strengthening of civilian agencies in Veracruz by the late 1940s, but a less clear trend in Guerrero. Gillingham, "Force and Consent."

24. Boils, *Los militares y la política*, 82; Alegre, "Contesting the Mexican Miracle," 248–50.

25. MA Report on DF Police, May 4, 1944, NARA, MIDRF, box 2553, file "May–June"; B. Muse, "Memorandum: Observations on Visit to Mexico," to G-2, March 31, 1943, NARA, MIDRF, box 2534, file "March–April." For a discussion of corruption and impunity in the DF police, see Davis, "The Political and Economic Origins."

26. MA to G-2, September 17, 1943, NARA, MIDRF, box 2553, file "Sept.–Dec."; Taracena, *La vida en México*, 2:107; Geraldo, *Sobre las armas*, 121–22.

27. Del Villar, *Where the Strange Roads Go Down*, 41.

28. Inspector Jesús González Valencia and Fernando López Portillo, DF, November 20, 1948, AGN, DGIPS, caja 18, exp. 6.

29. Jean Meyer, *La Cristiada*, 269; personnel tables in AGN, MAV, 550/19 and 298/22349; Santos, *Memorias*, 447; Flores Arellano and Wences Román, *María de la O*, 68–70; Anituy Rebolledo Ayerdi, "Trotsky Nunca Estuvo en Acapulco," *El Sur Acapulco*, September 22, 2005, el-suracapulco.com.mx/anterior/2005/septiembre/22/pag2.htm (accessed March 8, 2010).

30. Geraldo, *Sobre las armas*, 47.

31. Consuelo Lizárraga, "Gente Mazatlán, Eusebio Olalde Hernández: Un hombre íntegro," *Periódico Noroeste*, May 14, 2008, http://www.noroeste.com.mx/movil/index.php?id=11&id2=&txt1=GENTE&txt2=MAZATL%C3%81N&id_pub=375822 (accessed June 20, 2008); Delegado 36, Culiacán, Sinaloa, to DGIPS, May 27, 1950, AGN, DGIPS, caja 803, exp. 2.

32. Geraldo, *Sobre las armas*, 1–22, 101–2; Ríos Thivol, Senguio, Michoacán, September 4, 1947, AGN, DGIPS, caja 84, exp. 1.

33. Ronfeldt, *Atencingo*, 33–104.

34. Crider, "Material Struggles," 2. On the 1940s, see Gauss, "Working-Class Masculinity."

35. Vaughan, *Cultural Politics in Revolution*, 100–102; Bautista, *El esfuerzo de los poblanos*.

36. Pansters, *Power and Politics in Puebla*, 77–100. On the failure of Puebla's textile manufacturers to improve technology, see Gauss, *Made in Mexico*, 131–68.

37. Román Pérez, Comisario Ejidal, Ejido del Maíz, Coazintla, Veracruz, to Alemán, June 2, 1947, AGN, DGIPS, caja 16, exp. 31; Liga Nacional Campesina "Ursulo Galván," "Folleto Numero 1: Sobre el caso ejidal de Palma Sola, Ver.," AGN, DGIPS, caja 16, exp. 31; Santos, *Memorias*, 719; Geraldo, *Sobre las armas*, 107–15.

38. Márquez Carillo, *Tiempo y su sombra*, 105–6; Ronfeldt, *Atencingo*, 49, 130–31; Barbosa Cano, *La CROM*, 68; Romano Moreno, *Anecdotario estudiantil*, 1:201–2; various reports, January–May 1949, AGN, DGIPS, caja 801, exp. 2-1/49/496 "Puebla 1949." For Coca and Jaramillo, see also Cárdenas, *Apuntes*, 468, 765.

39. Military personnel tables in AGN, MAC, 606.3/91, and MAV 298/22349, and 550/19; tables on military and police deployments, 1966–7, Mayor Salvador More Garrido, 25 military zone, Puebla, Puebla, January 7, 1967, AGN, SDN, caja 166, exp. 0544.

40. Military personnel tables in AGN, MAC, 606.3/91, and MAV 298/22349 and 550/19; Bravo Izquierdo, *Soldado del pueblo*, 316–19, 321–22; Bautista, *El esfuerzo de los poblanos*, 44.

41. Tables on military and police deployments, 1966–67, Mayor Salvador More Garrido, 25 military zone, Puebla, Puebla, January 7, 1967, AGN, SDN, caja 166, exp. 0544.

42. Fernando Ruiz, Sección 77, Sindicato de Trabajadores de la Industria Azucarera y Similares de la República Mexicana, Atencingo, to Gobernación, Puebla, November 8, 1947, AGN, MAV, 432.2/3; various correspondence, December 1953–May 1954, Coalición de Obreros y Campesinos de Puebla, Puebla, to Ruiz Cortines, AGN, ARC, 542.1/436, caja 800.

43. Various correspondence, Xicotepec to Manuel Ávila Camacho, Jan.–July 1943, AGN, MAC, 544.4/44.

44. G. Ray, U.S. Embassy, to SD, with four enclosed pamphlets, January 13, 1943, NARA, MIDRF, box 2512, file "recruitment"; various correspondence, Pres. Municipal, Villa Juárez, to Manuel Ávila Camacho, March–July 1943, AGN, MAC, 50/444; Ignacio Martínez, Juzgado de Defensa Social, Chiautla, Puebla, to Alemán, January 19, 1948, AGN, MAV, 542.1/526.

45. Various reports, January–May 1949, AGN, DGIPS, caja 801, exp. 2-1/49/496 "Puebla 1949." The *aftosa* campaign is the subject of an ongoing research project by the author.

46. Blas Chumacero, DF, to Manuel Ávila Camacho, August 14, 1943, AGN, MAC, 432/553.

47. Various reports, January–May 1949, AGN, DGIPS, caja 801, exp. 2-1/49/496 "Puebla 1949."

48. Communidad de Tlalchichuca (approximately 400 signatures), Puebla, to Alemán, April 18, 1948, Betancourt to Alemán, June 22, 1948, and Representante de Quimixtlán, Puebla, to Alemán, April 18, 1948, AGN, MAV, 542.1/43.

49. Geraldo, *Sobre las armas*, 101–2.

50. Intercept of L. Carvajal, Comité Sinarquista, Tehuacán, Puebla, to Manuel Torres Bueno, DF, February 2, 1943, AGN, DGIPS, caja 744, exp. 2-1/43/210 "Puebla." The commander in question was probably General Arturo Campillo Seyde. Personnel tables, 1943, AGN, MAC, 606.3/91.

51. Crider, "Material Struggles," 277; Pedro Armas, Isaac Pedraza, FTP-CTM, Puebla, Puebla, to Manuel Ávila Camacho, July 23, 1943, AGN, MAC, 432/553; various correspondence from Captain Ozuna Rojas, Head of Consejo Municipal, Atlixco, to Col. Ochoa Moreno, Cavalry Commander, Atlixco, 1945, AHSDN, X/111/1-435 (Ochoa Moreno); Confed. Campesina Puebla "General Miguel Alemán," to Alemán, July 11, 1949, AGN, MAV, 542.1/947, caja 543; various correspondence, 1948–50, AHSDN, XI/111/2-1392 (Martínez Cairo); Romano Moreno, *Anecdotario estudiantil*, 1:294–95.

52. *Séptimo censo general de población.*

53. See reported comments of Captain Ozuna Rojas, head of Tehuacán's municipal council, in Pedro Armas, Isaac Pedraza, FTP-CTM, Puebla, Puebla, to Manuel Ávila Camacho, July 23, 1943, AGN, MAC, 432/553.

54. Faustino Casarez Canongo, Presidente Municipal Provisional, Huehuetlán El Chico, Puebla, to Manuel Ávila Camacho, March 27, 1943, AGN, MAC, 541/757, caja 673. For similar tactics used to "exterminate" armed groups around Teziutlán in the late 1930s, including the systematic burning of peasant homes, see Inspector Gustavo Pérez Aldama, Teziutlán, to Gobernación, September 1, 1938, AGN, DGIPS, caja 140, exp. 3. These tactics echoed those of the CROM's gunmen around Atlixco in the mid-1930s. Crider, "Material Struggles," 371–77.

55. Author's calculation based on 113 complaints collected from AGN: MAC, MAV, ARC, DGG, DGIPS. I have not included in this calculation the five members of the municipal council of Honey who were killed in 1946 because I could not find a military record for the officer accused of killing them, one Lieutenant Gayosso Téllez. For some complaints that Gayosso was but one of several well-known *pistoleros* sporting military titles protected by infantry commander General Demetrio Barrios, see Herón Animas Pérez, Tulancingo, Hidalgo, to Alemán, July 14, 1947, and Lucio Cruz Gómez, Honey, to Alemán, August 16, 1947, in AGN, MAV, 541/214, caja 528.

56. McCormick, "The Political Economy of Desire," 204–59; Ronfeldt, *Atencingo*, 130–31; Ravelo Lecuona, *Los jaramillistas*, 121–23.

57. Rafael Ávila Camacho, Puebla, to Ruiz Cortines, July 7, 1953, AGN, ARC, 556.4/12, caja 932.

58. Author's calculation based on ninety-two petitions collected from AGN: MAC, MAV, ARC, DGG, DGIPS. The remaining petitions concerned local elections (5 percent); disarmament (2 percent); union disputes (1 percent); defense of officers' reputations from public criticism (4 percent). In 22 percent of cases, I was unable to find sufficient additional information that would permit a definitive categorization of the context for the petition.

59. The remainder were sent by *ejidal* authorities (16 percent), CNC-affiliated peasant groups (8 percent), independent peasant groups (5 percent), CTM-affiliated unions (5 percent), members of the militia (2 percent), the state government (1 percent), unions not affiliated with the CTM (1 percent).

60. Secretaría de Gobernación, Puebla, to Comandante de la 25/a Zona Militar, May 21, 1947, transcribing Juez de Paz, and Presidente Municipal, Canoas Altas, Ciudad Serdán, to Alemán, April 28, 1947, AGN, MAV, 404.1/1122, caja 226. See also Report by General Bravo, Puebla, to Defensa Nacional, June 14, 1947, AHSDN, X-2/III/456 (Demetrio Barrios Cabrera), 696; Col. Nava Castillo, Atlixco, Puebla, to Defensa Nacional, July 23, 1949, AHSDN, XI/III/2-1392 (Martínez Cairo), 1398; Bernardo Chávez, Secretario General de Gobierno, Puebla, to Alemán, January 11, 1946, transcribing report by Presidente Municipal de Tlalchichuca, December 8, 1945, AGN, MAV, 542.1/43; Antonio J. Hernández, Matamoros, Puebla, to Alemán, July 3, 1949; and Dip. Fed. Agustín Pérez Caballero, DF, to Alemán, August 25, 1949, AGN, MAV, 544.4/20.

61. Delegado RVS, Acatlán, November 15, 1949, AGN, DGIPS, caja 801, exp. 2-1/49/496 "Puebla 1949."

62. Geraldo, *Sobre las armas*, 190–248.

63. Gayosso Ríos, *Mi palabra*, 110–14.

64. Requests from the Atencingo *ejidatarios* and the National Sugar Workers Union for military protection from the CROM and local pistoleros can be found in various correspondence, July 1948–May 1949, MAV 432.2/3, caja 309. For complaints about harassment and intimidation by the federal army units stationed at Atencingo in the 1950s, see McCormick, "The Political Economy of Desire," 204–59.

65. Vecinos de Yagostura, Hueytamalco, Ex-distrito Teziutlán, Puebla, to Ruiz Cortines (date illegible); Jacinto López, Lázaro Rubio Félix, UGOCM, DF, to Ruiz Cortines, May 27, 1954, AGN, ARC, 542.1/436.

66. Nickel, "Agricultural Laborers in the Mexican Revolution."

67. This narrative of the dispute is taken from Ing. Juan Hernández, Cámara Agrícola y Ganadera de Puebla y Tlaxcala, Puebla, to Manuel Ávila Camacho, December 28, 1944, AGN, MAC, 404.1/275; Comisariado Ejidal, San Hipólito Soltepec, Puebla, to Manuel Ávila Camacho, January 11, 1944, AGN, MAV, 404.1/1813; Rafael Galicia, Pres. Consejo Ejidal, San Hipólito Soltepec, to Manuel Ávila Camacho, September 15, 1941, and various correspondence, Liga Central de Comunidades Agrarias de la República, DF to MAC, January–February, 1944, AGN, MAV, 404.1/275, caja 217; *Diario Official*, July 24, 1937, 2–5.

68. Open Letter to the President of the Republic (175 signatures), San Hipólito Soltepec, Puebla, April 15, 1950, AGN, MAV 404.1/275, caja 217.

69. Ibid.

70. Various correspondence, Cámara Agrícola, Puebla, to Alemán, 1950, AGN, MAV 404.1/275, caja 217.

71. *La Opinión*, March 5, 1935; *El Universal*, June 30, 1935.

72. Valencia Castrejón, *Poder regional*, 75.

73. Romano Moreno, *Anecdotario estudiantil*, 1:311.

74. *El Universal*, April 28, 1939.

75. Ronfeldt, *Atencingo*, 260n78.

76. Modesto M. Gutiérrez, Secretary General, Confederación Campesina Miguel Alemán, Puebla, to Commandante de la 25/a Zona Militar, July 1949, AGN, MAV, 542.1/952, caja 543. For a similar case of reticence from the zone command, see José Narváez Cano, Secretario General de Gobierno, Puebla, to Presidente Municipal, Cuapiaxtla, Puebla, November 12, 1947, transcribing complaint from "Lázaro Cárdenas," Valsequillo, Puebla, to Alemán, October 29, 1947, AGN, MAV, 544.4/20.

77. Barbosa Cano, *La CROM*, 441–50.

78. María Gregoria, Mazacoatlán, Puebla, to Manuel Ávila Camacho, July 17, 1942, AGN, MAC, 556.63/90. For similar arguments about the need for military policing to be authorized by civilian authorities, see Liga Central de Comunidades Agrarias de la República, DF, to Alemán, July 22, 1948; and Cecilio Pérez, Comisariado Ejidal, Soltepec, Puebla, to Alemán, July 21, 1948, AGN, MAV, 404.1/275.

79. Author's calculation based on 113 complaints collected from AGN: MAC, MAV, ARC, DGG, DGIPS. Four percent of complaints concerned disarmament. In a number of cases, however, complaints just spoke vaguely of abuses or *atropellos* either permitted or inflicted by soldiers, and I was unable to find sufficient additional information that would permit a more detailed categorization (21 percent). Judging by

the military file of Colonel Maximiliano Ochoa, the low number of complaints about extortion and larceny in the AGN may be because people tended to send these kinds of complaints directly to the army. Ochoa's file contains seven such complaints from Puebla between 1940 and 1946. AHSDN, X/III/1-435 (Ochoa Moreno).

80. Comunidad de Tlalchichuca (approximately 400 signatures), to Alemán, April 18, 1948, and Representante de Quimixtlan, Puebla, to Alemán, April 18, 1948, AGN, MAV, 542.1/43; Confederación Campesina Miguel Alemán, Puebla, Puebla, to Ruiz Cortines, and Gen. Rafael Ávila Camacho, Puebla to Ruiz Cortines, February 20, 1953, AGN, ARC, 556.4/2.

81. Franco G. Melgar, Fidel Cabrera Santos, Yolanda Carballo Vda. de Plañez, Wulfrano Mansillo, and Jovita Mérida Vda. de Encarnación, Tlacuilotepec, Puebla, to Alemán and Defensa Nacional, X-2/III/456 (Barrios Cabrera), 678–80. On the Barrios brothers' conflicts with mestizos while commanders in the Sierra Norte de Puebla in the 1920s, see Brewster, *Militarism, Ethnicity and Politics*.

82. Various correspondence, Liga Central de Comunidades Agrarias de la República, DF, to Manuel Ávila Camacho, January–February, 1944, AGN, MAV, 404.1/275, caja 217.

83. Author's calculation based on database of 113 complaints collected from AGN: MAC, MAV, ARC, DGIPS, DGG.

84. Margarito P. Villanueva y demás, Comité Ejecutivo Agrario, San Francisco Tzompahuacán, Chietla, Puebla, to Ruiz Cortines, January 3, 1957, AGN, ARC, 404.1/6268, caja 356; Uvaldo Ramos and Jesús Quiroz, Huauchinango, Puebla, to Defensa Nacional, June 11, 1942, AHSDN, X/III/1-435 (Ochoa Moreno), 972.

85. Vecinos, Cuautilulco, Zacatlán, to Manuel Ávila Camacho, December 14, 1942, AGN, MAC, 542.2/368, caja 702.

86. Ing. Rubén Ortiz, Puebla, Puebla, to Manuel Ávila Camacho, June 8, 1945, AGN, MAC, 556.64/689, caja 880.

87. Pansters, *Power and Politics in Puebla*, 98–101; Manjarrez, *Puebla: el rostro olvidado*, 97–168. For complaints about military officers illegally taking land from a political outsider, see Miguel Almazán, Puebla, Puebla, to Manuel Ávila Camacho, April 10, 1946, AGN, MAC, 404.1/1696.

88. For example, see Ing. Juan Hernández, Cámara Agrícola y Ganadera de Puebla y Tlaxcala, Puebla, to Manuel Ávila Camacho, December 28, 1944, AGN, MAC, 404.1/275. See also comments transcribed in General de Brigada DEM, Jefe EM, Alberto Violante Pérez, DF, to Oficial Mayor, Presidencia de la República, DF, July 6, 1953, AGN, ARC, 404.1/1016, caja 299.

89. Estado Mayor del Secretario, Defensa Nacional, to State Governor, Puebla, August 24, 1942, transcribing report by General Brigadier Constantino Rivera Díaz, Comandante de la 28 Regimiento de Caballería, Colima, August 8, 1942, AGN, MAC, 542.1/137; Report by 25 Military Zone, Puebla, to Manuel Ávila Camacho, May 1945, AGN, MAC, 432/553, caja 403; Col. Nava Castillo, Atlixco, Puebla, to Defensa Nacional, July 23, 1949, AHSDN, XI/III/2-1392 (Martínez Cairo), 1398; Report by General Bravo, Puebla, to Defensa Nacional, June 14, 1947, AHSDN, X-2/III/456, 696; Gen. Div. Jefe EM Tomás Sánchez Hernández, Defensa Nacional, to Ruiz Cortines, May 11, 1956, AGN, ARC, 556.63/115, caja 945.

90. Gunther, *Inside Latin America*, 48; various correspondence, MA to G-2, October–November 1938, USMIR, reel 2, 136–47; XA-1, Report, August 26, 1955, AHSDN, X/lll/1-435 (Ochoa Moreno), leg. 13, 161.

91. Niblo, *Mexico in the 1940s*, 107; "Extracto de Antecedentes," AHSDN, X/lll/1-435 (Ochoa Moreno).

92. Nava Castillo to Manuel Ávila Camacho, 1942, AGN, MAC, 556.63/90; Lindoro Hernández to Defensa Nacional, July 17, 1942, in AHSDN, X/lll/1-435 (Ochoa Moreno); Moisés Vergara, Huauchinango, September 14, 1942, AHSDN, X/lll/1-435 (Ochoa Moreno), 631.

93. Lindoro Hernández to Manuel Ávila Camacho, July 17, 1942, in AHSDN, X/lll/1-435 (Ochoa Moreno).

94. Various correspondence, 1942–43, AGN, MAC, 556.63/90.

95. General Anacleto López Morales, 25 Military Zone, Puebla, to Defensa Nacional, December 14, 1945, AHSDN, X/lll/1-435 (Ochoa Moreno), 1348.

96. Various correspondence, February–August 1945, in AHSDN, X/lll/1-435 (Ochoa Moreno), 1235–40; Barbosa Cano, *La CROM*, 87; Juana de la Rosa Hernández, San Miguel Tecuanipa, Puebla, to Manuel Ávila Camacho, May 30, 1946, AGN, MAC, 556.63/13.

97. Juana de la Rosa Hernández, San Miguel Tecuanipa, Puebla, to Manuel Ávila Camacho, May 30, 1946, AGN, MAC, 556.63/13.

98. Manuel Villa, Comisariado Ejidal, Tochimilco, Puebla, to Defensa Nacional, January 7, 1946, AHSDN, X/lll/1-435 (Ochoa Moreno), 1361.

99. "Extracto de antecedentes," AHSDN, X/lll/1-435 (Ochoa Moreno); Parra, Javier, and Hernández Díaz, *Violencia y cambio social*, 139–54.

100. Report for Inter-Secretarial Commision by Ing. Joaquín de Zayas Coto, Mayor Manuel Olguín Serrano, and Lic. Jesús Cárdenas Martínez, November 24, 1949, AGN, MAV, 432.2/3.

101. See Porfirio Jaramillo, Sociedad Cooperativa Ejidal de Atencingo y Anexas, Puebla, to Alemán, February 6, 1950, AGN, MAV, 432.2/3; Ronfeldt, *Atencingo*, 67–105.

102. Hermenegildo J. Aldana, Secretary General, Sindicato Nacional Azucarero, Atencingo via Chietla, to Alemán, December 29, 1947, and Fernando Ruiz, Sección 77, Sindicato de Trabajadores de la Industria Azucarera y Similares de la República Mexicana, Atencingo, to Gobernación, Puebla, November 8, 1947, AGN, MAV, 432.2/3. On union control of municipal offices in the 1930s, see Crider, "Material Struggles," 172–74, 348.

103. "Lista de los Pre-Candidatos a Diputados," August 1947, and Ramón Mentado, Pres. Com. Distrital Pro-Viveros Muñive, Izúcar de Matamoros, Puebla, to Alemán, April 12, 1949, AGN, MAV, 544.4/20.

104. Various correspondence, June 1948–December 1951, AHSDN, XI/lll/2-1392 (Martínez Cairo), 1333–98; Peral, *El pelelismo*, 145–76.

105. Col. Nava Castillo, Atlixco, Puebla, to Defensa Nacional, July 23, 1949, AHSDN, XI/lll/2-1392 (Martínez Cairo), 1398.

106. Juan Caccia Bernal, DF, July 31, 1950, AGN, DGIPS, caja 801, exp. 8.

107. Peral, *El pelelismo*, 145–76.

108. Various reports, February 1950, AGN, DGIPS, caja 801, exp. 2–1/49/496 "Puebla 1949."

109. Manuel Gómez Torres y demás, "Unión Matamorense," Matamoros, Puebla, to General Gilberto R. Limón, Defensa Nacional, June 26, 1948, AHSDN, XI/111/2-1392 (Martínez Cairo), 1390.

110. Hermenegildo Mijares, M. González, and R. Camaño, Matamoros, Puebla, to Defensa Nacional, February 23, 1949, AHSDN, XI/111/2-1392 (Martínez Cairo), 1394.

111. "La Legalidad del Despotismo," April 20, 1949, pamphlet reproduced in Peral, *El pelelismo*, 173.

112. *El Sol de Puebla*, May 5, 1949. On Jenkins, see Paxman, "William Jenkins."

113. Peral, *El pelelismo*, 160–61, 166.

114. Márquez Carillo, *Tiempo y su sombra*, 78, 90; electoral reports, April 1947, AGN, MAV, 544.4/20.

115. Reproduced in Peral, *El pelelismo*, 151.

116. Arnulfo Pérez and six co-signatures, Matamoros, Puebla, to Defensa Nacional, September 8, 1951, AHSDN, XI/111/2-1392 (Martínez Cairo), 1390.

117. Taracena, *La vida en México*, 2:232; General de Brigada Comandante José Heredia Aceves, 25 Zona Militar, Puebla, to Estado Mayor, Defensa Nacional, May 1948, AHSDN, XI/111/2-1392 (Martínez Cairo), 1424.

118. Pamphlets "Abofeteando a un Cínico," April 30, 1949, and "La Legalidad del Despotismo," April 20, 1949, reproduced in Peral, *El pelelismo*, 173. Neither Martínez Cairo's army file nor intelligence reports provide any information on the colonel's claim to have been a member of the Presidential Guard.

119. *El Universal*, October 21, 1950.

120. *El Sol de Puebla*, May 5, 1949. The army started to investigate the affair only after this letter was published. SDN, XI/111/2-1392 (Martínez Cairo) 1333.

121. *El Sol de Puebla*, May 5, 1949; "La Legalidad del Despotismo," April 20, 1949, reproduced in Peral, *El pelelismo*, 173.

122. For some examples of complaints elsewhere that used a similar moral tone, see Pedro Armas, Isaac Pedraza, FTP-CTM, Puebla, to Manuel Ávila Camacho, July 23, 1943, AGN, MAC, 432/553; Agustín Moncada, Reynaldo Gutiérrez, and Guadalupe Vivas Calderón, Oriental, Puebla, to Ruiz Cortines, March 20, 1956, AGN, ARC, 556.63/115, caja 945.

123. *El Sol de Puebla*, May 5, 1949.

124. Pamphlet "Abofeteando a un Cínico," April 30, 1949, reproduced in Peral, *El pelelismo*, 173.

125. Various correspondence, February 1949, AHSDN, XI/111/2-1392 (Martínez Cairo), 1400–1.

126. *Últimas Noticias de Excélsior*, October 20, 1950; clipping "Ayuntamiento depuesto por el pueblo amotinado," AGN, DGIPS, caja 801, exp. 8; Peral, *El pelelismo*, 175–76.

127. "Cayó de su pedestal uno de los odiados caciques," *El Sol de Puebla*, October 20, 1950. See also *Jueves de Excélsior*, October 26, 1950; *Últimas Noticias de Excélsior*, October 20, 1950; Peral, *El pelelismo*, 166; Simpson, *Many Mexicos*, 342.

128. *La Prensa*, October 25, 1950.

129. *Últimas Noticias de Excélsior*, October 20, 1950; clipping "Ayuntamiento depuesto por el pueblo amotinado," AGN, DGIPS, caja 801, exp. 8; Peral, *El pelelismo*, 175–76.

130. Vicente Sánchez, Matamoros, n.d., 1950, to Defensa Nacional, AHSDN, XI/III/2-1392 (Martínez Cairo) 1516.

131. Confederación Campesina Miguel Alemán, Puebla, to MAV, July 11, 1949, AGN, MAV, 542.1/947, caja 543.

132. Various correspondence, 1951–52, AHSDN, XI/III/2-1392 (Martínez Cairo) 1544–54; *La Opinión*, October 20, 1950; Ronfeldt, *Atencingo*, 140.

133. See discussion of Colonel Guerrero's tenure as head of the Atencingo complex in Ronfeldt, *Atencingo*, 105–44.

134. Vélez Pliego, "La sucesión," 56–57.

135. Azcué Bilbao, *El movimiento*, 13.

136. Vélez Pliego, "La sucesión," 55; Beltrán González, *Mejores anecdotas del H. Colegio Militar*, 104–6; *Puebla en marcha*, May 1940; various reports, 1949, AGN, DGIPS, caja 104, exp. 1, and caja 801, exp. 2-1/49/496 "Puebla 1949."

137. Silva Andraca, *Puebla y su universidad*, 40–42, 55–56; Azcué Bilbao, *El movimiento*, 14.

138. Azcué Bilbao, *El movimiento*, 14–17; Silva Andraca, *Puebla y su universidad*, 40–42; Rivera Terrazas, *Documentos universitarios*, 67–68.

139. Azcué Bilbao, *El movimiento*, 14.

140. Ibid.

141. Ibid.; Silva Andraca, *Puebla y su universidad*, 90–92.

142. Azcué Bilbao, *El movimiento*, 15.

143. Silva Andraca, *Puebla y su universidad*, 55.

144. Azcué Bilbao, *El movimiento*, 15–16.

145. Vélez Pliego, "La sucesión," 55–59.

146. Gillingham, "Maximino's Bulls," 210.

147. Azcué Bilbao, *El movimiento*, 15–16.

148. Smith, "Inventing Tradition at Gunpoint."

149. Jiménez Castillo, *Huancito*, 155–56; Schryer, "A Ranchero Elite."

Chapter 6

1. *Revista del Ejército y Marina*, cited in Nunn, *The Time of the Generals*, 117.

2. Chambers, "'With His Life He Paid for This Pension'"; Blight, *Race and Reunion*; Mann, *Native Sons*.

3. "Characteristics of the leaders of the Mexican Cavalry," extracted from G-2 files, August 15, 1926, NARA, MIDRF, box 2555, file "5990–6000."

4. *El Sol de Puebla*, May 5, 1949; various correspondence, Martínez to Defensa Nacional, 1960–65, SDN, XI/III/2-1392 (Martínez Cairo).

5. Alan Knight cited in Benjamin, *La Revolución*, 46.

6. Vicente Estrada, quoted in Tobler, "Shaping of the Revolutionary State," 493. On Obregón's 1920 coalition, see Lieuwen, *Mexican Militarism*, 64.

7. Hall, "Álvaro Obregón"; O'Malley, *The Myth of the Revolution*, 41–55; Buchenau, *Plutarco Elías Calles*, xxi.

8. *Diario Oficial*, August 17, 1917; Guzmán Navarro, "Las pensiones militares," 48–49.

9. Various correspondence, Gumersindo Esquer, Navajoa, Sonora, and Obregón, December 1920 to February 1923, AGN, OC, 805-E-4.

10. Obregón to Comisión Investigadora de Pensiones, July 1, 1924, AGN, OC, 805-E-4. On the brothers' military service and ties to Obregón, see Gill, "Los Escudero de Acapulco."

11. Francisca Abundes Viuda de Figueroa, Huitzuco, Guerrero, to Ortiz Rubio, June 15, 1930, AGN, POR, caja 30, exp. 37. See also memo from F. A. Borquez, Secretaría de Hacienda, to Obregón, April 25, 1921; C. S. Urbina, Oficial Mayor de la Sec. Hac. y Crédito Público, to Obregón, June 16, 1921; General Jacinto Pérez Treviño, Piedras Negras, Coahuila, to Obregón, October 13, 1921, AGN, OC, 826-P-1.

12. Treviño, *Memorias*, 45; Plasencia de la Parra, *Historia y organización*, 185.

13. López de Nava Camarena, *Mis hechos de campaña*, III, 127–28.

14. Klingemann, "Triumph of the Vanquished," 133, 144.

15. Guzmán Navarro, "Las pensiones militares," 56.

16. Miller, *In the Shadow of the State*, 215–220; Benjamin, *La Revolución*, 140.

17. Guzmán Navarro, "Las pensiones militares," 56.

18. MA to G-2, January 25, 1927, USMIR, reel 6, 77. For a detailed discussion of disputes over the recognition of military ranks and service in the 1920s, see Plasencia de la Parra, *Historia y organización*, 194–99.

19. Manuela C. Vda. de Espinosa, Cuernavaca, Morelos, to Obregón, December 26, 1921, and June 12, 1922; and Genovevo de la O, cited in Obregón to Espinosa, January 10, 1922, AGN, OC, 826-E-2.

20. General Gavira, Dept. EM, to Amaro, December 14, 1925; and Amaro to Guadalupe Díaz Vda. de Díaz, December 16, 1925, APECFT, FJA, 03/05, leg. 10.

21. Womack, *Zapata*, 180–83.

22. Eulalia Vda. De García, Guayameo, Mina, Guerrero, to Amaro, May 15, 1926, APECFT, FJA, 03/05, leg. 14.

23. Amaro to García, May 31, 1926, APECFT, FJA, 03/05, leg. 14. For background, see Knight, *The Mexican Revolution*, 2:283, 396.

24. Guzmán Navarro, "Las pensiones militares," 55–57.

25. Cano, "Unconcealable Realities of Desire," 43–44.

26. López de Nava Camarena, *Mis hechos de campaña*, 183.

27. Salas suggests that Valentina Ramírez, who fought under Ramón Iturbe from 1917 to 1920, received a pension, but it is not clear when this was granted or on what grounds. Elizabeth Salas, *Soldaderas in the Mexican Military*, 50.

28. Arce Vda. De Pérez, DF, to Obregón, November 9, 1921, AGN, OC, 826-P-1.

29. Concepción P. Vda. de Avalos, Mazatlán, Sinaloa, to Amaro, December 15, 1928, APECFT, FJA, 03/05, leg. 2.

30. Amaro to Matilde Durán Vda. de Garza, León, Guanajuato, January 25, 1925, APECFT, FJA, 03/05, leg. 14.

31. Matilde Durán Vda. de Garza, León, Guanajuato, to Amaro, February 22, 1925, APECFT, FJA, 03/05, leg. 14.

32. Amaro to Matilde Durán Vda. de Garza, León, Guanajuato, February 28, 1925, APECFT, FJA, 03/05, leg. 14.

33. Matilde Durán Vda. de Garza, León, Guanajuato, to Amaro, March 10, 1925, APECFT, FJA, 03/05, leg. 14.

34. Cravioto Leyzaola, *Historia documental*, 3:94.

35. Ibid., 3:218.

36. Casasola, *Historia gráfica*, 3:1564, 1566; *Anales gráficos de la historia militar*, 476; Department of the Treasury project "Veteranos de la Intervención Francesa," March 3, 1922, AGN, OC, 731-P-12; Torrea, *El Asilo del Honor*.

37. Plasencia de la Parra, "Conmemoración de la hazaña épica de los Niños Héroes."

38. Matilde Echeveste, DF, to Obregón, May 10 and July 31, 1923, and Obregón to Echeveste, May 19, 1923; Antonio Esquivel, DF, to Obregón, September 10, 1923, both in AGN, OC, 805-E-4.

39. That is, from May 24, 1846, until February 2, 1848, and from December 8, 1861, until July 21, 1867. Guzmán Navarro, "Las pensiones militares," 59.

40. Knight, "Ideology of the Mexican Revolution."

41. *Time*, May 19, 1941. On prerevolutionary disputes over veterans, see McNamara, *Sons of the Sierra*, 93–155; McNamara, "Saving Private Ramírez."

42. Nicéforo Guerrero, Presidential Secretary, to Celso Basurto, DF, August 13, 1931, AGN, POR, caja 30, exp. 37 (1931).

43. For revolutionary condemnations of Porfirian militarism, see *Diario de los Debates*, December 27, 1917, and August 26, 1918.

44. *Homenaje a un viejo soldado republicano*, 28.

45. Ibid.

46. Ibid., 38.

47. Ibid., 37–39.

48. See copy of speech given by Enrique Pérez Arce at Colegio Civil "Rosales," Culiacán, December 22, 1927, ibid., 16–17.

49. Telegram from retired Colonel José Manterola and retired Division General Angel García Peña, ibid., 26–29.

50. Telegram from General Manuel M. Guasque, ibid., 28.

51. Telegram from Angel García Conde, ibid., 25.

52. Telegram from Manuel Haro, Offices of *El Universal*, Guadalajara, ibid., 33.

53. Benjamin, *La Revolución*, 117–36.

54. *Anales gráficos de la historia militar*, 1200. See also Benjamin, *La Revolución*, 115.

55. Calles, *Manifiesto que lanza a sus compañeros*; *Acta constitutiva y estatutos de la Unión de Veteranos de la Revolución*.

56. The Gold Shirts were not strictly a veterans group, but they were led by many who claimed to be veterans and made ample use of this discourse in public pronouncements. Gojman de Backal, *Camisas, escudos y desfiles militares*, 234–35, 240, 246.

57. Inspector V-72, November 16, 1936, AGN, DGIPS, caja 73, exp. 3.

58. Campbell, "The Radical Right in Mexico," 120–98, 267–80. Campbell suggests that the secular radical right took this fragmentary form because it lacked the co-ordinating influence of national institutions such as the Catholic Church. See also Fernández Boyolí and Marrón de Angelis, *Lo que no se sabe*, 11–31.

59. Cited in Sherman, *The Mexican Right*, 74.

60. Inspector V-72, November 16, 1936, AGN, DGIPS, caja 73, exp. 3; list of UNVR members, August 1940, AGN, DGIPS, caja 16, exp. 6.

61. Bantjes, *As If Jesus Walked on Earth*, 83.

62. Sherman, *The Mexican Right*, 74.

63. *Excélsior*, February 1, 1940. The group was entitled Unifier of the Veterans of the Revolution.

64. *El Nacional*, December 5, 1936; MA to G-2, December 11, 1936, USMIR, reel 5, 64–66.

65. The Cuautla lodge obliged, although the list they sent is not in the AGN file. José López Guillemin, Logia "Alborada del Sur," no. 68, to Cárdenas, December 9, 1935, and July 6, 1936; Luis I. Rodríguez, DF, to Secretaría de Educación Pública, July 20, 1936, AGN, LC, 534/64, caja 687.

66. *Reglamento del ceremonial militar*.

67. Various correspondence from Sección Femenil Militar del Partido Revolucio-nario Mexicano, to Cárdenas, 1939, AGN, LC 151.2/1301; draft of "Ley de Retiros y Pensiones Del Ejército y Armada Nacionales," 1940, in CESU, FFU, caja 8.

68. Mario Gill, "Zapata," 310; various correspondence, 1941–42, AGN, MAC, 201.5/27.

69. Various reports, January–November 1940, AGN, DGIPS, exp. 3, caja 99.

70. Katz, *Life and Times of Pancho Villa*, 790. See also Vargas-Lobsinger, *La Comarca Lagunera*, 185–89.

71. Navarro Valdez, *El cardenismo en Durango*, 144–45. See also discussion of Cardenismo in Parra, *Writing Pancho Villa's Revolution*, 120–36.

72. PHO 1/9, Francisco Gil Piñon, interviewed by A. O. Bonfil and E. Meyer, in Chihuahua, Chihuahua, August 3, 1972.

73. Navarro Valdez, *El cardenismo*, 116, 243.

74. Ibid., 243–47.

75. *Anales gráficos de la historia militar*, 550. See also MA to G-2, March 14, 1937, USMIR, reel 4, 736.

76. Brunk, *The Posthumous Career*, 113.

77. Bantjes, *As If Jesus Walked on Earth*, 198; Gojman de Backal, *Camisas, escudos y desfiles militares*, 250–51.

78. See Cor. G. Vizcarra, DF, to Cárdenas, February 7, 1938, and General José García Lugo, UNVR, Torreón, Coahuila, to Cárdenas, February 10, 1938, in AGN, LC, 534/64, caja 687; Michaels, "Las elecciones de 1940," 121–25.

79. *New York Times*, February 19, 1939.

80. *Instructivo de la comisión pro-veteranos*.

81. Rocha, "The Faces of Rebellion." None of the six women discussed by Rocha received a pension.

82. "Ley de Retiros y Pensiones Del Ejército Y Armada Nacionales," in CESU, FFU, caja 8, 10. See also Guzmán Navarro, "Pensiones militares," 63.

83. *La Prensa*, April 15, 1939.

84. *Instructivo de la comisión pro-veteranos.*

85. Lieutenant Margarito Reyes Calderón, Atoyac, Guerrero, to Manuel Ávila Camacho, August 14, 1942, AGN, MAC, 418.2/47.

86. Cor. Gabino Vizcarra, DF, to Manuel Ávila Camacho, March 6, 1941, AGN, MAC, 544.2/11; Legion Mexicana, La Siberia, Atoyac, Veracruz, to Alemán, January 2, 1947, AGN, MAV, 133.2/2. See also various correspondence, 1947–48, AGN, MAV, 418.2/333, 135.2/287, and 503.11/300.

87. Gojman de Backal, *Camisas, escudos y desfiles militares*, 266, 493–501.

88. See pamphlet "A los Veteranos de la Revolución," by Agrupaciones de Veteranos de la Revolución al Servicio del Estado, DF, November 18, 1948, enclosed in AGN, DGIPS, caja 18, exp. 6.

89. Unsigned report, August 17, 1948, AGN, DGIPS, caja 24, exp. 3; Ríos Thivol, DF, February 28, 1949, AGN, DGIPS, caja 24, exp. 3.

90. See reports from Inspector Jesús González Valencia and Fernando López Portillo, DF, November 17–20, 1948, AGN, DGIPS, caja 18, exp. 6.

91. *Diario Oficial*, February 8, 1949.

92. Delegación de Veteranos de la Revolución, Los Mochis, Sinaloa, to Alemán, May 31, 1947, AGN, MAV, 120/50, caja 82.

93. Inspector P.S. "Equis," DF, November 9, 1950, AGN, DGIPS, caja 84, exp. 2.

94. Servín, *Ruptura y oposición*, 373–74.

95. *La Prensa*, December 23, 1950, AGN, DGIPS, caja 805, exp. 1.

96. Arnulfo Domínguez Casales, Acapulco, Guerrero, to Alemán, April 28, 1949, AGN, MAV, 120/50, caja 82, exp. 4; Benjamín J. Villa, DF, to Alemán, March 7, 1949; and Delegación de Veteranos de la Revolución, Cuautla, Morelos, to Alemán, April 5, 1949, both in AGN, MAV, 120/50, caja 82, exp. 5; various correspondence, Frente Zapatista de la República to Ruiz Cortines, 1953–54, AGN, ARC, 556/53/394, caja 936.

97. Editorial by General Manuel J. Solís, head of the army's historical archive, *El Legionario*, March 1951, 9.

98. See "Instructivo a los Commandantes de la Legion de Honor," *El Legionario*, June 1951, 33.

99. "Observaciones de un legionario en campaña," *El Legionario*, July 1951, 35–36; "La preparación de la batalla de Zacatecas," *El Legionario*, July 1952, 24–28; General Adolfo Terrones Benítez, "La última batalla de Torreón, Chih.," *El Legionario*, April 1956, 36–39. On the "battle piece," see Keegan, *The Face of Battle*, 28–29.

100. "Código moral del legionario," *El Legionario*, July 1951, 2; Christian D. Larson, "Credo optimista," *El Legionario*, April 1951, 20; General Manuel de J. Solís, "Amor propio del legionario mexicano," *El Legionario*, July 1951, 31–32; General Rafael Benavides, "Los generales," *El Legionario*, August 1951, 40; Liborio Domínguez López, "Alegría, bondad, optimismo," *El Legionario*, April 1952, 64–65.

101. "Palabras de Prof. Mario Hernández Torres," *El Legionario*, March 1951, 8.

102. Veterans employed in government bureaucracies gathered in their own groups. See Bloque de Veteranos de la Revolución del Dept. Agrario, DF, to Alemán, January 23, 1947; Agrupaciones de Veteranos de la Revolución, Trabajadores del Estado, DF, to Alemán, December 27, 1946, AGN, MAV, 120/50, caja 82.

103. Inspector Jesús González Valencia and Fernando López Portillo, DF, November 20, 1948, AGN, DGIPS, caja 18, exp. 6.

104. For example, see J. Saldaña, Montemorelos, Nuevo León, to Ruiz Cortines, July 9, 1956, AGN, ARC, 201.5/39, caja 282, exp. 6.

105. For correspondence from veterans allied to Morelos's Jaramillistas, see Grupo de Veteranos de Puebla to Ruiz Cortines, October 1955 (exact date illegible), AGN, ARC, 702.2/34, caja 1147.

106. Captain Juan de la O Gardea and Rafael Chávez Vela, Legion de Veteranos de la Revolución División del Norte, to Ruiz Cortines, August 3, 1957, in AGN, ARC, 503.11/154, caja 587. This narrative of the dispute is taken from Mayor Esteban Mendiola and Francisco Leyva, Unificación de Veteranos de la Revolución División del Norte, to Ruiz Cortines, December 17 and 22, 1954; Dirección de Colonización, DF, to Ruiz Cortines, April 10, 1956; Jacinto López, Secretary General, UGOCM, DF, to Ruiz Cortines, October 1, 1956; Juan Agustín Ramírez, President, Union Nacional de Defensa Campesina, DF, to Ruiz Cortines, November 1, 1956.

107. Rocha, "The Faces of Rebellion," 17.

108. Diego and José Angel Ortega, DF, to Ruiz Cortines, January 29, 1956, AGN, ARC, 545.22/79, caja 869. See also assorted correspondence, February 1953–58, AGN, ARC, 201.5/39, caja 282.

109. AHSDN, XI/111/3-1049 (Martínez Castro), 30–45.

110. Grupo de Veteranos de Puebla to Ruiz Cortines, October 1955 (exact date illegible), AGN, ARC, 702.2/34, caja 1147; Klingemann, "Triumph of the Vanquished," 188–89.

111. Francisco Gil Piñon, interviewed by A. O. Bonfil and E. Meyer, in Chihuahua, Chihuahua, August 3, 1972, PHO 1/9; Colonel Roberto Sánchez Aguilar, interviewed by América Teresa Briseño, February 13–March 13, 1973, PHO 1/38; Ten. Cor. E. Angeles Meraz, interviewed by América Teresa Briseño, December 8–11, 1972, Mexico City, PHO, 1/31; Tiburcio Cuéllar Montalvo, interviewed by Eugenia Meyer, March 8, 1973, Mexico City, PHO, 1/45.

112. "Asunto relativo a la autorización que solicita el C.Comte. de la VI R.M. para aceptar el nombramiento de presidente honorario de los Veteranos Revolucionarios de la Div. del Norte," Grupo Jurídico, EMS, May 13, 1955, AHSDN, I-444 (Tapia Freyding), 2819.

113. *El Legionario*, October 1951, 27. See also Legion Mexicana Civil, Guadalajara, to Ruiz Cortines, October 4, 1957, AGN, ARC, 703.4/1199, caja 1259; Columna Militar de Precursores y Veteranos de la Revolución, DF, to Ruiz Cortines, May 17, 1954, AGN, ARC, 556.64/171, caja 947.

114. Confederación Nacional de Veteranos de la Revolución, DF, to ARC, October 3, 1953, AGN, ARC, 136.3/507.

115. Unión Confederada de Veteranos de la Revolución, Tres Valles, San Luis Potosí, to Alemán, April 26, 1950, AGN, MAV, 120/50, caja 82, exp. 6.

116. General and Senator Porfirio Neri Arizmendi, DF, to Ruiz Cortines, November 1958, AGN, ARC, 556/53/394, caja 936. See also assorted correspondence from Confederación de Veteranos Revolucionarios de la División del Norte, DF, to Ruiz Cortines, July 1954, AGN, ARC, 111/405, caja 12.

117. Florescano, *National Narratives in Mexico*, 349.

118. On the PARM leadership's basically loyal relationship to Ruiz Cortines and later the PRI, see DFS reports: May 7, 1953, 9-12-53, H-32, L-1; March 8, 1954, 48-6-954, H-95, L-1; April 28, 1957, 10-26-957, H-38, L-2.

119. *La Prensa*, March 1, 1939.

120. E. Victoria Peña, Sec. Gen. Sindicato Hidráulicos, DF, to Alemán, April 27, 1950, AGN, MAV, 120/50, caja 82, exp. 6; editorial by Joel F. Torres, *Excélsior*, February 27, 1948.

121. Monsiváis, "Foreword"; Kluckhohn, *The Mexican Challenge*, 216; Gruening, *Mexico and Its Heritage*, 647.

122. "Zipezape entre veteranos," *Novedades*, March 6, 1962; "El veterano más veterano de los veteranos," *El Universal*, April 4, 1964.

123. Various clippings, 1964, AGN, SDN, caja 97, exp. 81.

124. Memo, Torreón, Coahuila, 1952, AGN, DGIPS, caja 2014-B, exp. 29. On the founding of the PARM, see Taylor to Foreign Office, March 10, 1954, NA, FO 371/109026, 35.

125. Benjamin, *La Revolución*; Vaughan, *Cultural Politics in Revolution*; O'Malley, *The Myth of the Revolution*.

Conclusion

1. Carriedo, "The Man Who Tamed Mexico's Tiger."

2. Krauze, *La presidencia imperial*, 66.

3. Knight, "Habitus and Homicide," 108.

4. Del Villar, *Where the Strange Roads Go Down*, 100.

5. Knight, "Habitus and Homicide."

6. Adelman, "Problem of Persistence in Latin American History."

7. Jean Meyer, "Grandes compañias."

8. Grandin, "Coming to Terms," 4.

9. Schmidt, "Making It Real," 25.

10. Jeffrey Rubin cited in Knight, "Historical Continuities in Social Movements," 95; Knight, "Cardenismo"; Knight, "The Weight of the State."

11. Collier, *The New Authoritarianism*.

12. Pion-Berlin, "Latin American National Security Doctrine"; Schamis, "Reconceptualizing Latin American Authoritarianism"; Remmer, "Neopatrimonialism"; Pereira, *Political Injustice*; Finchelstein, *Transatlantic Fascism*.

13. Stepan, *The Military in Politics*, 25.

14. Smallman, *Fear and Memory*.

15. Mares, *Violent Peace*, 8. See also Resende Santos, *Neorealism*.

16. Huggins, Haritos-Fatouros, and Zimbardo, *Violence Workers*.

17. Aguayo, *La charola*, 72, 112; Scherer García and Monsiváis, *Parte de guerra*, 43–44.

18. Sierra Guzmán, *El enemigo interno*, 31–70. For a rare account of debates in the army about counterinsurgency in the 1970s, see Veledíaz, *El general sin memoria*.

19. Grandin, "Coming to Terms." On state violence and public secrets in Colombia, see Tate, *Counting the Dead*.

20. Moloeznick, "The Militarization of Public Security."

21. *El Universal*, March 21 and April 2, 2009; Ferreyra and Segura, "Examining the Military in the Local Sphere."

22. Aguayo and Treviño, "Neither Truth nor Justice," 61.

23. López-Montiel, "The Military," 81–82; Moloeznick, "The Militarization of Public Security."

BIBLIOGRAPHY

Archival Sources

London
  National Archives
    Foreign Office Reports
    War Office
Mexico City
  Archivo de la Palabra, Instituto Mora
  Archivo de la Secretaría de Educación Pública
  Archivo General de la Nacíon
    Dirección Federal de Seguridad
    Dirección General de Gobierno
    Dirección General de Investigaciones Políticas y Sociales
    Fondo Enrique Díaz Delgado y García, Fototeca
    Ramo Presidentes: Obregón-Calles, Emilio Portes Gil, Pascual Ortiz Rubio,
      Abelardo L. Rodríguez, Lázaro Cárdenas, Manuel Ávila Camacho,
      Miguel Alemán Valdés, Adolfo Ruiz Cortines, Adolfo López Mateos
    Secretaría de la Defensa Nacional
  Archivo Histórico de la Secretaría de la Defensa Nacional
  Biblioteca del Ejército
  Biblioteca Miguel Lerdo de Tejada, Archivos Económicos
  Centro de Estudios Sobre la Universidad, Universidad Nacional Autónoma
      de México
    Fondo Francisco Urquizo
    Fondo Heriberto Jara
  Fideicomiso Archivos Plutarco Elías Calles y Fernando Torreblanca
    Fondo Joaquín Amaro
  Hemeroteca Nacional
Washington, D.C.
  National Archives and Records Administration
    Record Group 84, Consular Reports
    Record Group 165, Military Intelligence Division Regional Files (Mexico)
    Record Group 319, Records of Army Staff
    Records Relating to the Internal Affairs of Mexico, U.S. State Department,
      1944–54 (Microfilm)
    United States Military Intelligence Reports, 1920–41 (Microfilm)

217

Periodicals

Diario de los Debates de la Cámara de Diputados del Congreso de los Estados Unidos Mexicanos (Mexico City: LV Legislatura, Comité de Biblioteca, 1994)
Diario Oficial (Mexico City)
Excélsior (Mexico City)
El Maestro Rural (Mexico City)
Mañana (Mexico City)
Memorias de la Secretaría de Educación Pública
Memorias de la Secretaría de Guerra y Marina
Memorias de la Secretaría de la Defensa Nacional
El Nacional (Mexico City)

New York Times (New York)
Novedades (Mexico City)
La Opinión (Puebla)
Periódico Noroeste (Mazatlán)
La Prensa (Mexico City)
Puebla en marcha (Puebla)
Regeneración (Mexico City)
El Soldado (Mexico City)
El Sol de Puebla (Puebla)
El Sur Acapulco (Acapulco)
Time (New York)
Últimas Noticias de Excélsior (Mexico City)
El Universal (Mexico City)
El Universal Gráfico (Mexico City)
El Veterano (Mexico City)

Other Primary Sources

Acta Constitutiva y Estatutos de la Unión de Veteranos de la Revolución. Mexico City: n.p., 1932.

Alamillo Flores, Luis. *Memorias: luchadores ignorados al lado de los grandes jefes de la Revolución Mexicana*. Mexico City: Extemporáneos, 1976.

Alemán y el ejército. Mexico: Estado Mayor Presidencial, 1950.

Almada, Pedro. *Con mi cobija al hombro*. Mexico: Editorial Alrededor de América, 1936.

Almada, Pedro, and Francisco Díaz Babio. "La estrategia nacional: como memoria de la carta estratégica general." Unpublished manuscript in Bancroft Library, University of California, Berkeley, 1934.

Amezcua, José Luis. *Estudio de los sistemas de reclutamiento y bases para un proyecto de sistema en México*. Mexico: Secretaría de la Defensa Nacional, 1940.

Anales gráficos de la historia militar de México. Mexico City: Editorial Gustavo Casasola, 1973.

Azcárate, Juan F. *Escencia de la Revolución*. Mexico: Costa-Amic, 1966.

Azcué Bilbao, Karmele, ed. *El movimiento estudiantil poblano, 1952–1957: entrevista con Francisco Arellano Ocampo*. Puebla: Archivo Histórico Regional Universitario, Universidad Autónoma de Puebla.

Bautista, Gonzalo. *El esfuerzo de los poblanos en 4 años, 1941–1944*. Puebla: n.p., 1944.

Beals, Carleton. *Mexican Maze*. Philadelphia: J.B Lippincott, 1931.

Beltrán González, J. Antonio. *Mejores anecdotas del H. Colegio Militar*. Mexico City: n.p., n.d.

Blasco Ibáñez, Vicente. *Mexico in Revolution*. New York: E. P. Dutton, 1920.

Bosques, Gilberto. *The National Revolutionary Party of Mexico and the Six-Year Plan.* Mexico City: Bureau of Foreign Information of the National Revolutionary Party, 1937.

Bravo Izquierdo, Donato. *Soldado del pueblo.* Puebla: n.p., 1964.

Cabrera, Luis. *El servicio militar obligatorio.* Mexico City: n.p., 1940.

Calderón, Ricardo. *El ejército y sus tribunales.* Mexico City: Ediciones Lex, 1944.

Calles, Plutarco Elías. *Manifiesto que lanza a sus compañeros y al pueblo del estado en general.* Mexico: n.p., 1932.

Cárdenas, Lázaro. *Apuntes: una selección.* Mexico City: Centro de Estudios de la Revolución Mexicana "Lázaro Cárdenas"; Universidad Nacional Autónoma de México, 2003.

Carrasco Cuéllar, Juan. *Hacia la república socialista de trabajadores: obra de lectura para soldados, obreros y campesinos; oratoria revolucionaria socialista.* Mexico City: DAPP, 1938.

Casasola, Gustavo. *Historia gráfica de la revolución mexicana.* 5 vols. Mexico City: Editorial Casasola, 1967.

Castillo Ramírez, María Gracia, Alma Dorantes González, and Julia Tuñon Pablos. *La noble tarea de educar: recuerdos y vivencias de una maestra jalisciense.* Mexico: Instituto Nacional de Antropología e Historia, 2000.

Corona del Rosal, Alfonso. *Moral militar y civismo.* Mexico: Estado Mayor Presidencial, 1952.

———. *Moral militar y civismo: obra de texto en el Colegio Militar y en el Centro de Instrucción para Jefes y Oficiales.* Mexico: Anáhuac, 1938.

Correa, Eduardo. *El balance del avila camachismo.* Mexico City: n.p., 1946.

Cravioto Leyzaola, Adrián. *Historia documental del Heróico Colegio Militar: através de la historia de México.* 3 vols. Mexico: Costa-Amic, 2001.

Del Villar, Mary and Fred. *Where the Strange Roads Go Down.* New York: Macmillan, 1953.

Díaz Escobar, Alfredo Félix. *Alemán y la democracia mexicana (ideario de orientación política y social).* Mexico City: Comité Nacional de Orientación Política, 1947.

Dillon, Emile Joseph. *President Obregón, a World Reformer.* London: Hutchinson and Co., 1923.

Fernández Boyolí, Manuel, and Eustaquio Marrón de Angelis. *Lo que no se sabe de la rebelión cedillista.* Mexico City: DAPP, 1938.

García, Rubén. *El servicio militar obligatorio.* Santiago de Chile: Balcells and Co., 1927.

———. *¿Qué y cómo es el servicio militar obligatorio?* Mexico City: Centro Revolucionario de Estudios Políticos, 1933.

Garza Guajardo, Celso. *Los conscriptos de la clase de 1924.* Monterrey, Nuevo León, Mexico: Editorial Nogales, 1992.

Gayosso Ríos, Filadelfo. *Mi palabra: (a la vera de Tlacuilo).* Mexico City: Plaza y Valdés, 2004.

Génesis de la Escuela Superior de Guerra. Mexico City: Secretaría de Guerra y Marina; Biblioteca de la Dirección General de Educación Militar, 1933.

Geraldo, Arturo. *Sobre las armas*. Tijuana, B.C., Mexico: Impresora Contreras, 1993.

González Luna, Efraín. *Servicio militar: derechos del soldado*. Mexico: Acción Nacional, 1943.

Goodfriend, Arthur. "Ejército Mexicano." *Infantry Journal* (May 1947): 48–49.

Gruening, Ernest. *Mexico and Its Heritage*. New York: Century Co., 1928.

Gunther, John. *Inside Latin America*. New York: Harper and Brothers, 1941.

Historia documental de la CNOP. 3 vols. Mexico City: Instituto de Capitación Política, 1984.

Homenaje a un viejo soldado republicano: aniversario del hecho glorioso de San Pedro, 22 Diciembre, 1864–1927. Mexico: n.p., 1928.

Informe del Secretario de la Defensa Nacional. Mexico City: Secretaría de la Defensa Nacional, 1938.

Instructivo de la comisión pro-veteranos de la revolución. Mexico City: Secretaría de la Defensa Nacional, 1939.

Jaramillo, Rubén. *Autobiografía y asesinato*. Mexico City: Editorial Nuestro Tiempo, 1978.

Kluckhohn, Frank L. *The Mexican Challenge*. New York: Doubleday, 1939.

López de Nava Camarena, Rodolfo. *Mis hechos de campaña: testimonios del General de División Rodolfo López de Nava Baltierra, 1911–1952*. Mexico City: Instituto Nacional de Estudios Históricos de la Revolución Mexicana; Secretaría de Gobernación, 1994.

Los alojamientos militares en la república: dictamen presentado por el presidente de la "Comisión Consultora de Cuarteles y Edificios Militares de la República Mexicana" al c. Secretario de Comunicaciones y Obras Públicas, General e Ingeniero Pascual Ortiz Rubio. Mexico City: Departamento Universitario y de Bellas Artes, Dirección de Talleres Gráficos, 1921.

Los estudios de la Escuela Superior de Guerra. Mexico City: Secretaría de Guerra y Marina; Biblioteca de la Dirección General de Educación Militar, 1934.

Los pinceles de la historia: la arqueología del régimen, 1910–1955. Mexico City: Patronato del Museo Nacional de Arte; Banamex; CONACULTA, INBA, 2003.

Mondragón, Rafael. "El servicio militar obligatorio: aspecto social." *Boletín Jurídico Militar* 11:5–6 (May 1943): 223–45.

Pani, Alberto. *El cambio de regímenes en México y las asonadas militares: síntesis histórica*. Paris: Editorial de Livre Libre, 1930.

Paz, Eduardo. *El servicio militar obligatorio a la nación mexicana y al ejército*. Mexico City: Talleres del Departamento de Estado Mayor, 1908.

Peral, Miguel Ángel. *El pelelismo en México: biografía de un político con anverso y reverso*. Mexico City: Editorial Pac, 1951.

Prewett, Virginia. "The Mexican Army." *Foreign Affairs* 1, no. 3 (1941): 609–20.

———. *Reportage on Mexico*. New York: E. P. Dutton and Co., 1941.

Quezada, Abel. *El sistema: los mejores cartones, 1943–1988*. Mexico: Planeta, 1999.

Quiles Ponce, Enrique. *Henríquez y Cárdenas ¡Presentes! Hechos y realidades en la campaña henriquista*. Mexico City: Costa-Amic Editores, 1980.

Ravelo Lecuona, Renato. *Los jaramillistas: la gesta de Rubén Jaramillo narrada por sus compañeros*. 1978. Reprint, Cuernavaca, Morelos, Mexico: Editorial la Rana del Sur, 2007.

Reglamento de las comandancias de las zonas militares. Mexico City: DAPP, 1937.

Reglamento del ceremonial militar. Mexico City: DAPP, 1937.

Rivera Terrazas, Luis, ed. *Documentos universitarios*. Puebla: Universidad Autónoma de Puebla, 1983.

Romano Moreno, Armando. *Anecdotario estudiantil*. 2 vols. Puebla: Universidad Autónoma de Puebla, 1985.

Salas, Gustavo. *El servicio militar obligatorio. Apuntes sobre la reorganización del ejército*. Guadalajara, Mexico: Talleres Lino-Tipográficos, Escuela de Artes y Oficios del Estado, 1922.

Sánchez Lamego, Miguel Ángel. *¿Debe tener México militares profesionales, científicos o de ocasión?* Mexico City: Secretaría de la Defensa Nacional, 1943.

Santos, Gonzalo N. *Memorias*. Mexico City: Grijalbo, 1986.

Seis años de actividad nacional. Mexico City: Secretaría de Gobernación, 1946.

Septimo censo general de población: Estado de Puebla. Mexico: Secretaría de Economía, 1950.

Sexto censo general de población. Mexico: Secretaría de Economía, 1940.

Soto Oliver, Nicolás. *Entre soldados y cabos—a la ley de herodes*. Pachuca, Hidalgo: Gobierno del Estado de Hidalgo, Instituto Hidalguense de Cultura, 1993.

Suárez Suárez, Rosendo. *Breve historia del ejército mexicano*. Mexico City: Editorial Anáhuac, 1938.

Taracena, Alfonso. *La vida en México bajo Ávila Camacho*. 2 vols. Mexico City: Editorial Jus, 1976.

Teja Zabre, Alfonso. *Breve historia de México*. Mexico City: Secretaría de Educación Pública, 1935.

Torrea, Juan Manuel. *El Asilo del Honor*. Mexico City: Victoria, 1923.

Treviño, Jacinto B. *Memorias*. Mexico City: Editorial Orion, 1961.

Un soldado en cada hijo te dió. (El servicio militar nacional). Mexico City: Secretaría de Educación Pública, 1943.

Urquizo, Francisco L. *Charlas cuarteleras*. Mexico City: Editorial Muñoz, 1955.

———. *Tres de Diana*. Mexico City: Publicaciones Mundiales, 1947.

Vega González, Roberto. *Cadetes mexicanos en la Guerra de España*. Mexico City: Colección Málaga, 1977.

Secondary Sources

Ackroyd, William S. "Military Professionalism, Education, and Political Behavior in Mexico." *Armed Forces and Society* 18, no. 1 (1991): 81–96.

Adelman, Jeremy. "Introduction: The Problem of Persistence in Latin American History." In *Colonial Legacies: The Problem of Persistence in Latin American History*, edited by Jeremy Adelman, 1–14. New York: Routledge, 1999.

———. "Spanish-American Leviathan? State Formation in Nineteenth-Century Spanish America." *Comparative Studies in Society and History* 40, no. 2 (1998): 391–408.

Aguayo, Sergio. *La charola: una historia de los servicios de inteligencia en México*. Mexico City: Grijalbo, 2001.

Aguayo, Sergio, and Javier Treviño Rangel. "Neither Truth nor Justice: Mexico's De Facto Amnesty." *Latin American Perspectives* 33, no. 2 (2006): 56–68.

Aguilar Camín, Héctor. "The Relevant Tradition: Sonoran Leaders in the Revolution." In *Caudillo and Peasant in the Mexican Revolution*, edited by David Brading, 92–123. Cambridge: Cambridge University Press, 1980.

Agustín, José. *Tragicomedia mexicana: la vida en México de 1940 a 1970*. 2 vols. Mexico City: Editorial Planeta Mexico, 1990.

Alegre, Robert Francis. "Contesting the Mexican Miracle: Railway Men and Women Struggle for Democracy, 1943–1959." Ph.D. diss., Rutgers, State University of New Jersey, 2007.

Alonso, Ana María. *Thread of Blood: Colonialism, Revolution and Gender on Mexico's Northern Frontier*. Tucson: University of Arizona Press, 1995.

Anguiano Equihua, Victoriano. *Lázaro Cárdenas: su feudo y la política nacional*. Mexico City: Editorial Eréndira, 1951.

Ankerson, Dudley. *Agrarian Warlord: Saturnino Cedillo and the Mexican Revolution in San Luis Potosí*. DeKalb: Northern Illinois University Press, 1984.

Archer, Christon. "The Politicization of the Army of New Spain during the War of Independence, 1810–1821." In *The Origins of Mexican National Politics, 1808–1847*, edited by Jaime Rodríguez, 11–37. Wilmington, Del.: SR Books, 1997.

Arellano Cruz, Artemio. "Las defensas rurales como fuerza militar de protección de los derechos agrarios." Law thesis, Universidad Nacional Autónoma de México, 1950.

Astorga Almanza, Luis Alejandro. *El siglo de las drogas: el narcotráfico, del Porfiriato al nuevo milenio*. Mexico: Plaza y Janés, 2005.

Bantjes, Adrian A. *As If Jesus Walked on Earth: Cardenismo, Sonora and the Mexican Revolution*. Wilmington, Del.: Scholarly Resources, 1998.

Barbosa Cano, Fabio. *La CROM de Luis N. Morones a Antonio J. Hernández*. Puebla: ICUAP, Universidad Autónoma de Puebla, 1980.

Beattie, Peter. *The Tribute of Blood: Army, Honor, Race and Nation in Brazil, 1864–1945*. Durham: Duke University Press, 2001.

Bellingeri, Marco. *Del agrarismo armado a la guerra de los pobres: ensayos de guerilla rural en el México contemporáneo, 1940–1974*. Mexico: Casa Juan Pablos, 2003.

Benjamin, Thomas. *La Revolución: Mexico's Great Revolution as Memory, Myth and History*. Austin: University of Texas Press, 2000.

Benjamin, Thomas, and Mark Wasserman, eds. *Provinces of Revolution: Essays on Regional Mexican History, 1910–1929*. Albuquerque: University of New Mexico Press, 1990.

Berghahn, Volker R. *Militarism: The History of an International Debate, 1861–1979*. New York: St. Martin's Press, 1982.

Bermúdez, Antonio, and Octavio Véjar Vázquez. *No dejes crecer la hierba . . . El gobierno avilacamachista*. Mexico City: B. Costa-Amic, 1969.

Bethel, Leslie, and Ian Roxborough, eds. *Latin America between the Second World War and the Cold War, 1944–1948*. Cambridge: Cambridge University Press, 1992.

Blight, David W. *Race and Reunion: The Civil War in American Memory*. New York: Belknap Press, 2001.

Bliss, Katherine Elaine. *Compromised Positions: Prostitution, Public Health, and Gender Politics in Revolutionary Mexico City*. University Park: Pennsylvania State University Press, 2002.

Boils, Guillermo. *Los militares y la política en México*. Mexico City: Ediciones "El Caballito," 1975.

Boyer, Christopher R. *Becoming Campesinos: Politics, Identity and Agrarian Struggle in Postrevolutionary Michoacán, 1920–1935*. Stanford: Stanford University Press, 2003.

Brandenburg, Frank. *The Making of Modern Mexico*. New York: Prentice Hall, 1964.

Brewster, Keith. *Militarism, Ethnicity and Politics in the Sierra Norte de Puebla, 1917–1930*. Tucson: University of Arizona Press, 2003.

Brunk, Samuel. *Emiliano Zapata! Revolution and Betrayal in Mexico*. Albuquerque: University of New Mexico Press, 1995.

———. *The Posthumous Career of Emiliano Zapata: Myth, Memory, and Mexico's Twentieth Century*. Austin: University of Texas Press, 2008.

Buchenau, Jürgen. *Plutarco Elías Calles and the Mexican Revolution*. Lanham, Md.: Rowman and Littlefield, 2007.

Camp, Roderic A. *Generals in the Palacio: The Military in Modern Mexico*. Oxford: Oxford University Press, 1992.

———. *Mexican Political Biographies, 1935–1993*. Austin: University of Texas Press, 1995.

———. *Mexico's Military on the Democratic Stage*. Westport, Conn.: Praeger Security International, 2005.

Campbell, Hugh G. "The Radical Right in Mexico, 1929–1949." Ph.D diss., University of California, Los Angeles, 1968.

Cano, Gabriela. "Unconcealable Realities of Desire: Amelio Robles's (Transgender) Masculinity in the Mexican Revolution." In *Sex in Revolution: Gender, Politics and Power in Modern Mexico*, edited by Jocelyn Olcott, Mary Kay Vaughan, and Gabriella Cano, 35–56. Durham: Duke University Press, 2006.

Caplan, Karen D. *Indigenous Citizens: Local Liberalism in Early National Oaxaca and Yucatán*. Stanford: Stanford University Press, 2010.

Caplow, Deborah. *Leopoldo Méndez: Revolutionary Art and the Mexican Print*. Austin: University of Texas Press, 2007.

Carriedo, Robert. "The Man Who Tamed Mexico's Tiger: General Joaquín Amaro and the Professionalization of Mexico's Revolutionary Army." Ph.D. diss., New Mexico University, 2005.

Casanova, Pablo González. *Democracy in Mexico*. New York: Oxford University Press, 1970.

Centeno, Miguel Ángel. *Blood and Debt: War and the Nation-State in Latin America*. University Park: Pennsylvania State University Press, 2002.

———. "The Disciplinary Society in Latin America." In *The Other Mirror: Grand Theory through the Lens of Latin America*, edited by Miguel Ángel Centeno and Fernando López-Alves, 289–308. Princeton: Princeton University Press, 2001.

Chambers, Sarah. "'With His Life He Paid for This Pension': The Politics of Military Pensions in Chile, 1817–1850." Paper presented at Annual Meeting of the American Historical Association, January 2006.

Collier, David, ed. *The New Authoritarianism in Latin America*. Princeton: Princeton University Press, 1980.

Córdova, Arnaldo. *La ideología de la Revolución Mexicana: la formación del nuevo régimen*. Mexico City: Ediciones Era, 1973.

Craib, Raymond. *Cartographic Mexico: A History of State Fixations and Fugitive Landscapes*. Durham: Duke University Press, 2004.

Crider, Gregory. "Material Struggles: Workers' Strategies during the Institutionalization of the Revolution in Atlixco, Puebla, Mexico." Ph.D. diss., University of Wisconsin, 1996.

Davis, Diane. "The Political and Economic Origins of Violence and Insecurity in Contemporary Latin America: Past Trajectories and Future Prospects." In *Violent Democracies in Latin America*, edited by Desmond Arias and Daniel Goldstein, 35–62. Durham: Duke University Press, 2010.

Davis, Diane, and Anthony W. Pereira. "New Patterns of Militarized Violence and Coercion in the Americas." *Latin American Perspectives* 111, no. 27 (2000): 3–17.

Dawson, Alexander S. *Indian and Nation in Revolutionary Mexico*. Tucson: University of Arizona Press, 2004.

Deas, Malcolm. "The Man on Foot: Conscription and the Nation-State in Nineteenth Century Latin America." In *Studies in the Formation of the Nation-State in Latin America*, edited by James Dunkerley, 77–93. London: Institute of Latin American Studies, 2002.

de la Peña, Guillermo. "Populism, Regional Power, and Political Mediation: Southern Jalisco, 1900–1980." In *Mexico's Regions: Comparative History and Development*, edited by Eric Van Young, 191–223. San Diego: University of California, San Diego; Center for U.S.-Mexican Studies, 1992.

De Palo, William. *The Mexican National Army, 1822–1852*. College Station: Texas A & M University Press, 1997.

Dulles, John W. F. *Yesterday in Mexico: A Chronicle of the Revolution, 1919–1936*. Austin: University of Texas Press, 1961.

Estrada Correa, Francisco. *Sin reconocimiento oficial: la biografía de Miguel Henríquez Guzmán, el último liberal mexicano*. Mexico City: Editorial Consuelo Sánchez y Asociados, 2006.

Fallaw, Ben. *Cárdenas Compromised: The Failure of Reform in Postrevolutionary Yucatán*. Durham: Duke University Press, 2001.

———. "Militaries and Paramilitaries in Postrevolutionary Zacatecas, 1915–1940." Paper presented at Latin American Studies Association Conference, San Francisco, 2012.

———. "Varieties of Mexican Revolutionary Anticlericalism: Radicalism, Iconoclasm and Otherwise, 1914–1935." *The Americas* 65, no. 4 (2009): 481–509.

Fallaw, Ben, and Terry Rugeley, eds. *Forced Marches: Soldiers and Military Caciques in Modern Mexico*. Tucson: University of Arizona Press, 2012.

Fein, Seth. "Myths of Cultural Imperialism and Nationalism in Golden Age Mexican Cinema." In *Fragments of a Golden Age: The Politics of Culture in Mexico since 1940*, edited by Gilbert M. Joseph, Anne Rubenstein, and Eric Zolov, 159–98. Durham: Duke University Press, 2001.

Ferreyra, Aleida, and Renata Segura. "Examining the Military in the Local Sphere: Colombia and Mexico." *Latin American Perspectives* 27, no. 2 (2000): 18–35.

Finchelstein, Federico. *Transatlantic Fascism: Ideology, Violence and the Sacred in Argentina and Italy, 1919–1945*. Durham: Duke University Press, 2010.

Fiscalía Especial para Movimientos Sociales y Políticos del Pasado. *Informe histórico a la sociedad mexicana* (leaked draft version). http://www.gwu.edu/~nsarchiv/NSAEBB/NSAEBB180/index.htm (accessed February 2006).

Flores Arellano, Mélida, and América Wences Román. *María de la O, una mujer ejemplar*. Chilpancingo, Mexico: Universidad Autónoma de Guerrero; CEHAM, 1992.

Florescano, Enrique. *National Narratives in Mexico: A History*. Norman: University of Oklahoma Press, 2006.

Forment, Carlos. *Civic Selfhood and Public Life in Mexico and Peru*. Vol. 1 of *Democracy in Latin America, 1760–1900*. Chicago: Chicago University Press, 2003.

Fowler, Will. *Forceful Negotiations: The Origins of the Pronunciamiento in Nineteenth-Century Mexico*. Lincoln: University of Nebraska Press, 2010.

———. *Military Political Identity and Reformism in Independent Mexico: An Analysis of the Memorias de Guerra (1821–1855)*. London: Institute of Latin American Studies, 1996.

García de León, Antonio. *Fronteras interiores: Chiapas, una modernidad particular*. Mexico: Oceano, 2002.

Garduño Valero, Guillermo J. R. "El ejército mexicano, el poder incógnito." *Iztapalapa* 34 (1994): 91–106.

Gauss, Susan. *Made in Mexico: Regions, Nation and the State in the Making of Mexican Industrialism, 1920s–1940s*. University Park: Pennsylvania State University Press, 2010.

———. "Working-Class Masculinity and the Rationalized Sex: Gender and Industrial Modernization in the Textile Industry in Post-Revolutionary Puebla." In *Sex in Revolution: Gender, Politics and Power in Modern Mexico*, edited by Jocelyn Olcott, Mary Kay Vaughan, and Gabriella Cano, 181–98. Durham: Duke University Press, 2006.

Gill, Mario. "Los Escudero de Acapulco." *Historia Mexicana* 3, no. 2 (1953): 291–308.

———. *El Sinarquismo: su origen, su esencia, su misión*. Mexico City: Comité de Defensa de la Revolución, 1944.

———. "Zapata: su pueblo y sus hijos." *Historia Mexicana* 2, no. 2 (1952): 294–312.

Gillingham, Paul. "Force and Consent in Mexican Provincial Politics: Guerrero and Veracruz, 1945–53." D.Phil. diss., Oxford University, 2005.

———. "Maximino's Bulls: Popular Protest after the Mexican Revolution." *Past and Present* 206 (2010): 175–211.

———. "Military Caciquismo in the PRIísta State: General Mange's Command in Veracruz, 1937–1959." In *Forced Marches: Soldiers and Military Caciques in Modern Mexico*, edited by Ben Fallaw and Terry Rugeley. Tucson: University of Arizona Press, 2012.

Gillingham, Paul, and Benjamin Smith, eds. *Soft Authoritarianism in Mexico, 1940–1955*. Duke University Press, forthcoming.

Gilly, Adolfo. *El cardenismo, una utopia mexicana*. Mexico City: Ediciones Era, 2001.

Gojman de Backal, Alicia. *Camisas, escudos y desfiles militares: los Dorados y el antisemitismo en México, 1934–1940*. Mexico City: Escuela Nacional de Estudios Profesionales Acatlán; Fondo de Cultura Económica, 2000.

González, Hugo Pedro. *Portesgilismo y alemanismo en Tamaulipas*. Ciudad Victoria, Tamaulipas: Universidad Autónoma de Tamaulipas, 1983.

Grandin, Greg. "Coming to Terms with the Violence of Latin America's Long Cold War." In *A Century of Revolution: Insurgent and Counterinsurgent Violence during Latin America's Long Cold War*, edited by Gilbert Joseph and Greg Grandin, 1–44. Durham: Duke University Press, 2010.

Greenberg, James B. *Blood Ties: Life and Violence in Rural Mexico*. Tucson: University of Arizona Press, 1989.

Guardino, Peter. *The Time of Liberty: Popular Political Culture in Oaxaca, 1750–1850*. Durham: Duke University Press, 2005.

Guzmán Navarro, Enrique. "Las pensiones militares en México." Law thesis, Universidad Nacional Autónoma de México, 1951.

Haber, Stephen H., Armando Razo, and Noel Maurer, eds. *The Politics of Property Rights: Political Instability, Credible Commitments, and Economic Growth in Mexico, 1876–1929*. Cambridge: Cambridge University Press, 2003.

Hale, Charles. "José María Luis Mora and the Structure of Mexican Liberalism." *Hispanic American Historical Review* 45, no. 2 (1965): 196–227.

Hall, Linda B. "Álvaro Obregón and the Politics of Mexican Land Reform." *Hispanic American Historical Review* 60, no. 2 (1980): 213–38.

Harrison, Donald. "United States–Mexican Military Collaboration during World War II." Ph.D. diss., Georgetown University, 1976.

Henderson, Timothy. *The Worm in the Wheat: Rosalie Evans and Agrarian Struggle in the Puebla-Tlaxcala Valley, 1906–1927*. Durham: Duke University Press, 1998.

Hernández, Rogelio. *Amistades, compromisos y lealtades: líderes y grupos políticos en el Estado de México, 1942–1993*. Mexico: Colegio de México, 1998.

Hernández Chávez, Alicia. *Historia de la Revolución Mexicana, 1934–1940: La mecánica cardenista*. Mexico City: Colegio de México, 1979.

———. "Militares y negocios en la Revolución Mexicana." *Historia Mexicana* 34, no. 2 (1984): 181–212.

———. "Origen y ocaso del ejército porfiriano." *Historia Mexicana* 39, no. 1 (1989): 257–96.

Huggins, Martha K., Mika Haritos-Fatouros, and Phillip G. Zimbardo. *Violence Workers: Police Torturers and Murderers Reconstruct Brazilian Atrocities.* Berkeley: University of California Press, 2001.

Irigoin, Alejandra, and Regina Grafe. "A Stakeholder Empire: The Political Economy of Spanish Imperial Rule in America." LSE Working Paper No. 111/88. 2008.

Jiménez Castillo, Manuel. *Huancito: organización y práctica política.* Mexico City: Instituto Nacional Indigenista, 1985.

Johnson, John J. *The Military and Society in Latin America.* Stanford: Stanford University Press, 1964.

Joseph, Gilbert M. "Rethinking Mexican Revolutionary Mobilization: Yucatán's Seasons of Upheaval, 1909–1915." In *Everyday Forms of State Formation: Revolution and the Negotiation of Rule in Modern Mexico,* edited by Gilbert M. Joseph and Daniel Nugent, 135–69. Durham: Duke University Press, 1994.

Joseph, Gilbert M., and Daniel Nugent, eds. *Everyday Forms of State Formation: Revolution and the Negotiation of Rule in Modern Mexico.* Durham: Duke University Press, 1994.

Katz, Friedrich. *The Life and Times of Pancho Villa.* Stanford: Stanford University Press, 1998.

Keegan, John. *The Face of Battle.* London: Penguin, 1978.

Klingemann, John Eusebio. "Triumph of the Vanquished: Pancho Villa's Army in Revolutionary Mexico." Ph.D. diss., University of Arizona, 2008.

Knight, Alan. "Cardenismo: Juggernaut or Jalopy?" *Journal of Latin American Studies* 26, no. 1 (1994): 73–107.

———. "Habitus and Homicide: Political Culture in Revolutionary Mexico." In *Citizens of the Pyramid: Essays on Mexican Political Culture,* edited by Wil Pansters, 107–29. Amsterdam: Thela, 1997.

———. "Historical Continuities in Social Movements." In *Popular Movements and Political Change in Mexico,* edited by Joe Foweraker and Ann Craig, 78–104. Boulder: L. Rienner Publishers, 1990.

———. "The Ideology of the Mexican Revolution, 1910–40." *Estudios Interdisciplinarios de América Latina y el Caribe* 8, no. 1 (1997): 77–110.

———. *The Mexican Revolution.* 2 vols. Cambridge: Cambridge University Press, 1986.

———. "Political Violence in Post-revolutionary Mexico." In *Societies of Fear: The Legacy of Civil War, Violence and Terror in Latin America,* edited by Kees Koonings and Dirk Krijt, 105–24. New York: Zed Books, 1999.

———. "Popular Culture and the Revolutionary State in Mexico, 1910–1940." *Hispanic American Historical Review* 74, no. 3 (1994): 393–444.

———. "Racism, Revolution and *Indigenismo*: Mexico 1910–1940." In *The Idea of Race in Latin America, 1870–1940,* edited by Richard Graham, 71–114. Austin: University of Texas Press, 1990.

———. "The Weight of the State in Modern Mexico." In *Studies in the Formation of the Nation-State in Latin America*, edited by James Dunkerley, 212–53. London: Institute for the Study of the Americas, 2002.

Krauze, Enrique. *General Misionero Lázaro Cárdenas*. Mexico: Fondo de Cultura Económica, 1987.

———. *La presidencia imperial: ascenso y caída del sistema político mexicano (1940–1996)*. Mexico City: Tusquets Editores, 2002.

LaFrance, David. "The Military as Political Actor (and More) in the Mexican Revolution: The Case of Puebla in the 1920s and 1930s." Paper Presented at the Meeting of the Latin American Studies Association, San Juan, Puerto Rico, March 15–18, 2006.

———. *Revolution in Mexico's Heartland: Politics, War and State-Building in Puebla, 1913–1920*. Wilmington, Del.: Scholarly Resources, 2003.

Lear, John. *Workers, Neighbors and Citizens: The Revolution in Mexico City*. Lincoln: University of Nebraska Press, 2001.

Lewis, Oscar. *Life in a Mexican Village: Tepoztlán Revisited*. Urbana: University of Illinois Press, 1951.

Lieuwen, Edwin. "The Depoliticization of the Mexican Revolutionary Army, 1915–1940." In *The Modern Mexican Military: A Reassessment*, edited by David Ronfeldt, 51–62. San Diego: Center for US-Mexican Relations, 1984.

———. *Mexican Militarism: The Political Rise and Fall of the Revolutionary Army*. Albuquerque: University of New Mexico Press, 1968.

Lockhart, James, and Stuart Schwartz. *Early Latin America: A History of Colonial Spanish America and Brazil*. Cambridge: Cambridge University Press, 1983.

López, Rick. *Crafting Mexico: Intellectuals, Artisans and the State after the Revolution*. Durham: Duke University Press, 2010.

López-Montiel, Ángel Gustavo. "The Military, Political Power, and Police Relations in Mexico City." *Latin American Perspectives* 27, no. 2 (2000): 79–94.

Loyo Camacho, Marta. *Joaquín Amaro y el proceso de institucionalización del Ejército Mexicano, 1917–1931*. Mexico City: Universidad Nacional Autónoma de México, 2003.

Lozoya, Jorge Alberto. *El ejército mexicano*. Mexico City: Colegio de México, 1965.

Lutz, Catherine. "Militarization." In *A Companion to the Anthropology of Politics*, edited by David Nugent and Joan Vincent, 318–31. Oxford: Blackwell-Wiley, 2004.

Macías-González, Víctor M. "Presidential Ritual in Porfirian Mexico." In *Heroes and Hero Cults in Latin America*, edited by Samuel Brunk and Ben Fallaw, 83–108. Austin: University of Texas Press, 2006.

Mallon, Florencia. *Peasant and Nation: The Making of Postcolonial Mexico and Peru*. Berkeley: University of California Press, 1995.

Manjarrez, Alejandro C. *Puebla: el rostro olvidado*. Cholula, Puebla: Imagen Pública y Corporativa S.A. de C.V., 1991.

Mann, Gregory. *Native Sons: West African Veterans and France in the Twentieth Century*. Durham: Duke University Press, 2006.

Mares, David. *Violent Peace: Militarized Interstate Bargaining in Latin America.* New York: Columbia University Press, 2001.

Margiotta, Franklin D. "Civilian Control of the Military: Changing Patterns and Influence." In *Civilian Control of the Military: Theory and Cases from Developing Countries,* edited by Claude Welch, 213–53. Albany: State University of New York, 1976.

Markarian, Vania. "Los debates públicos sobre el movimiento estudiantil mexicano de 1968." *Anuario de Espacios Urbanos* (2001): 239–64.

Márquez Carillo, Jesús. *Tiempo y su sombra: política y oposición conservadora en Puebla, 1932–40.* Puebla: Gobierno del Estado de Puebla, 1997.

McAlister, Lyle. "Mexico." In *The Military in Latin American Socio-political Evolution: Four Case Studies,* 197–258. Washington, D.C.: Center for Research in Social Systems, 1970.

McCormick, Gladys. "The Political Economy of Desire in Rural Mexico: Authoritarianism and Revolutionary Change, 1935–1965." Ph.D. diss., University of Wisconsin, Madison, 2009.

McKee Irwin, Robert, Edward J. McCaughan, and Michele Rocío Nasser. "Introduction." In *The Famous 41: Sexuality and Social Control in Mexico, 1901,* edited by Robert McKee Irwin, Edward J. McCaughan, and Michele Rocío Nasser, 1–20. Basingstoke: Palgrave Macmillan, 2003.

McNamara, Patrick. "Saving Private Ramírez: The Patriarchal Voice of Republican Motherhood in Mexico." *Gender and History* 18, no. 1 (2006): 35–49.

———. *Sons of the Sierra: Juárez, Díaz and the People of Ixtlán, Oaxaca, 1855–1920.* Chapel Hill: University of North Carolina Press, 2007.

Meacham, J. Lloyd. "Mexican Federalism—Fact or Fiction?" In *Mexico Today: Annals of the American Academy of Political and Social Science* 208, edited by Arthur P. Whitaker, 23–38. Philadelphia: American Academy of Political and Social Science, 1940.

Medin, Tzvi. *El sexenio alemanista: ideología y praxis política de Miguel Alemán.* Mexico: Ediciones Era, 1990.

Méndez, Leopoldo. *Leopoldo Méndez y su tiempo: colección Carlos Monsiváis: el privilegio del dibujo.* Mexico City: Instituto Nacional de Bellas Artes, 2002.

Meyer, Jean. "Grandes compañias, ejércitos populares y ejército estatal en la revolución mexicana (1910–1930)." *Anuario de Estudios Americanos* 31 (1974): 1005–30.

———. *Historia de la Revolución Mexicana, 1924–1928: Estado y sociedad con Calles.* Mexico City: Colegio de México, 1977.

———. *La Cristiada: La guerra de los cristeros.* 3 vols. Mexico: Siglo XXI, 1994.

Meyer, Lorenzo. "Historical Roots of the Authoritarian State in Mexico." In *Authoritarianism in Mexico,* edited by José Luis Reyna and Richard S. Weinart, 3–22. Philadelphia: Institute for the Study of Human Issues, 1977.

Michaels, Albert. "Las elecciones de 1940." *Historia Mexicana* 21, no. 3 (1971): 80–134.

Miller, Nicola. *In the Shadow of the State: Intellectuals and the Quest for National Identity in Twentieth-Century Spanish America.* London: Verso, 1999.

Moloeznick, Marcos Pablo. "The Militarization of Public Security and the Role of the Military in Mexico." In *Police and Public Security in Mexico*, edited by David Shirk and Robert Donnelly, 65–92. San Diego: University Readers, 2010.

Monsiváis, Carlos. "Foreword: When Gender Can't Be Seen Amid the Symbols: Women and the Mexican Revolution." In *Sex in Revolution: Gender, Politics and Power in Modern Mexico*, edited by Jocelyn Olcott, Mary Kay Vaughan, and Gabriella Cano, 1–20. Durham: Duke University Press, 2006.

———. "Leopoldo Méndez: la radicalización de la mirada." In *Leopoldo Méndez y su tiempo: colección Carlos Monsiváis: el privilegio del dibujo*, 19–25. Mexico City: Instituto Nacional de Bellas Artes, 2002.

Moran, Daniel, and Arthur Waldron, eds. *The People in Arms: Military Myth and National Mobilization since the French Revolution*. Cambridge: Cambridge University Press, 2003.

Mottier, Nicole. "Drug Gangs and Politics in Ciudad Juárez: 1928–1936." *Mexican Studies/Estudios Mexicanos* 25, no. 1 (2009): 19–46.

Mraz, John. *Looking for Mexico: Modern Visual Culture and National Identity*. Durham: Duke University Press, 2010.

Navarro, Aaron. *Political Intelligence and the Creation of Modern Mexico, 1938–1954*. University Park: Pennsylvania State University Press, 2010.

Navarro Valdez, Pavel Leonardo. *El cardenismo en Durango: historia y política regional, 1934–1940*. Durango, Mexico: Instituto de Cultura del Estado de Durango, 2005.

Neufeld, Stephen. "Servants of the Nation: The Military in the Making of Modern Mexico, 1876–1911." Ph.D. diss., University of Arizona, 2009.

Newcomer, Daniel. *Reconciling Modernity: Urban State Formation in 1940s León, Mexico*. Lincoln: University of Nebraska Press, 2004.

Niblo, Stephen. *Mexico in the 1940s: Modernity, Politics and Corruption*. Wilmington, Del.: Scholarly Resources, 1999.

Nickel, Herbert J. "Agricultural Laborers in the Mexican Revolution (1910–1940): Some Hypotheses and Facts about Participation and Restraint in the Highlands of Puebla-Tlaxcala." In *Riot, Rebellion, and Revolution: Rural Social Conflict in Mexico*, edited by Friedrich Katz, 376–415. Princeton: Princeton University Press, 1988.

Nugent, Daniel. *Spent Cartridges of Revolution: An Anthropological History of Namiquipa, Chihuahua*. Chicago: University of Chicago Press, 1993.

Nunn, Frederick M. *The Time of the Generals: Latin American Predatory Militarism in World Perspective*. Lincoln: University of Nebraska Press, 1992.

———. *Yesterday's Soldiers: European Military Professionalism in South America, 1890–1940*. Lincoln: University of Nebraska Press, 1983.

Olcott, Jocelyn. *Revolutionary Women in Postrevolutionary Mexico*. Durham: Duke University Press, 2005.

O'Malley, Ilene V. *The Myth of the Revolution: Hero Cults and the Institutionalization of the Mexican State, 1920–1940*. Westport, Conn.: Greenwood Press, 1986.

Osten, Sarah. "Peace by Institutions: The Rise of Political Parties and the Making of the Modern Mexican State, 1920–1928." Ph.D. diss., University of Chicago, 2010.

Padilla, Francisco. *Lo que el tiempo no se llevó : los conflictos agrarios en el sur de Sinaloa durante el periodo cardenista, 1935–1940*. Culiacán: Dirección de Investigación y Fomento de la Cultura Regional; Universidad Autónoma de Sinaloa, 1993.

Padilla, Tanalís. *Rural Resistance in the Land of Zapata: The Jaramillista Movement and the Myth of the Pax Priísta, 1940–1962*. Durham: Duke University Press, 2008.

Pansters, Wil. *Power and Politics in Puebla: The Political History of a Mexican State, 1937–1987*. Amsterdam: CEDLA, 1990.

——. "Zones of State-Making: Violence, Coercion and Hegemony in Twentieth-Century Mexico." In *Violence, Coercion and State-Making in Twentieth-Century Mexico*, edited by Wil Pansters, 3–42. Stanford: Stanford University Press, 2012.

Parra, Max. *Writing Pancho Villa's Revolution: Rebels in the Literary Imagination of Mexico*. Austin: University of Texas Press, 2005.

Parra Mora, León Javier, and Jorge Hernández Díaz. *Violencia y cambio social en la región Triqui*. Oaxaca: Universidad Autónoma Benito Juárez de Oaxaca, 1994.

Paxman, Andrew. "William Jenkins, Business Elites, and the Evolution of the Mexican State, 1910–1960." Ph.D. diss., University of Texas at Austin, 2008.

Pensado, Jaime. "Political Violence and Student Culture in Mexico: The Consolidation of *Porrismo* during the 1950s and 1960s." Ph.D. diss., University of Chicago, 2008.

Pereira, Anthony. *Political Injustice: Authoritarianism and the Rule of Law in Brazil, Chile and Argentina*. Pittsburgh: University of Pittsburgh Press, 2005.

Piccato, Pablo. *City of Suspects: Crime in Mexico City, 1900–1931*. Durham: Duke University Press, 2001.

Pimentel, Stanley A. "The Nexus of Organized Crime and Politics in Mexico." In *Organized Crime and Democratic Governability: Mexico and the U.S.-Mexican Borderlands*, edited by John Bailey and Roy Godson, 33–57. Pittsburgh: University of Pittsburgh Press, 2000.

Pion-Berlin, David. "Latin American National Security Doctrine: Hard and Softline Themes." *Armed Forces and Society* 15, no. 3 (1989): 411–29.

Plasencia de la Parra, Enrique. "Conmemoración de la hazaña épica de los Niños Héroes: su origen, desarrollo y simbolismos." *Historia Mexicana* 178, no. 2 (1995): 241–79.

——. *Historia y organización de las fuerzas armadas en México, 1917–1937*. Mexico City: Universidad Nacional Autónoma de México, Instituto de Investigaciones Históricas, 2010.

Quintana, Alejandro. *Maximino Ávila Camacho and the One-party State: The Taming of Caudillismo and Caciquismo in Post-revolutionary Mexico*. New York: Lexington Books, 2010.

Ramírez Melgarejo, Ramón. "La bola chiquita: un movimiento campesino." In *Los campesinos de la tierra de Zapata, I: Adaptación, cambio y rebelión*, edited by Laura Helguera, Sinecio López, and Ramón Ramírez Melgarejo, 165–221. Mexico City: Centro de Investigaciones Superiores, Instituto Nacional de Antropología e Historia, 1974.

Rath, Thomas. "Gender and Military Reform in Postrevolutionary Mexico." Paper presented at Latin American Studies Association Conference, Toronto, 2010.

———. "'Que el cielo un soldado en cada hijo te dio . . .' : Conscription, Recalcitrance and Resistance in Mexico in the 1940s." *Journal of Latin American Studies* 37, no. 3 (2005): 507–32.

Redfield, Robert. *A Village That Chose Progress: Chan Kom Revisited*. Chicago: University of Chicago Press, 1950.

Reina, Leticia. *Las rebeliones campesinas en México, 1819–1906*. Mexico City: Siglo Veintiuno, 1980.

Remmer, Karen. "Neopatrimonialism: The Politics of Military Rule in Chile, 1973–1987." *Comparative Politics* 21, no. 2 (1989): 149–70.

Resende Santos, Joao. *Neorealism, States and the Modern Mass Army*. Cambridge: Cambridge University Press, 2007.

Reyes Peláez, Juan Fernando. "El largo brazo del estado: la estrategia contrain-surgente del gobierno Mexicano." In *Movimientos armados en México*, edited by Verónica Oikión Solano, 2:405–16. Mexico: El Colegio de Michoacán, 2006.

Robertson Sierra, Margarita. "La casa de nuestra cultura: el territorio de los nahuas de Ayotitlán." *Chiapas* 8 (1999): 93–102.

Rocha, Marta Eva. "The Faces of Rebellion: From Revolutionaries to Veterans in Nationalist Mexico." In *The Women's Revolution in Mexico, 1910–1953*, edited by Stephanie Mitchell and Patience A. Schell, 15–35. Lanham, Md.: Rowman and Littlefield, 2007.

Ronfeldt, David. *Atencingo: The Politics of Agrarian Struggle in a Mexican Ejido*. Stanford: Stanford University Press, 1973.

———. "The Mexican Army and Political Order since 1940." In *The Modern Mexican Military: A Reassessment*, edited by David Ronfeldt, 63–86. San Diego: Center for US-Mexican Relations, 1984.

Roseberry, William. "Hegemony and the Language of Contention." In *Everyday Forms of State Formation: Revolution and the Negotiation of Rule in Modern Mexico*, edited by Gilbert M. Joseph and Daniel Nugent, 355–66. Durham: Duke University Press, 1994.

Rouquié, Alain. *The Military and the State in Latin America*. Berkeley: University of California Press, 1987.

Rubenstein, Anne. *Bad Language, Naked Ladies and Other Threats to the Nation*. Durham: Duke University Press, 1998.

Rubin, Jeffrey. "Decentering the Regime: Culture and Regional Politics in Mexico." *Latin American Research Review* 31, no. 3 (1996): 85–126.

Salas, Elizabeth. *Soldaderas in the Mexican Military: Myth and History*. Austin: University of Texas Press, 1990.

Salmerón Sanginés, Pedro. "Los historiadores y la guerra civil de 1915: origen y persistencia de un canon historiográfico." *Historia Mexicana* 58, no. 4 (2009): 1305–68.

Sánchez Gutiérrez, Arturo. "La política en el México rural de los años cincuenta." In *The Evolution of the Mexican Political System*, edited by Jaime E. Rodríguez, 215–44. Wilmington, Del.: SR Books, 1993.

———. "Los militares en la década de los cincuenta." *Revista Mexicana de Sociología* 50, no. 3 (1988): 269–93.

Santoni, Pedro. "A Fear of the People: The Civic Militia of Mexico in 1845." *Hispanic American Historical Review* 68, no. 2 (1988): 269–88.

———. "'Where Did the Other Heroes Go?' Exalting the *Polko* National Guard Battalions in Nineteenth-Century Mexico." *Journal of Latin American Studies* 34, no. 4 (2002): 807–44.

Saragoza, Alex. *The Monterrey Elite and the Mexican State, 1880–1940.* Austin: University of Texas Press, 1988.

Schamis, Hector. "Reconceptualizing Latin American Authoritarianism in the 1970s: From Bureaucratic Authoritarianism to Neoconservatism." *Comparative Politics* 23 (1991): 201–20.

Scherer García, Julio, and Carlos Monsiváis. *Parte de guerra. Tlatelolco 1968. Documentos del General Marcelino García Barragán. Los hechos y la historia.* Mexico: Aguilar, 1999.

Schmidt, Arthur. "Making It Real Compared to What? Reconceptualizing Mexican History since 1940." In *Fragments of a Golden Age: The Politics of Culture in Mexico since 1940,* edited by Gilbert M. Joseph, Anne Rubenstein, and Eric Zolov, 23–68. Durham: Duke University Press, 2001.

Schryer, Frans. "A Ranchero Elite in the Region of Huejutla: The Career of General Juvencio Nochebuena of Atlapexco." In *Region, State and Capitalism in Mexico. Nineteenth and Twentieth Centuries,* edited by Wil Pansters and Arij Ouweneel, 158–73. Amsterdam: Center for Latin American Research and Documentation, 1989.

Schuler, Friedrich. *Mexico Between Hitler and Roosevelt: Mexican Foreign Relations in the Age of Lázaro Cárdenas, 1934–1940.* Albuquerque: University of New Mexico Press, 1998.

———. *Secret Wars and Secret Policies in the Americas, 1842–1929.* Albuquerque: University of New Mexico Press, 2011.

Scott, James. *Weapons of the Weak: Everyday Forms of Peasant Resistance.* New Haven: Yale University Press, 1987.

Serdán, Félix. *Memorias de un Guerrillero.* Mexico: Rizona, 2002.

Serrano, José Antonio. *El contingente de sangre: los gobiernos estatales y departamentales y los métodos de reclutamiento del ejército permanente mexicano, 1824–1844.* Mexico: Instituto Nacional de Antropología e Historia, 1993.

Servín, Elisa. "Reclaiming Revolution in the Light of the 'Mexican Miracle': Celestino Gasca and the *Federacionistas Leales* Insurrection of 1961." *The Americas* 66, no. 4 (2010): 527–57.

———. *Ruptura y oposición: El movimiento henriquista, 1945–1954.* Mexico City: Ediciones Cal y Arena, 2001.

Sherman, John W. *The Mexican Right: The End of Revolutionary Reform, 1929–1940.* Westport, Conn.: Praeger, 1997.

Sierra Guzmán, Jorge Luis. *El enemigo interno: contrainsurgencia y fuerzas armadas en México.* Mexico: Plaza y Valdés, 2003.

Silva Andraca, Héctor. *Puebla y su universidad*. Puebla: Editorial Universidad Autónoma de Puebla, 1980.

Simpson, Lesley Byrd. *Many Mexicos*. 4th ed., rev. Berkeley: University of California Press, 1966.

Skjelsbaek, Kjell. "Militarism, Its Dimensions and Corollaries: An Attempt at Conceptual Clarification." In *Problems of Contemporary Militarism*, edited by Asbjorn Eide and Marek Thee, 77–105. New York: St. Martin's Press, 1980.

Skurski, Julie, and Fernando Coronil. "Introduction: States of Violence and the Violence of States." In *States of Violence*, edited by Julie Skurski and Fernando Coronil, 1–31. Ann Arbor: University of Michigan Press, 2006.

Smallman, Shawn. *Fear and Memory in the Brazilian Army and Society, 1889–1954*. Chapel Hill: University of North Carolina Press, 2002.

Smith, Benjamin. "Heliodoro Charis Castro and the Soldiers of Juchitán: Indigenous Militarism, Local Rule and the Mexican State." In *Forced Marches: Soldiers and Military Caciques in Modern Mexico*, edited by Ben Fallaw and Terry Rugeley. Tucson: University of Arizona Press, 2012.

———. "Inventing Tradition at Gunpoint: Culture, Caciquismo and State Formation in the Región Mixe, Oaxaca (1930–1959)." *Bulletin of Latin American Research* 27, no. 2 (2008): 215–34.

———. *Pistoleros and Popular Movements: The Politics of State Formation in Postrevolutionary Oaxaca*. Lincoln: University of Nebraska Press, 2009.

Sosa Elízaga, Raquel. *Los códigos ocultos del cardenismo: un estudio de violencia política, el cambio social y la continuidad institucional*. Mexico City: Plaza y Valdés, 1996.

Stepan, Alfred. *The Military in Politics: Changing Patterns in Brazil*. Princeton: Princeton University Press, 1971.

Tate, Winifred. *Counting the Dead: The Culture and Politics of Human Rights Activism in Colombia*. Berkeley: University of California Press, 2007.

Taussig, Michael. *The Magic of the State*. New York: Routledge, 1997.

Thompson, Guy. "Los indios y el servicio militar en el México decimonónico. ¿Leva o ciudadanía?" In *Indio, nación y comunidad en el México del Siglo XIX*, edited by Antonio Escobar Ohmstede, 207–52. Mexico City: Centro de Estudios Mexicanos y Centroamericanos; Centro de Investigaciones y Estudios Superiores en Antropología Social, 1993.

Thompson, Guy, with David G. LaFrance. *Patriotism, Politics and Popular Liberalism in Nineteenth-Century Mexico: Juan Francisco Lucas and the Puebla Sierra*. London: Rowman and Littlefield, 2002.

Tobler, Hans-Werner. "Las paradojas del ejército revolucionario: su papel social en la reforma agraria mexicana, 1920–1935." *Historia Mexicana* 21, no. 1 (1971): 38–79.

———. "Peasants and the Shaping of the Revolutionary State, 1910–40." In *Riot, Rebellion, and Revolution: Rural Social Conflict in Mexico*, edited by Friedrich Katz, 487–518. Princeton: Princeton University Press, 1988.

Torres Ramírez, Blanca. *Historia de la Revolución Mexicana: 1940–52: México en la Segunda Guerra Mundial*. Mexico City: Colegio de México, 1979.

Valencia Castrejón, Sergio. *Poder regional y política nacional en México: el gobierno de Maximino Ávila Camacho en Puebla (1937–1941)*. Mexico City: Instituto Nacional de Estudios Históricos de la Revolución Mexicana, 1996.

Vanderwood, Paul. *Disorder and Progress: Bandits, Police and Mexican Development*. Lincoln: University of Nebraska Press, 1981.

———. *Juan Soldado: Rapist, Murderer, Martyr, Saint*. Durham: Duke University Press, 2004.

Vargas-Lobsinger, María. *La Comarca Lagunera, México: de la revolución a la expropriación de las haciendas, 1910–1940*. Mexico City: Universidad Nacional Autónoma de México, 1999.

Vaughan, Mary Kay. *Cultural Politics in Revolution: Teachers, Peasants, and Schools in Mexico, 1930–40*. Tucson: University of Arizona Press, 1997.

Vaughan, Mary Kay, and Stephen Lewis, eds. *The Eagle and the Virgin: Nation and Cultural Revolution in Mexico, 1920–1940*. Durham: Duke University Press, 2006.

Vázquez, Josefina Zoraida. "Iglesia, ejército y centralismo." *Historia Mexicana* 39, no. 1 (1989): 205–34.

———. "Political Plans and Collaboration Between Civilians and the Military, 1821–1846." *Bulletin of Latin American Research* 15, no. 1 (1996): 19–38.

Veledíaz, Juan. *El general sin memoria: una crónica de los silencios del Ejército Mexicano*. Mexico: Debate, 2010.

Vélez Pliego, Alfonso. "La sucesión rectoral, las lecciones de la historia y las tareas actuales del movimiento universitario democrático." *Crítica: revista de la Universidad Autónoma de Puebla* 1 (1978): 41–90.

Vera Salvo, Ramón. *Historia de la cuestión agraria mexicana: estado de Zacatecas*. Mexico: Gobierno del Estado de Zacatecas; Universidad Autónoma de Zacatecas; Centro de Estudios Históricos del Agrarismo en México, 1990.

Vinson, Ben, III. *Bearing Arms for His Majesty: The Free-Colored Militia in Colonial Mexico*. Stanford: Stanford University Press, 2001.

Vinson, Ben, III, and Matthew Restall. "Black Soldiers, Native Soldiers: Meanings of Military Service in the Spanish American Colonies." In *Beyond Black and Red: African-Native Relations in Colonial Latin America*, edited by Matthew Restall, 15–52. Albuquerque: University of New Mexico Press, 2005.

Wager, Stephen J. "The Mexican Army, 1940–1982: The Country Comes First." Ph.D. diss., Stanford University, 1992.

Warman, Arturo. "The Political Project of Zapatismo." In *Riot, Rebellion, and Revolution: Rural Social Conflict in Mexico*, edited by Friedrich Katz, 321–37. Princeton: Princeton University Press, 1988.

Wasserman, Mark. *Persistent Oligarchs: Elites and Politics in Chihuahua, Mexico, 1910–1940*. Durham: Duke University Press, 1993.

Whetten, Nathan. *Rural Mexico*. Chicago: University of Chicago Press, 1948.

Whitehead, Lawrence. "State Organization in Latin America since 1930." In *Latin America: Economy and Society since 1930*, edited by Leslie Bethell, 381–440. Cambridge: Cambridge University Press, 1998.

Womack, John. *Zapata and the Mexican Revolution*. New York: Vintage, 1968.

INDEX

Izúcar de Matamoros, 66, 109–10, 113, 125, 134–40

Jalisco, 25, 69, 119, 136; military commanders in, 26, 45, 89, 92, 97, 104, 105
Japan, 57–58, 65
Jaramillo, Porfirio, 123, 126, 134
Jaramillo, Rubén, 65, 72
Jenkins, William, 137, 140

Land reform. *See* Agrarian reform
La Prensa, 128, 138, 139, 161
León massacre, 93–94, 138, 168
Leyva Velázquez, Gabriel, 112, 128–29
Liberalism, 15, 20, 21, 22, 29, 55, 130, 138
Lieuwen, Edwin, 4, 5, 26
Limón, Gilberto, 91, 99–100, 104, 139
Lombardo Toledano, Vicente, 41, 51, 100
López, Anacleto, 87, 96, 101, 103, 110, 134
López de Nava, Rodolfo, 26, 105, 149
López de Santa Anna, Antonio, 20, 74
Lucas, Juan Francisco, 73, 106
Lynching, 122, 127, 139

Macías Valenzuela, Pablo, 90–91, 92, 102
Madero, Francisco, 18, 20, 55–56, 145, 146, 148, 151, 153, 159; family of, 155
Mange, Alejandro, 26, 28, 43, 87, 89, 102, 103
Marijuana, 22, 74
Martín del Campo, Carlos, 48–49
Martínez, Miguel Z., 94–96, 101–2, 121–22
Martínez Cairo, Salvador, 134–40, 145
Martínez Castro, José, 112, 131, 163
Mestizaje, 60, 72
Mexican Legion of Honor, 161–62, 163
Mexican Revolution (1910–20), 9, 13, 18–21, 29; legacy of, 3; historical memory of, 11, 73, 146–66 passim; U.S. role in, 17, 18, 152, 159; mobilization during, 18–19, 145; and Cardenismo, 33, 34–35; and local autonomy, 55; in state of Puebla, 106
Mexico City, 15, 44, 66, 73, 76, 95, 113, 137, 144, 153; during Mexican Revolution, 13, 19; national government in, 25; debates about army in, 31–32, 42, 51, 57, 98; mayor of, 34; schools in, 45, 48, 49; and recruitment, 56, 62, 68–69, 76; feminists from, 67; parades in, 75, 108, 153; foreigners in, 83; military forces in, 84–85, 104–5, 116, 120; intelligence agents in, 99; police in, 120, 121; muralist movement in, 147; veterans in, 147, 155, 158, 164–65
México (state), 64, 66, 81, 91, 104, 121
Meyer, Jean, 6, 26, 169
Michoacán, 25, 28, 37, 43, 45, 122, 143; recruitment in, 28, 63, 67, 68, 69, 71, 75; military commanders in, 41, 47, 87, 103, 121; militia in, 43, 117; revolutionary warfare in, 149
Militarism, 3, 9, 15, 22, 34, 37, 46, 94, 167; and Military College, 151; in Latin America, 167, 170
Militarization: in contemporary Mexico, 3, 6, 172
Military
—budget, 5, 16, 18, 26, 102
—conscription, 10; debates about policy, 21, 55–61, 80; implementation of, 54, 61–64, 77–80; protest against, 54, 62–80, 137, 168, 169. *See also* Press-gang
—corruption, 5, 25–26, 33, 37, 43, 91–93, 98, 100–107 passim, 110, 114, 129, 131, 135, 148, 168, 169; during conscription, 62–64
—discipline, 17, 22, 26, 38, 75–76; military justice, 20–21, 63, 90–91, 110, 132; desertions, 28, 41, 55, 56–57, 75–76, 116, 169; impunity, 121–22, 132–33, 140, 142, 168–69, 172

Nava Castillo, Antonio, 109, 111, 112–13, 134, 135, 136, 139
Navarro, Juan J., 152–53
Navy, 17, 33
Nayarit, 69, 92, 105, 121, 122
New Spain, 14
Niños héroes de Chapultepec, 74, 151
Nuevo León, 23, 41, 68–69, 90, 103, 163

Oaxaca, 28, 67, 72, 73, 81, 119, 120, 142–43, 156; military commanders in, 101, 134
Obregón, Álvaro, 19, 22, 23, 24, 57, 84, 146, 147, 148, 150, 151
Ochoa Moreno, Maximiliano, 133–34, 171, 205–6 (n. 79)
Olachea Avilés, Agustín, 92, 105
Ortiz, Eulogio, 26, 28
Ortiz Rubio, Pascual, 40
Otero Pablos, Ignacio, 43

Partido Auténtico de la Revolución Mexicana (PARM), 164–65, 168
Partido Nacional Revolucionario (PNR), 22, 27, 153, 154
Partido Revolucionario Institucional (PRI), 52, 82, 93, 97, 142; historiography, 4–5, 169–70; and military, 78, 82, 99, 103, 105, 115, 143, 167–72; and elections, 93, 97; in state of Puebla, 113, 135; and veterans, 161, 164–65
Piña Soria, Santiago, 100
Pistoleros, 7, 90, 91, 126, 127, 128, 131, 134, 135, 171, 294 (n. 55)
Police, 7, 105, 113, 120–22, 124, 135–38, 139, 143, 170–71, 172, 201 (n. 23). *See also* Military: policing role
Political violence, 5–8, 123, 143, 170–71. *See also* Counterinsurgency; Military: policing role
Popular Graphic Workshop, 31, 32
Porfiriato, 16–18, 55, 151, 152
Portes Gil, Emilio, 27, 100

Postrevisionism, 4, 6. *See also* Gramsci, Antonio
Presidential general staff, 84–85, 87, 100, 171
Presidential guard, 17, 84–85, 99, 117, 138
Press, 31, 47, 63; and military sector, 40; and militia, 51; and conscription protests, 63, 65–66, 69; and *civilismo*, 81, 94; censorship of, 105, 144; and state of Puebla, 107, 129, 137–39, 141; and veterans, 155–56, 161, 164–65
Press-gang, 17, 18, 21, 28, 35, 55, 56, 68, 74, 152. *See also* Military: conscription
Prieto Laurens, Jorge, 24
Professionalism: military, 5, 29, 56
Pronunciamientos, 14, 22
Propaganda, 47, 50–51, 63, 69, 72, 74, 75, 81, 114
Prostitution, 20, 22, 47, 76, 149
Puebla (city), 66, 107, 108, 110, 112, 117, 123–24
Puebla (state), 1, 45, 73, 81, 156; as case study, 9; anticlericalism in, 22; military commanders in, 26, 87, 89, 104, 106–14, 169; politics in, 44, 106–14; conscription in, 62–63, 64, 66, 69, 72, 76, 78; military policing in, 116, 119, 122–43, 151; veterans in, 163

Querétaro, 69
Quevedo, Rodrigo, 44, 87, 96, 102, 104, 110
Quintana Roo, 69

Ramos Santos, Matías, 26, 105–6, 114
Rebellions: of Cedillo, 41, 86; against conscription, 64–66, 79, 116, 121, 124; of Celestino Gasca, 81; in 1950s, 119. *See also* Military: rebellions
Recruitment. *See* Military: conscription, enlisted men, officer corps; Press-gang
Red Battalions, 19